The Good Retirement Guide 2025

The Good Retirement Guide 2025

Everything you need to know about health, property, investment, leisure, work, pensions and tax

39TH EDITION

Edited by Jonquil Lowe

KoganPage

Thirty-ninth edition published in Great Britain and the United States in 2025 by Kogan Page Limited

2nd Floor, 45 Gee Street
London
EC1V 3RS
United Kingdom

8 W 38th Street, Suite 902
New York, NY 10018
USA

www.koganpage.com

Kogan Page books are printed on paper from sustainable forests.

ISBNs
Hardback   978 1 3986 1879 4
Paperback   978 1 3986 1877 0
eBook   978 1 3986 1878 7

ISSN 0959-2237

British Library Cataloguing-in-Publication Data
A CIP record for this book is available from the British Library.

Typeset by Integra Software Services, Pondicherry
Print production managed by Jellyfish
Printed and bound by CPI Group (UK) Ltd, Croydon CR0 4YY

Contents

This edition of the Good Retirement Guide went to press just after the new Labour government had been elected and before it had held its first Budget. A Budget update and a directory of useful organizations and contacts is available online at:

www.koganpage.com/GRG2025
and there is a QR code at the back of the book as well.

CHAPTER ONE

Are you looking forward to retirement?

Coping with the cost-of-living crisis over the last few years has stretched most people's finances. However, we often overlook the value of public services for our budgets. A study for the Institute of Fiscal Studies estimated that public services and infrastructure (as opposed to cash benefits) were worth £7,600 per person in 2019/20. Traditionally, Labour governments have prioritized public services but the new government has inherited constrained public finance. Among its manifesto promises are improvements to the National Health Service and public transport, which, if delivered, can save us spending on private healthcare and make travel more affordable – as well as greener and more reliable. The manifesto was silent on whether delayed social care reforms to cap care costs would go ahead and subsequently they were axed. However, the manifesto does pledge to tackle local delivery of social care with a focus on improving access and support in your own home.

Whether protecting yourself against inflation, planning for care costs, reducing your carbon footprint or tackling the myriad decisions that transitioning to retirement entails, this stage of your life can feel bewildering. But, with information, guidance and advice, you can improve your confidence and ensure that the plans you make are flexible and robust so that you stay on track for achieving a happy and fulfilling retirement, whatever life and the economy throws at you. And that's where *The Good Retirement Guide* can help.

How to use this book

The Good Retirement Guide is packed with information, suggestions and advice on every aspect of retirement and beyond.

Whichever aspect of retirement concerns you most, the first step is of course to do some figure work. Chapter 2 deals with money in general and contains a very practical budget planner. It will help you to have a clear idea of how much you spend and on what, how much you will need to live comfortably in retirement, and whether you have a shortfall that you'd like to try to fill. Throughout, the chapter takes inflation into account.

The main way to ensure you have enough income in retirement is to save while you are working, so Chapter 3 is all about pensions, first building up your savings and then understanding your options when you want to start drawing money out, including how you may be protected against rising prices. It also deals with the various tax angles relating to pension schemes. The wider picture of tax is discussed in Chapter 4, which looks at income tax and capital gains tax, and ceasing to pay National Insurance contributions once you reach State Pension age, while Chapter 15 looks at issues such as making a will and inheritance tax.

In the course of your preparation, you will want to maximize the value of your assets. Chapter 5 deals with investments and the many types on offer, why you might consider buying an annuity, and investment strategies if you opt to draw a pension direct from your invested funds (called 'drawdown'). There is also guidance on where to get advice to assist you in this complex field.

Around 7 in 10 retirees own their own home, according to the Department for Work and Pensions. If that includes you, it is probably your most valuable asset alongside your pension savings. It may be that downsizing is the answer to living well in retirement, but Chapter 6, *Your home*, will help you weigh it against other options, such as equity release or home improvements.

And, whether you own or rent, the chapter includes ideas on energy efficiency (to reduce your carbon footprint as well as keeping down bills) and staying safe in your home.

Many dream of retiring abroad, maybe to a place where they have spent many happy holidays. Chapter 7 looks at the practicalities of making such dreams come true!

When it comes to leisure activities, there are opportunities throughout the country for almost every kind of sport and hobby, many with over-55s especially welcome. Chapter 8 has a wealth of ideas, while Chapter 13 offers tips on taking trouble-free holidays.

For some, retirement offers the opportunity to start a new career – and the government is encouraging retirees to return to work. There are 1.1 million people under age 65 who are already retired. To make returning to work more attractive, the government has changed the tax rules so that you can more easily build up extra pension (see Chapter 3 for more on this). This could be an attractive option if the recent bout of high inflation has damaged your financial plans. If tempted to become a mature entrepreneur, Chapter 9, *Starting your own business*, provides good advice to help you decide whether this course of action is right for you, while Chapter 10 has suggestions for looking for paid jobs.

More than any other group, older people are the social glue of most communities. They are often the linchpins of local clubs and charities. Whether you can spare only the occasional day or can help on a regular basis, Chapter 11, *Voluntary work*, has an abundance of suggestions.

Your health is the subject of Chapter 12, which contains information and advice on how to keep well. Notwithstanding unexpected illness, good health as you grow older is to a large extent in your own hands, and a healthy lifestyle can make all the difference.

If you are caring for elderly parents, the range of organizations that can provide you with back-up is far more extensive than you might realize. These are listed in Chapter 14, *Caring for elderly parents*.

Pre-retirement courses

Whatever age you are due to retire, taking a pre-retirement course will help you plan well for the next stage in your life. Some employers or workplace pension schemes run in-house courses (often run by outside specialists, such as Age UK), but if your organization doesn't offer such help, or if you are self-employed, there are a number of independent organizations that can help, for example:

- **Civil Service College** (Directory, p 6) runs face-to-face courses in London for people who work in the public sector or civil service in the UK and abroad.

- **Experience Matters** (Directory, p 6) is aimed at people aged 50 and over. It offers one-to-one coaching either face-to-face or by phone, as well as workshops on topics ranging from relationships to managing elderly parents.
- **Prime Cymru** (The Prince's Initiative for Mature Enterprise) (Directory, p 45) is a charity dedicated to providing people in Wales over the age of 50 with support to find employment or set up their own business.

Help with the cost-of-living crisis

Although inflation has dropped back to more modest levels, we are all still living with prices that are now permanently around 20 per cent higher than they were three years ago. Not everyone has had similar increases in their pay and pensions, so your budget may be tight. Throughout the book, you will find ideas and tips that can help you protect your standard living in the face of higher prices. Here are some websites that you may find especially helpful:

- **Cooking on a Bootstrap** (Directory, p 31) This is the website of Jack Monroe who, as well as offering advice on shopping and cooking nutritiously for less, is an ardent campaigner against injustice and poverty. Check out Monroe's moving TED talk, also on the site.
- **Energy Saving Trust** (Directory, p 7). Comprehensive guidance on reducing your energy usage.
- **GOV.UK** (browse benefits) (Directory, p 2). Make sure you claim any state help to which you are entitled, including help with housing, heating and low income. There is more information in Chapter 2.
- **MoneySavingExpert,** Cost of living help guide (Directory, p 9). Wide range of down-to-earth suggestions from the site's journalists and users, including benefits, claiming extra government support, eating, heating and more.

New focus for the retired

There are many organizations and websites representing the interests of retired people. The over-50s are an increasingly large and important section of the population, so it is not surprising to find numerous local and national sources of advice and information on issues that affect their lives. Here are some useful websites:

- **Age UK** (Directory, p 3) is the largest charitable organization providing information, advice, products and services to people to improve later life.
- **GOV.UK** (throughout the Directory) is the UK government's website for all issues relating to the government, including State Pensions and tax.
- **Midlife MOT** (Directory, p 32) is a government site with resources aimed at those in their 40s to 60s to support planning for retirement.
- **National Pensioners Convention** (Directory, p 33) is the campaigning voice for UK pensioners – for dignity, financial security and fulfilment for all older people.
- **Pension Wise** (Directory, p 9) is a government site focusing on your private (non-state) pension options as you approach retirement.
- **Retirement Expert** (Directory, p 6) offers expert advice and information on all issues related to retirement.

Financial advice

There are many aspects of retirement, such as planning how much income you'll need, pension choices, and investment decisions, where you may want the help of a professional financial adviser. There are a number of organizations that supply directories you can use to find an adviser near you (which can be found in the Directory, p 8), such as:

- **Chartered Institute for Securities and Investment (Wayfinder)**
- **MoneyHelper**
- **Personal Finance Society (PFS) (Find An Adviser)**
- **Personal Investment Management and Financial Advice Association (PIMFA)**
- **Society of Later Life Advisers (SOLLA)**
- **Unbiased**
- **VouchedFor**

Check that any adviser is genuine and properly regulated by checking a firm's entry on the Financial Services Register before doing business (Directory, p 9).

Dealing with a regulated firm ensures that you have access to a proper complaints procedure and compensation scheme if things go wrong. Regulated firms must also hold relevant qualifications and abide by rules that aim to ensure they meet a good standard of business conduct. Since July 2023, these rules have included a 'Consumer Duty'. This is an overarching principle that requires all regulated firms, including financial advisers, to act to deliver good outcomes for you as the consumer. This includes, for example, ensuring that you get suitable products and services that offer you fair value for money and appropriate customer support. Under the Duty, firms must act in good faith, avoid causing you foreseeable harm, and enable and support you in pursuing your financial objectives.

Reporting scams

Pensions and investments are fertile areas for scams and fraud (see Chapter 5) and fraudsters also use multiple ways to persuade you to divulge information that can be used to empty your bank account or use your credit card for a spending spree. It is already illegal for UK firms to cold call you about pensions and, in 2023, the government consulted on extending this 'cold calling' ban to most other financial products. However, in mid-2024, it was still unclear when this ban would be brought into effect. Once the ban takes effect, you will know that any call, text, mail or visit that you get out of the blue trying to sell you a financial product must be a scam. In the meantime, if you are approached out of the blue by anyone claiming they can give you investment or pension advice and/or offering you deals that sound too good to be true, do not do business.

Also be alert to common tactics used by fraudsters, such as texts saying you owe money on undelivered mail or to the tax authority, you are owed a tax refund, or you need to hand over personal or banking details to get help paying energy bills. Do not reply to such emails and never click on any links.

Another disturbing ploy is where you receive a text purportedly from a family member saying they're using a friend's phone as they've lost theirs and need you to send money urgently. Worryingly, the increasingly wide availability of artificial intelligence (AI) means you might even be targeted with fake voicemails and videos. Don't be fooled. If in doubt, check by contacting your relative on their usual number or by another trusted means.

Report the scam to Action Fraud: 0300 123 2040 (Directory, p 8). Over the three years to the end of 2025, the government is phasing in a raft of changes to tackle fraud and online crimes. These will include replacing Action Fraud (date unknown) with a new easier-to-use reporting service, better support if you are a victim of fraud and an increased chance of getting back any money you've lost.

Don't feel ashamed if you've been taken in by a scam – remember that fraudsters are experts at manipulating our emotions and behaviours. They deliberately create a sense of urgency and panic which makes it very hard to think rationally at the time.

You can also help the authorities keep track of scams by forwarding suspicious emails to report@phishing.gov.uk. Forward suspicious texts to 7726 (easy to remember because it spells SPAM on your keypad).

Additional resources

Throughout this guide, you will find many signposts to places where you can get relevant and helpful additional support and information. These signposts take the form of pointers to the relevant page in the directory of resources, which you can download from www.koganpage.com/GRG2025.

CHAPTER TWO

Money and budgeting

While retirement may be when you cease work, you should not allow your money to retire as well. It is important that it continues to work hard for you, so that you've got the financial security and flexibility you need. There are many money-related decisions to be made when you retire: get them right, and your income could increase year by year; fail to plan, and you might be faced with making personal cutbacks at a time when you should be relaxing and enjoying yourself.

Having a plan

With people living longer, secure pensions from salary-related pension schemes fading fast and new pension freedoms that reduced the use of annuities for a time, more pensioners are directly exposed to the three great risks of retirement: longevity risk (outliving your savings), inflation risk (the buying power of your money falling over time) and investment risk (being exposed to the ups and downs of the stock market). Inflation risk especially has recently been on all our minds. Chapters 3 and 5 look at the pension and investment choices you can make to help to ensure the income you have coming in is guarded against these risks. This chapter focuses on working out how much income you will need in retirement and checking whether you are on track to achieve that goal. Throughout, you will be guided to take inflation into account.

Inflation means a sustained rise in prices. It can happen, as we are all too aware, because of a sudden rise in the global price of energy or other key commodities. But, even in more normal times, the relentless upward drift of prices over time also means your money buys less today than it did in the past. Even low rates of inflation have a big impact on prices over a long period: for example, if inflation averaged 2 per cent a year (the official target for the UK), £100 after 25 years would buy only the same as £61 today, meaning you'd have to cut your spending by over a third. So you should always factor inflation into longer-term financial planning.

When inflation is high, it becomes all the more important to check that you are getting all the income and government help you're entitled to and to look at adjustments to save on spending. This chapter will help you do that.

There are many ideas on what makes a good financial plan, but the core elements are the same. In order of priority, a typical person should normally aim to:

1 Sort out any problem debts.
2 Stay in your workplace pension scheme. (Since your employer must contribute on your behalf, opting out is like turning down part of your pay!) If you are not an employee, save through your own pension plan.
3 Get term life assurance if anyone is financially dependent on you.
4 Build up at least three months' worth of outgoings in accessible savings, such as a cash Individual Savings Account (ISA), to cover emergencies.
5 Buy a home if you are ready to settle somewhere.
6 Save and invest to achieve other goals.

Everyone's circumstances and resources are different, so you may have a slightly different plan and, if you're already retired, maintaining an inflation-resilient income from your pensions will often be a high priority. How much that retirement income should be is personal to you, depending on the lifestyle you want. But, as a rough guide, the Pensions and Lifetime Savings Association (Directory, p 33) suggests a single person needs between £14,400 and £43,100 a year and a couple between £22,400 and £59,000 (assuming you own your home outright).

Unaffordable debts undermine your financial security and make it impossible to achieve your goals. If you have problem debts, you should urgently consult one of the free, independent money advice agencies, such as Citizens Advice (Directory, p 3), National Debtline (Directory, p 3) or StepChange (Directory, p 3). These impartial, non-judgemental organizations can efficiently help you deal with your creditors, without stigma, and identify any additional sources of income you may be eligible for. Debt problems get worse if you ignore them, so be honest with yourself that there is a problem. Warning signs include borrowing to buy day-to-day essentials, taking out new loans to pay off old ones and being afraid to open your post.

With debt sorted, you are ready to put your money to work for a good retirement.

Doing the sums – budgeting

A budget is a record of all your income and spending. It can be used in two ways:

- **To understand your current finances.** Knowing how much you spend, and on what, is essential. While you have records of formal bills, it's very easy to overlook casual and ad hoc purchases. A tip some people recommend is keeping track of your expenditure by means of a 'spending diary'. Whether you use a notebook, a spreadsheet or an app on your phone, the result is the same. Put down everything you spend over a period of, say, one month, so you can see what you are spending on and how much; it's then quite easy to see if these are essentials and/or whether they are costing too much. Keeping a spending diary on a more permanent basis can be an aid to controlling your spending. In the same way that a food diary can help you stick to a healthy diet, the act of writing down what you spend each day can make you think twice about buying non-essentials.
- **To plan your future finances.** Armed with your current budget, you can project how your income and spending may change in retirement, or as retirement progresses.

The next section will take you through the exercise of drawing up a budget. You can use this to assess your current finances and to plan for the future.

Creating a budget

The first step is to create a cash flow statement using Tables 2.1 and 2.2. In column 2 of each table, simply collate the relevant information about income and spending, noting how regularly each item occurs. For example, you might be paid monthly but spend on food every week, and a holiday just once a year, while you might spread council tax payments over 10 months.

In column 3 of each table, you need to convert each item to a common time period, say monthly. The easiest way to do this is to work out what you'd spend over a year and divide by 12. For example, for weekly payments, multiply by 52 and divide by 12 (or multiply by 4.3).

Use column 4 to think about how your income might change in retirement. There are ideas in this chapter to help you do this.

There are a growing number of online and phone apps that will help you draw up a budget based on your current spending, and this can be automated to some degree if you allow the app to link directly to your bank account, credit card and any other financial accounts. If you prefer, there are online budget templates where you simply enter your own figures. For example, you could use the Budget Planner from **MoneyHelper** (Directory, p 9), as well as its Pension Calculator (Directory, p 9) for checking whether you might have a pension-income shortfall in retirement.

INCOME

Start by entering your income in Table 2.1. The documents that will help you do this include, for example, statements from your employer or pension provider and bank. Enter the 'before tax' amounts.

TABLE 2.1   Calculating your total net income

Income before tax	Current income	Current monthly budget	Future monthly budget
Example: work bonus	*£600 every six months*	*£100 (= 600 × 2÷12)*	*£0*
State Pension			

(continued)

TABLE 2.1 (Continued)

Income before tax	Current income	Current monthly budget	Future monthly budget
Occupational pension(s)			
Personal pension(s)			
State benefits			
Income from savings and investments			
Earnings from work or self-employment			
Other income (e.g. rental)			
TOTAL before tax			
Less: income and (if any) National Insurance			
TOTAL NET INCOME			
(Amount A)			

The biggest change when you retire is likely to be replacing all or part of your earnings with pensions. Chapter 3 explains how you can get statements that will help you estimate your future pension income. Take care to note whether those pensions will increase during retirement to help you cope with inflation. If not, in Table 2.2 consider extra regular saving.

If you carry on working in retirement, be aware that once you reach State Pension age, although you still pay income tax (if your income is high enough), National Insurance contributions stop – see Chapter 4.

SPENDING

Now complete Table 2.2 with the amounts you spend. The documents that may help include bank and credit card statements, till receipts and your spending diary if you've had a go at keeping one.

TABLE 2.2   Calculating your total spending

Spending	Current spending	Current monthly budget	Future monthly budget
Example: Council tax	*£140 a month for 10 months*	*£117 (= 140 × 10÷12)*	*£100*
Food			
Alcohol and tobacco			
Other weekly shop items			
Eating out, takeaways			
Rent or mortgage			
Service charge			
Council tax (or rates)			
Home insurance			
Electricity and gas			
Water			
Broadband, phone, TV			
Miscellaneous services (e.g. boiler contract)			
Furniture and appliances			
Garden costs			
Car costs			
Other transport			
Clothes			
Personal care (e.g. hairdresser)			
Health costs			
Pet costs			
Postage			

(continued)

TABLE 2.2   (Continued)

Spending	Current spending	Current monthly budget	Future monthly budget
Gifts and donations			
Holidays			
Subscriptions (e.g. clubs, gym, magazines)			
Hobbies, entertainment			
Loan repayments*			
Regular saving			
Other			
TOTAL SPENDING			
(Amount B)			

*Note: Take care not to count twice any items you pay for with your credit card or other borrowing. If you pay off your card balance in full every month, put £0 for credit cards (under Loan repayments) and record each item bought under the relevant headings. If you pay back a loan or card by making a minimum or regular payment each month, record that sum under Loan repayments but do not include the items purchased under the separate headings. However, if this means the amount you owe is increasing and out of control, see earlier for guidance on tackling problem debts.

Thinking ahead to post-retirement, you might save on work-related costs such as travel and lunches out. On the other hand, you might spend more on home heating and holidays. As retirement progresses, you might need to spend more on health. You might plan to move to a smaller home (with lower council tax and other bills) but, if you move to a retirement complex, you might start paying service charges for the first time. Chapter 6 has guidance on homes.

DOES YOUR BUDGET WORK?

In Table 2.3 insert Amount A from Table 2.1 and subtract Amount B from Table 2.2. If your current budget is negative, you are either running down savings or running up debts and need to take steps to get your finances back into balance. Similarly, if you have a future budget deficit, you need to think how you can boost your income or manage on less by cutting your spending.

TABLE 2.3   Your budget position

	Current monthly budget	Future monthly budget
Total net income (Amount A from Table 2.1)		
Less: Total spending (Amount B from Table 2.2)		
BUDGET SURPLUS/DEFICIT		

Possible ways to cut spending

There are two main ways to reduce spending: cut out non-essential items and switch to cheaper essential ones.

Revisit Table 2.2 and first identify those items that you could classify as non-essential. This will vary from one person to another, but likely candidates include, say, alcohol, tobacco, meals out, takeaways, entertainment, holidays and donations.

Some of the biggest savings on essential items are to be had by shopping around for cheaper substitutes. In normal times, this includes gas and electricity. But when energy prices surge as they did in 2022, beware of switching if you currently have a fixed-rate deal. If you do want to shop around, the energy regulator Ofgem (Directory, p 7) has a list of approved price comparison websites that can help you do this: use 'Search' to find the section called *Switch supplier or energy tariff*.

While we're on the subject of energy bills, you might be thinking about changing to a smart meter. In the past, the main use of a smart meter has been to show you which appliances and activities gobble the most energy, which can prompt you to cut your energy usage. However, as more people switch to smart meters, energy providers have an increasingly detailed knowledge of patterns of energy usage. This is enabling them to offer 'time-of-use tariffs'. The simplest form is a static tariff that offers cheaper energy during a set period each day (like the Economy 7 deals that have been around for decades). But nowadays dynamic tariffs are also on offer that offer lower charges for periods when energy use is predicted to be lower or the supply of renewables higher (for example, because wind or sun are forecast). A time-of-use tariff could save you money – and help you reduce your carbon footprint – if you can be flexible about when you run your washing machine, charge your electric vehicle, and so on.

Price comparison websites are also a good way of finding cheaper insurance. Try the following, which can be found in the Directory, p 32:

- **Compare the Market**
- **Confused.com**
- **GoCompare**
- **MoneySuperMarket**

Comparison websites do not necessarily cover the whole market and may feature companies that pay them commission more highly than others, so always check deals on at least two sites. Bear in mind, too, that some companies like DirectLine do not market themselves on comparison sites at all. Some smartphone apps do regular shopping around and switching for you.

Be aware that if you are claiming state benefits for people on a low income (such as Pension Credit or Universal Credit – see below), you might be eligible for special low prices for gas, electricity, water, phone and broadband – check with the provider. If you get Pension Credit and you're over 75, you can get a free TV licence – visit TV Licensing (Directory, p 26) or call 0300 790 6117.

If you buy postage stamps in bulk, note that you can still swap left-over old stamps for new barcoded ones through the Royal Mail Stamp Swap-Out Scheme (Directory, p 32).

While we are on the subject of new technology, it's worth thinking about *how* you pay for items. Paying with cash has been in decline for over a decade, although, according to the British Retail Consortium, there was a small reversal during the cost-of-living crisis as more households reverted to cash budgeting. Even so, cash now accounts for only 19 per cent of transactions, compared with 76 per cent for cards (especially debit cards). Over two-thirds of card transactions are now made by contactless payment, and there are new payment options such as Open Banking. The government has passed legislation to ensure everyone can carry on accessing cash in future. However, there is no requirement for shops and other sellers to continue accepting cash. Increasingly the places where you can use cash may dwindle.

Open Banking (available only with internet and mobile banking) is still a relatively new, secure way to pay direct from your bank account without using a debit card. It also allows trusted third parties, with your permission, to connect to your bank account to view your transactions. Trusted providers could, for example, be lenders who can assess from your transactions history whether you can afford a new loan or price comparison services that can use your current payments for energy or insurance to find you better deals (see Directory, p 32).

The cheapest and best loans and other deals may become unavailable unless you can search, apply and pay electronically. Therefore, you might want to look into using online or mobile banking, if you don't already. If you already use the internet, your bank's website is a good place to get information. If you lack confidence in your IT skills, many banks will offer help, or check if your local Age UK (Directory, p 6) runs training courses. Also, see Chapter 10 for widely available computer courses, many of which are free.

Possible ways of boosting your retirement income

There are basically four ways to give your retirement finances a boost: your home, work, investments and state benefits (and other state support).

Your home

Seven out of ten people aged 65 and over own their home outright, and a further 8 per cent are homeowners with a mortgage or shared ownership, according to the government's 2021 census. Your home is not just a place to live, it offers several different options for boosting your income: moving somewhere smaller, taking in lodgers or raising money on your home through equity release. All the possibilities are explored in Chapter 6, *Your home.*

Work

Your employer may allow you to switch to part-time working. This can be an attractive option if you like your job, because work is not just about earning money but can also be a source of intellectual stimulus, social contact, identity and self-esteem. By law, most jobs do not have a compulsory retirement age, but there is usually a normal pension age. However, you may be able to defer your work pension (and/or your State Pension) if continuing to work means you don't need it yet (see Chapter 3) and this can boost your pension when its does start (see Chapter 3) and help to keep down your tax bill while working (see Chapter 4).

Retirement for you may offer the chance of a job change or setting up on your own. When you do the figures, it is as well to err on the side of caution with regard to any additional income this will provide: there is a lot more information on work, and how to get it, in Chapters 9 and 10.

Investments

Investing is not just the preserve of the rich. Increasingly, people are reaching retirement with a sizeable pension pot and need to decide how best to use it to provide an income. There is a mind-boggling array of financial products, and if managing your own investments is something you haven't done before, it can be fascinating and rewarding for some but daunting for others. You will see in Chapter 5 the various forms invest-ment can take.

State benefits

You may be entitled to money or other benefits from the state.

There are two main types of benefits: contributory, where your entitle-ment is due to having paid National Insurance contributions; and non-contributory, where your entitlement depends either on low income and savings (means-tested benefits) or your circumstances regardless of income. Some state benefits are taxable and others tax-free – see Chapter 4.

If you are under State Pension age, claiming benefits is doubly important because it not only provides financial help now but also protects your even-tual State Pension (explained in Chapter 3).

The main contributory benefit is State Pension and you'll find details about this in Chapter 3. Paying National Insurance may also entitle your surviving wife, husband, civil partner or, if a parent, unmarried partner to bereavement benefits if you die – see Chapter 15.

The following sections give a brief outline of some of the other more common benefits which you might be able to claim. The benefit system is complex and you can get information and advice from these organizations (see Directory, pp 2–3), some of which include calculators to help you work out what you are entitled to, which are free to use and anonymous:

- **Age UK:** Benefit details and calculator
- **Citizens Advice:** Benefit details
- **entitledto:** benefits calculator

- **GOV.UK:** Benefit details and how to claim
- **Independent Age:** Information and a helpline for older people experiencing financial hardship.
- **Policy in Practice:** Benefits calculator which can be combined with budgeting tools
- **Turn2us:** Benefit details and calculator

ATTENDANCE ALLOWANCE

This is a non-contributory, non-means-tested allowance. You may be eligible if you are over State Pension age and have a physical or mental disability that means you need help from others. The aim is to help you cope with the extra costs this involves, but you decide how to use the cash.

There are two rates: £72.65 a week (in 2024/25) if you need help during the day or night and £108.55 if both apply or you are terminally ill. You apply online, by post using a detailed claim form that you can download from the GOV.UK website or order by calling 0800 731 0122.

In Scotland, an equivalent benefit called Pension Age Disability Payment (PADP) was piloted during 2024 and is due to be rolled out across the whole of Scotland from April 2025. In 2024, it was worth between £290 and £434, depending on the extent of disability. If you currently get Attendance Allowance, you will automatically be moved on to PADP.

If you are under State Pension age you may instead be eligible to claim Personal Independence Payment (PIP) or its Scottish equivalent (see below).

CARER'S ALLOWANCE

If you are caring for at least 35 hours a week for someone who gets Attendance Allowance, PIP or certain other disability-related benefits, you may be able to claim Carer's Allowance. This provides £81.90 a week (in 2024/25). However, the rules are quite complex:

- If the person has more than one carer, only one of you can claim.
- You're not eligible if you are getting State Pension, have after-tax earnings of more than £151 (after tax, National Insurance and some expenses) a week or are studying for 21 hours a week or more.
- If you go over the earnings limit, you lose the whole of your Carer's Allowance (it is not gradually tapered away). The government Department for Work and Pensions (DWP) should alert you if this is the case, but has been very slow in doing so. As a result, many carers have found that they owe large repayments. The government is investigating this scandal, but as yet it is unclear whether they will take action to help carers in this position.

- Getting Carer's Allowance can cause a reduction in other benefits you or the person being cared for gets, but can increase others such as Pension Credit (see below). Use one of the benefit calculators listed earlier in this section to check how other benefits may be affected.

Claim online on the GOV.UK website, download the form and post it to the address on the form, or contact the Carer's Allowance Unit on 0800 731 0297. If you live in Scotland, you may be eligible for Carer's Allowance Supplement – contact Social Security Scotland (Directory, p 5).

COUNCIL TAX REDUCTION OR SUPPORT

Council Tax Reduction (also called Council Tax Support) is a means-tested benefit to help people on a low income pay some or all of their council tax. The help is given as a reduction in your council tax bill. Each local council sets up its own scheme, so the amount of help you get varies not just with your income and savings, but also where you live. You can claim this even if you don't get other benefits. Contact your local council to make a claim – find details at GOV.UK (Directory, p 2).

Regardless of your income and savings, you might qualify for a reduction in council tax if you live alone or have a disability or an exemption for certain types of property – there are details in Chapter 6.

HELP WITH A MORTGAGE

If you are getting Pension Credit or Universal Credit and still have a mortgage, you may be able to get help paying some or all of your mortgage interest through a scheme called Support for Mortgage Interest (SMI). This help used to be given as an increase in your benefit payments. However, since 6 April 2018, that arrangement has been replaced. Now, if you opt for SMI, the help is treated as a loan which has eventually to be repaid to the government with interest, usually when you sell your home (though the loan can be transferred if you move).

If you are getting Pension Credit, SMI starts at the same time as your Pension Credit claim. In other cases, there is a nine-month waiting period. SMI covers interest only (not any capital repayments) and is limited to interest on a maximum of £100,000 of your loan if you are on Pension Credit, or £200,000 otherwise.

When you apply for Pension Credit or Universal Credit, you'll also be offered an SMI loan if you are eligible.

HELP WITH RENT

If you are on a low income and you are under State Pension age, a claim for Universal Credit will normally include help with your rent. If you are over State Pension age you may instead be able to get Housing Benefit. In Northern Ireland, whatever your age, Housing Benefit can help you pay your rent and also your rates bill.

If you rent from your local council or a housing association, Housing Benefit is based on the rent you pay. However, if you are deemed to be living in a home that is larger than you need, what you get is reduced: by 14 per cent if you have one spare bedroom and 25 per cent if two or more. Couples are assumed to share a room unless that's impossible because of disability.

If you rent privately, Housing Benefit is based on either what you actually pay or a Local Housing Allowance (LHA), whichever is the lower. The LHA that applies to you depends on the number of bedrooms you can claim for and the area in which you live. It is normally based on the 30 per cent of cheapest rents in an area and capped at a maximum amount, so it seldom covers your full rent.

Claim Housing Benefit in your Pension Credit claim or from your local council. Contact details are available from GOV.UK (Directory, p 18). Government data shows that one in five pensioners who are eligible for housing benefit are not claiming it, losing out on £1.3 billion.

JOBSEEKER'S ALLOWANCE

If you're under State Pension age, have been paying National Insurance and lose your job, you might qualify for Jobseeker's Allowance (JSA). For over-25s, the amount is £90.50 a week (in 2024/25) paid for up to six months. After that, you might qualify for Universal Credit (see below). Apply for JSA online on the GOV.UK website or contact Jobcentre Plus on 0800 055 6688.

PENSION CREDIT

This is the main means-tested benefit for people over State Pension age, but if you are in a couple and one of you is younger, for new claims since 16 May 2019 you instead have to claim Universal Credit (which is less generous). There are two parts to Pension Credit.

The Guarantee Credit tops up your income to a minimum level. In 2024/25, the standard amount is £218.15 a week for a single person and £332.95 for a couple, but you may get extra sums, for example if you have a disability, you are a carer or to help with some housing costs.

Only people who reached State Pension age before 6 April 2016 can now claim the Savings Credit. This is for people who have saved some money of their own for retirement. The maximum amount is £17.01 a week for a single person and £19.04 for a couple. You may qualify just for Savings Credit or for the Guarantee Credit as well.

Government data shows that 4 out of 10 people eligible for Pension Credit don't claim it, meaning that pensioners are losing out on £2.1 billion every year. Shockingly, these figures have been getting worse, not better. Even if the amount you can get is small, it's still important to claim, because Pension Credit acts as a gateway to other help, such as winter fuel payment (from 2024/25), utility company low tariffs for low-income households and the free TV licence for over-75s. Apply online on the GOV.UK website or contact the Pension Credit Claim Line (0800 99 1234).

PERSONAL INDEPENDENCE PAYMENT (PIP)

This is a non-contributory, non-means-tested benefit for adults under State Pension age who have a physical or mental disability and aims to help with the extra costs you incur as a result. The amount depends on the extent to which a person's daily living and/or mobility is affected and is determined after a medical assessment.

PIP has two components: a daily living component (£72.65 a week or £108.55 in 2024/25) and a mobility component (£28.70 a week or £75.75). A person can be entitled to either one or to both components.

In Scotland, PIP has been replaced with an equivalent benefit called Adult Disability Payment (ADP). The amounts are the same as for PIP but the assessment process is designed to be fairer.

UNIVERSAL CREDIT

This is the key means-tested benefit for people of working age whether in work or out of work. In 2024/25, the standard allowance is £393.45 a month for a single person aged 25 or over and £617.60 for a couple. However, there are lots of supplements you might qualify for, according to your dependants, disability, being a carer, housing costs and so on. You are normally expected to claim online on the GOV.UK website but, if you cannot, contact the Universal Credit Helpline on 0800 328 5644.

WINTER FUEL PAYMENT

This was previously paid to nearly all pensioner households, but from winter 2024/25 onwards it is a means-tested annual payment of £200 or £300, for households getting Pension Credit. It's normally given automatically if you are eligible; if not, call 0800 731 0160.

In Scotland, from winter 2025/26 onwards, Winter Fuel Payment will be replaced by the Pension Age Winter Heating Payment from the Scottish government, paid at the same rates, and with the same means-tested eligibility criteria.

If you are getting Pension Credit, you should also automatically get a Cold Weather Payment (Winter Heating Payment in Scotland) if there is a cold spell lasting more than a week. See GOV.UK (Directory, p 19).

Unclaimed or lost money

Make sure that you have not lost track of any money, for example in old bank and savings accounts or unclaimed lottery prizes. Gretel estimates that there are up to £78 billion of unclaimed assets in the UK.

Banks, building societies and National Savings & Investments and other financial providers normally try to track down account owners but where this is unsuccessful, long-unused accounts and investments are transferred to a government-backed Dormant Assets Scheme, where the money is used for good causes. However, if you discover that your money has been transferred to the scheme, you have the right to claim it back. You do this through My Lost Account (Directory, p 36).

The Dormant Assets Act 2022 extended the scheme to other types of assets, such as unused pension schemes, life insurance and other investments. Useful sites to help you trace these types of lost assets are:

- **Gretel** (Directory, p 36)
- **Investment Association Unclaimed Assets Portal** (Directory, p 36)
- **Pension Tracing Service** (Directory, p 33)

Be alert to scams. The websites mentioned above are free, independent services. Be wary of other sites that charge and may deliberately use confusingly similar names, and never respond to unsolicited emails, texts or phone calls claiming to be able to reunite you with missing money.

Spending and saving for later

While starting retirement may seem a time to be cautious about splashing out, there are some big outlays that may make sense and save you money later on. Conversely, you may want to set money aside in earlier retirement to help you cope with spending later on, particularly inflation and possible care costs.

Many people have the option to take a tax-free lump sum from a pension scheme as they start retirement (see Chapter 3), making this an ideal time to consider some big-ticket items like making home improvements, buying a car and paying off debts.

Home improvements

If you plan to remain in the same property, would making some changes or improvements be sensible now either to reduce your bills later on or make your home more age-friendly? These could include installing double glazing, insulating the loft, modernizing the kitchen, installing a downstairs shower room or converting part of the house to a granny flat. You might also decide now is a good time to switch to more environmentally friendly forms of heating – you can find out more about that in Chapter 6.

If you think you might move in the next few years, be aware that you might not recoup the cost of any improvements you've made. In a survey by NAEA Propertymark, estate agents reckoned those most likely to add value are a loft conversion to create an extra bedroom or a new kitchen.

Purchasing a car

There are a variety of reasons why you might be thinking about buying a car now. For example, while in work you may have had a company car, or you might want something smaller and more economical if you will no longer be commuting.

Company car owners should first check whether they are entitled to purchase their present car on favourable terms. A number of employers are quite happy to allow this.

A complication is whether to stick with traditional fuel or make the switch to an electric car. The government is committed to phasing out the sale of new petrol and diesel cars – the previous government said by 2035, but the new government plans to reinstate the original phase-out date of 2030. But, for now, electric and hybrid cars are costly to buy, although usually cheaper to run. However, a survey by Ford Motors found lack of charging points was putting off half of UK buyers and, because of that shortage, some local authorities have started fining people who stay too long at public charging points. So, you might decide it's worth hanging on to your existing car a bit longer until the electric market is better developed.

Electric vehicles are greener to run, but that is offset to some extent by the carbon emissions involved in making the cars. Studies suggest that taking all factors into account, after about 20,000 to 25,000 miles of driving, switching to an electric car is the greener option.

Paying off credit cards and loans

This is, generally speaking, a good idea, since delay is unlikely to save you money. However, one precaution is to check the small print of your agreement for any charge on early repayment, which is common with fixed-term personal loans. Similarly, if you have a mortgage, particularly one with a fixed or discounted interest rate, there may be a charge for paying off the mortgage before the period of the special deal has finished. So you may want to hold off paying it off for a while. After that, there is normally just a 'sealing fee' (also called a 'deeds fee') to cover the lender's legal costs involved in the mortgage coming to an end. At this point, you'll receive any deeds to your property that your lender had in its keeping. If your ownership of the property is recorded in the Land Registry, you might think the deeds are unimportant. However, they often contain additional information that is not held by the Land Registry, such as covenants about how the property may be used, who is responsible for boundaries and so on. So keep your deeds in a safe place.

Inflation

Some of your retirement income may increase each year in line with inflation – for example, your State Pension and some company pension schemes (Chapter 3 has details). However, if you will be relying for at least part of your income on sources that are not inflation-proofed, you need to decide how you will maintain your standard of living over the years as prices rise.

One option is to carry on saving during the early years of retirement so that you can gradually draw on this pot of money later on. Chapter 5 has suggestions on where to save and invest.

Care

Increasingly, people are fit and well when they reach retirement and with luck that will continue for a long time. However, the reality is that the chance of developing health conditions does increase with age.

A government report estimated that around 1 in 10 people now aged 65 will face future long-term care costs of more than £100,000. On the ther hand, a quarter of this age group will end up spending little or nothing on care. It is a total lottery and you have no real way of knowing if you will be one of the lucky ones. Legislation to protect people from catastrophic care costs was passed but has now been abandoned, so you could end up paying a lot. Therefore, it makes sense to plan ahead for how you might meet care costs later on if the worst does happen. Your plan might be to set aside some savings now, or perhaps be prepared to sell your home or use equity release to fund care if the need does arise. There is more information in Chapters 6 and 14.

Money if you are made redundant

We live in uncertain times and many people fear being made redundant. Much of the information in the earlier part of this chapter is equally valid whether you become redundant or retire in the normal way. However, there are several key points with regard to redundancy that it could be to your advantage to check.

From your employment

YOU MAY BE ENTITLED TO STATUTORY REDUNDANCY PAY

Your employer is obliged to pay the legal minimum, which is calculated on your age, length of service and weekly pay. To qualify, you will need to have worked for the organization for at least two years, with no age restriction. Redundancy pay is 1.5 weeks' pay for each year worked if you are 41 or older, based on pay up to a maximum of £700 a week (£729 in Northern Ireland) in 2024/25 and a maximum of 20 years. There is a calculator on GOV.UK to help you work out your entitlement: Calculate your statutory redundancy pay (Directory, p 46).

EX GRATIA PAYMENTS

Many employers are prepared to be more generous and will pay you more than just the statutory amount. As long as it's not more than £30,000, redundancy pay is not taxable. Any payment over this limit is subject to income tax. Redundancy pay means genuine compensation for loss of your job. It does not include, for example, pay in lieu of notice or holiday pay, which will be taxed just like any other earnings (see Chapter 4).

BENEFITS THAT ARE NOT PART OF YOUR PAY

Redundancy may mean the loss of several valuable benefits such as a company car, life assurance and health insurance. Your employer might agree to include your company car as part of your redundancy pay. Some insurance companies allow preferential rates to individuals who were previously insured with them under a company scheme.

HOLIDAY ENTITLEMENT

You could be owed holiday entitlement, for which you should be paid.

WORKPLACE PENSION

There are different types of workplace pension. If yours is a personal pension (see Chapter 3), it will continue even though you leave your employer, though any contributions your employer was paying into it on your behalf will stop and your own contributions can of course no longer be deducted direct from your pay packet. Contact your pension provider if you want to arrange another way to pay into it.

If you belong to a company pension, you will cease to be an active member when you leave, but will usually have what is called a 'deferred pension' that you will be able to claim when you reach retirement. However, if you are already close to retiring, your employer might offer an early or enhanced pension to encourage employees to opt for voluntary redundancy. Check the redundancy terms being offered with your firm's human resources department.

Your mortgage

If you have a mortgage and are worried about keeping up the repayments, you should contact your mortgage lender as soon as possible. It may agree to a more flexible repayment system and, if you do fall into arrears, must explore ways to help you pay – this is called the Pre-Action Protocol for Possession Claims based on Mortgage or Home Purchase Plan Arrears in Respect of Residential Property (Directory, p 17). Repossession of your home must be treated by your lender as the last resort.

Check whether your mortgage package includes insurance against redundancy. Called Mortgage Payment Protection Insurance (MPPI), this will typically cover your mortgage interest (but not capital) payments for a maximum of one, occasionally two, years. You might be eligible for a state loan to help with your mortgage interest payments – see *Help with a mortgage* earlier in this chapter.

Other creditors/debts

Any creditors that you may have difficulty in paying (electricity, gas, a bank overdraft) should be informed as early as possible in the hope of agreeing easier payment terms. There could be an argument for paying off credit card bills immediately, even if this means using some of your redundancy pay (since the interest on the card is likely to be higher than the return you could get by putting the redundancy pay into a savings account or investments).

'Signing on'

Even if you are hoping to get another job very soon, you should register as unemployed with Jobcentre Plus without delay. This will ensure that you get National Insurance credits (see Chapter 3). This is important to protect your State Pension. You may also be eligible to claim Jobseeker's Allowance (see earlier in this chapter).

Further information about redundancy

MoneyHelper publishes a useful online guide to all aspects of redundancy online and as a printed guide which you can download or order (Directory, p 46). Another useful agency is Citizens Advice (Directory, p 2).

More money information

If you enjoy browsing the internet and this chapter has whetted your appetite for research on the matter of retirement planning, the following websites cover a broad range of topics relating to your finances and retirement:

- **Citizens Advice** (Directory, p 2)
- **Financing Retirement** (Directory, p 9)
- **Low Incomes Tax Reform Group** (Directory, p 37)
- **MoneyHelper** (Directory, p 31)
- **MoneyWeek** (Directory, p 32)
- **This is MONEY** (Directory, p 32)
- **Which?** (Directory, p 32)

CHAPTER THREE

Pensions

You may be enrolled in, have access to or wish to consider a variety of pension schemes. Some important features to check include what any employer might pay in on your behalf and how the eventual pension may be protected against inflation.

The State Pension

First, let's consider the State Pension, which is by and large fully protected against inflation. The earliest you can claim it is at State Pension age. You do not have to stop work to claim your State Pension.

These days, women and men have had the same State Pension age, which has been increasing. If you were born between 6 September 1954 and 5 April 1960, your State Pension age is 66. After that, there is a further gradual rise to age 67 and, for people born after 5 April 1978, age 68 (though this may be brought forward). Any further rises are meant to depend on whether life expectancy increases. You can check your State Pension age and date online at GOV.UK (Directory, p 33).

Many workplace pension schemes align their normal pension age with State Pension age. Pension age is not the same as retirement age. Since October 2011 the default retirement age (which used to be 65) has been scrapped. Employers are no longer allowed to dismiss staff because of age.

Because some people retire and start drawing a workplace pension early, they can mistakenly assume it is possible to get an early State Pension. This is not correct – State Pension is never payable before State Pension age. However, if you're retiring early because of, say, ill health or the need to care for someone, you might be eligible to claim other state benefits (see Chapter 2).

Getting your State Pension

Your State Pension is not paid automatically; you need to claim it. You'll usually get a letter two months before your State Pension birthday inviting you to make a claim and telling you how to do this. If you don't receive a letter, you can still claim online at GOV.UK (Directory, p 33), or by post or phone by contacting the Pension Service: 0800 731 7898.

All State Pensions are taxable, even though they are paid without any tax deducted. This cannot be stressed enough – because of high inflation over the last few years and the government's freezing of the income limit below which you pay no tax, you may find that you now need to pay tax on your State Pension, even though you did not have to in the past. Chapter 4 explains how tax is collected on State Pensions if your income is high enough for you to pay tax.

State pensioners also get a £10 bonus paid shortly before Christmas, and this is tax-free. (The bonus was introduced and set at £10 back in 1972, when it could have bought a hearty family meal. To keep pace with inflation it would have needed to increase to £114 today.)

State Pensions are increased in April each year – but if you retire abroad see Chapter 7.

When you reach State Pension age, you decide whether or not to start drawing the State Pension. Retirement does not have to start on any particular date or on a single day. Many people prefer to stop working gradually by reducing hours or shifting to part-time work, so you might not need all your pensions straight away. By deferring your State Pension, you can have a bigger pension when it does start or, if you are covered by the old state scheme rules (see below), alternatively a lump sum.

Pensions are usually paid every four weeks direct into a bank account. This can be a bank or building society account or credit union account. Individuals who genuinely cannot use a bank account can ask the Pension Service to pay them by cheque, which can be cashed, for example, at the Post Office.

Your right to a State Pension

You build up your right to claim a State Pension by paying, or being credited with, National Insurance contributions (NICs). Each year that counts is called a 'qualifying year'. How many qualifying years you need during your working life (defined as the years from age 16 up to State Pension age) depends on when you reached or will reach State Pension age.

If you reached State Pension age before 6 April 2016, you are in the old State Pension scheme. There were two types of State Pension – basic and additional. From 6 April 2010, the number of qualifying years needed to get a full basic State Pension was reduced to 30 years for women and men (before this it was normally 39 and 44 years respectively). If you reach(ed) State Pension age on or after 6 April 2016, you are in the new single-tier State Pension system, and need 35 years to get the full amount and at least 10 qualifying years to get any State Pension at all. You can check your National Insurance record at GOV.UK (Directory, p 33).

Anyone trying to decide whether they can afford to retire should get a forecast of their State Pension from the Pension Service (Directory, p 33). It is worth getting an early estimate of what your pension will be, as there may be steps you can take to improve your NICs record as described below.

You stop paying National Insurance once you reach State Pension age.

PAYING NATIONAL INSURANCE CONTRIBUTIONS

If you are an employee, your employer will have automatically deducted Class 1 NICs from your salary, provided your earnings were above the 'primary threshold' (in 2024/25, this is £242 a week). Your employer hands these contributions to the government, which keeps a record of your qualifying years.

Self-employed people have in the past paid flat-rate Class 2 NICs to build up the State Pension. But, from 2024/25 onwards, these have been largely abolished and, although you pay nothing, you are treated as if you have paid NICs towards your State pension provided your profits from self-employment are at least £6,725 (the small profits threshold). If your profits are lower, you can still voluntarily pay Class 2 contributions at a flat rate of £3.45 in 2024/25. As a self-employed person, you may also be paying Class 4 NICs. These are purely a tax on your profits (between limits) and do not count towards the State Pension at all.

If you have gaps in your NICs record – for example, because you have been studying at university or taken some time out to travel – you can go back up to six years to fill the gaps by paying Class 3 voluntary

TABLE 3.1 Who can pay voluntary Class 3 contributions?

Who is eligible?	Time limit for paying them
Anyone	Six years after the year with the gap
A man born after 5 April 1951, or a woman born after 5 April 1953	Until 5 April 2025 to make up gaps between April 2006 and April 2016

contributions. Exceptionally, some people can fill gaps from longer ago – see Table 3.1. In 2024/25, Class 3 NICs cost £17.45 a week.

It will only be worth paying voluntary Class 2 or Class 3 NICs if you don't already have enough qualifying years for a full State Pension. You can check whether it is worth your while paying them by contacting the government's Future Pensions Centre (Directory, p 32).

LIVED OR WORKED OUTSIDE GREAT BRITAIN?

If you have lived in Northern Ireland or the Isle of Man, any contributions paid there will count towards your pension. The same should also apply in most cases if you have lived or worked in an EU country (and this continues to be the case post-Brexit), or any country whose social security is linked to Britain's by a reciprocal arrangement, in which case, parts of your pension may be paid from different sources. You can check your position by contacting the government's International Pension Centre (Directory, p 32).

CARING FOR CHILDREN OR ADULTS

If you were a carer for a child or a disabled person throughout any tax year after 1978 up until 5 April 2010, you may have got Home Responsibilities Protection. HRP reduced the number of qualifying years you needed for a full basic State Pension. HRP was awarded automatically if you got Child Benefit for a child under 16, but if you were caring for a disabled person or you were a foster carer, you usually had to complete an application form.

From 6 April 2010, HRP was replaced with weekly credits for parents and carers, called Carer's Credit. You can receive these credits for any weeks you are getting Child Benefit for a child under 12, you are an approved foster carer or you are caring for one or more sick or disabled people for at least 20 hours a week.

If you reach State Pension age on or after 6 April 2010, any years of HRP you have been awarded before April 2010 will have been converted to qualifying years of credits, up to a maximum of 22 years. However, it has come to light that, for some people (mainly women), HRP years are missing from their record, resulting in underpaid State Pension. Since autumn 2023, the government has started systematically reviewing cases to correct the position. They have said you should not contact them, but they will be in touch with you if it looks as if you are affected. There is a calculator on the GOV. UK site where you can check your past eligibility for HRP (see Directory, p 32 for more information).

Carer's Credits are awarded automatically if you are claiming Child Benefit, even if this is a 'nil claim'. You may want to make a nil claim because of the interaction between Child Benefit and the income tax system. Since April 2013, if you are getting Child Benefit and you or your partner (if you have one) have taxable income at or above a set limit (£60,000 in 2024/25), the higher earner has to pay extra income tax called a High Income Child Benefit Tax Charge. The effect is to claw back some or all of the Child Benefit. If you or your partner are caught by this tax charge, you'll have to declare it by completing a tax return each year. That can be inconvenient and you may have decided it's simpler just to stop getting the Child Benefit. In that case, though, you should still register for Child Benefit, but on the form put 'no' at the question that asks if you want to be paid the benefit. That way, you will still get Carer's Credits towards your State Pension.

Since 2011, the Carer's Credit that goes with Child Benefit can be transferred to someone else if they are caring for the child or children. For example, if you are a grandparent looking after your son's or daughter's children, you could apply to have their Carer's Credit transferred to you to help you build up your State Pension. Complete the application form for Specified Adult Childcare Credit at GOV.UK (Directory, p 33).

OTHER SITUATIONS WHEN YOU MAY GET CREDITS

If you have been in any of the following situations you will have been credited with contributions (instead of having to pay them):

- You were sick or unemployed (provided you sent in sick notes to your social security office, signed on at the unemployment benefit office or were in receipt of Jobseeker's Allowance).
- You were a man over the women's State Pension age, but under 65 and not working, during the period when women's State Pension age was lower than men's.
- You were entitled to maternity allowance, invalid care allowance or unemployability supplement.
- You were taking an approved course of training.

- You had left education but had not yet started working.
- (post-April 2000) Your earnings were between what is known as the lower earnings limit and the primary threshold. These usually change each year, and in 2024/25 are £123 and £242 a week, respectively.

MARRIED WOMEN AND WIDOWS

Under the old State Pension system, married women and widows who do not qualify for a basic pension in their own right or have built up a relatively low State Pension may be entitled to a basic pension based on their husband's NICs record, at about 60 per cent of the level to which he is entitled. In 2020, it came to light that up to 200,000 women who reached State Pension age before April 2016 may not have received this pension and other state pension elements to which they are entitled, worth an estimated £2.7 billion. The government is now reviewing these cases, and, if you think you might be affected, contact the Pension Service.

A dwindling number of women retiring today may have paid the married women's reduced-rate NICs (sometimes called the 'small stamp'). If this applies to you and you and/or your husband reach State Pension age on or after 6 April 2016, special rules mean you may still be able to claim a pension based on your husband's NICs record. Contact the Pension Service for more information.

State pensions and inflation

All state pensions are increased once a year, in April:

- The old basic pension and the new single-tier pension are currently covered by the 'triple lock', which means they increase each year in line with the higher of price inflation, earnings inflation, or 2.5 per cent. In its manifesto, the new government said it will retain the triple lock.
- The old additional pension is increased in line with price inflation.

Price inflation is measured as the annual change in the Consumer Price Index (CPI) up to the previous September and earnings inflation is the annual increase in average earnings over the previous May to July. The time lag between measuring the increases and paying the State Pension amounts isn't a problem when inflation is stable. But when inflation is rising, it takes a while for your pension to catch up with the cost-of-living increase you're experiencing.

Setting the time lag aside, what's important about state pensions is that – unlike most other pensions – they keep pace with, or even exceed, price inflation, however high prices rise.

How much is the old State Pension?

If you reached your State Pension age before 6 April 2016, your State Pension is paid under the old rules described in this section. Your pension may have two parts: a basic pension that most people get, and an additional pension mainly built up during periods when you worked as an employee. There is also a non-contributory, non-means-tested State Pension of £101.55 a week (2024/25) that you can claim from age 80 if your existing State Pension is less than that (or zero).

Basic State Pension

The full basic State Pension for a man or woman (2024/25) is £169.50 a week, and £271.05 for a married couple. These are the maximum amounts available. If you do not have enough qualifying years for the full basic State Pension, you will be entitled to a lower amount. The number of qualifying years you need for a full basic State Pension depends on when you reached State Pension age: if on or after 6 April 2010, you require 30 qualifying years to get a full basic State Pension and just one year to qualify for any pension. Each qualifying year of paid or credited contributions is therefore worth 1/30th of the full basic State Pension, up to a maximum of 30/30ths.

At present, the basic pension is increased annually, normally by the highest of price inflation, earnings or 2.5 per cent (called the 'triple lock').

Additional State Pension

If you spent some or all of your working years as an employee, you may have been building up an additional State Pension. (This was formerly known as SERPS – the State Earnings Related Pensions Scheme – but was replaced by the State Second Pension in April 2002.) The amount of additional pension you get depends on your earnings, your NICs record and whether you were 'contracted out' of the additional pension. Contracting out means that you were covered by a pension scheme at work, or a personal pension that you arranged yourself, which was designed to provide a pension that would replace your additional State Pension. In return, you either paid a lower rate of NICs or part of the NICs you had paid were given back by paying them into your pension scheme. It's common for people to have been contracted out for just part of their working life. So, at retirement, you may still get some additional pension, as well as the replacement pensions from the workplace and personal schemes.

In theory, the additional pension can be a substantial amount – £218.39 a week (2024/25) on top of the basic pension. In practice, because higher earners tend to have contracted out, the average amount is much lower, at around £20 to £30 a week.

There were other ways of building up some State Second Pension: for example if you earned below a certain amount set by the government, if you could not work through long-term illness or disability, or if you were a carer. You could not build up any additional pension during periods when you were self-employed.

The additional pension is increased each year in line with price inflation. (The 'triple lock' does not apply to this part of your pension.)

How much is the new State Pension?

If you reach your State Pension age on or after 6 April 2016, your State Pension is paid under the new rules described in this section. So this section applies to you if you are a woman born on or after 6 April 1953 or a man born on or after 6 April 1951. Eventually, everyone will get just this new State Pension. However, there are rules to protect your rights to the amount of pension you may already have built up under the old state scheme, so for a long time many people will get a transitional amount of State Pension that is higher than the full-rate new pension.

New State Pension

The full-rate new pension for a man or woman (2024/25) is £221.20 a week. Each person builds up their own entitlement, so – unlike the old state system – there is no rate for couples. This is the maximum available. If you do not have enough qualifying years for the full new pension, you will be entitled to a lower amount based on the number of qualifying years in your NICs record.

The number of qualifying years you need for a full new State Pension is 35, though you need 10 years to qualify for any pension. Once the new system is fully operational, provided the 10-year threshold is met, each qualifying year of paid or credited contributions is worth 1/35th of the full new State Pension up to a maximum of 35/35ths. (However, the calculation is a little different if you had also built up pension rights under the old state system – see below.)

The new pension up to the full rate is increased annually, currently by the highest of price inflation, earnings or 2.5 per cent (sometimes called the 'triple lock').

The full-rate new pension is higher than the old basic-rate State Pension. However, under the new system, there is no additional pension.

Protecting your old State Pension rights

Most people now covered by the new State Pension will have built up some pension under the old state scheme. To ensure they did not lose out under the switch to the new system, there are transitional rules. Broadly, they work as follows. On 6 April 2016, two calculations were made: first, the pension you had built up so far under the old system was worked out using the old system rules, and second, your qualifying years so far were used to calculate what your pension would have been if the new system had applied all along. In both cases, the calculation includes a deduction if you had been contracted out of the additional State Pension under the old system. You were then credited with the higher of the two amounts, and this is called your 'starting amount'.

If your starting amount on 6 April 2016 was higher than the full rate of the single-tier pension, your State Pension will be this higher amount. This amount is increased both up to the time you reach State Pension age and then once it starts to be paid. To do this, your starting amount is divided into two parts: the full-rate new pension, which currently increases each year in line with the triple lock, and the excess, which is your 'protected payment' and increases each year in line with price inflation. You cannot build up any more State Pension because you are already over the maximum full rate.

If your starting amount on 6 April 2016 is less than the full rate of the new pension, you can continue to build up more new State Pension until you reach the full rate. The whole of your pension increases each year by the triple lock.

REAL-WORLD EXAMPLE

On 16 April 2016, under the old state system rules Roshni, then aged 58, had built up a combined state basic and additional pension of £166.22 a week. On that date, based on her NICs to date but the new state system rules, she would already have been entitled to the full-rate new pension, which was then £155.65. This means her starting amount was £166.22 and, since it was higher than the full new rate, she cannot build up any more State Pension. Since then, £155.65 of Roshni's State

Pension has been increasing each year in line with the triple lock, and the excess – her protected payment of £10.57 a week – in line with price inflation. With these increases, by 2024/25, her expected weekly State Pension stood at £235.38.

Deferring your State Pension

You do not have to start your State Pension as soon as you reach State Pension age. You can put off the start – or cancel it (but only once) – and earn extra once it is paid. This can be useful if you're carrying on working and so do not need your State Pension yet or would lose a lot of it in tax.

If you defer the new State Pension, it is increased by 1 per cent for each nine weeks you defer it, i.e. an increase of 5.8 per cent a year. Ignoring tax, you would need to survive just over 17 years to get back as much in extra pension as you give up during the delay until it starts. If you defer the old State Pension, the increase is bigger at 10.4 per cent a year and you'd only need to survive 9 and a half years to get back as much as you had deferred. With the old State Pension (but not the new one), you also had the option to receive a lump sum rather than extra pension.

You can continue deferring your pension for as long as you like. The extra money will be paid to you when you eventually decide to claim your pension. The resulting extra pension is increased each year in line with prices and is taxable in the usual way. More information on deferring your State Pension is available online (Directory, p 33).

Advice about State Pensions and benefits

Bear in mind that, in addition to State Pension, you might be eligible for some of the state benefits described in Chapter 2. Information about all types of State Pensions and benefits is available at GOV.UK.

Any time and as often as you like before reaching State Pension age, you can get a statement of how much your State Pension is likely to be based on your NICs record to date. See the Directory (p 33) or call 0800 731 0175.

The Pension Service – part of the Department for Work and Pensions (DWP), the government department responsible for State Pensions and many state benefits – handles claiming and payments, and will explain what the state will provide when you retire and can let you know what pension-related benefits you may be entitled to. Visit gov.uk/contact-pension-service or phone 0800 731 0469.

If you think a mistake has been made, you can ask DWP to reconsider the Pension Service decision and, if you are still not satisfied, you then have the right to appeal and have your claim looked at by an independent tribunal. This is a formal process and you may want the help of a trained representative from, say, Citizens Advice or another benefits advice agency.

Private pensions

'Private pensions' means any pension schemes you have apart from a State Pension. They may be schemes you join through your workplace, or schemes that you arrange for yourself.

How much you can save

Private pension schemes are one of the most tax-efficient ways to save, because you get tax relief on the money you pay in, your savings build up tax-free and you can take out a quarter of those savings tax-free (the rest counts as taxable income). In fact, the tax reliefs on pension schemes cost the government £53 billion a year. To contain that cost, there are limits on the amount that you can save through pension schemes. These work in several ways.

First, tax relief on contributions is given only on contributions up to a maximum of £3,600 a year or an amount equal to 100 per cent of your UK earnings for the year, whichever is higher. This tax relief is given in one of two ways: *at source* or through the *net pay* method. With the at-source method, you deduct tax relief at the basic rate (2024/25: 20 per cent) from your contribution before handing it over to your pension provider. The provider then claims the same amount from HM Revenue & Customs (HMRC) and adds it direct to your pension savings. For example, suppose you want to pay £3,600 into your pension scheme: 20 per cent of £3,600 is £720. You deduct this from the £3,600 and hand over just £2,880 to your pension provider. The provider claims £720 from HMRC and adds it to your savings. The upshot is that £3,600 in total has gone into your scheme at a cost to you of £2,880. Under the at-source method – used for many workplace schemes and all schemes you arrange for yourself – you get this tax relief even if you are a non-taxpayer. If your top rate of tax is higher than the basic rate, you can claim extra tax relief by filling in a tax return (see Chapter 4 for how to do this).

The net-pay method is used by some workplace schemes. Your employer subtracts your pension contributions from your pay before working out how much income tax to deduct from your pay packet. This method is convenient because it automatically gives you all the tax relief you are due, without the need to complete a tax return. But, tax-wise, this method has not been great if your earnings are too low to have to pay tax, because you didn't get any tax relief at all, unlike the at-source method. However, since 2024/25, if you're a non-taxpayer, your net pay contributions do attract tax relief, which will be paid direct to your bank account. If this applies to you, you will be contacted after the end of the tax year with information on how to claim the relief. Bear in mind that, even without tax relief, you do still benefit from contributions paid in for you by your employer.

The second way that the government limits the amount you save through pension schemes is to set an Annual Allowance, which is the maximum amount by which your savings can increase each year. You can ask each pension scheme you have to tell you how much of your Annual Allowance it has used. In 2024/25, the standard Annual Allowance is £60,000. If you want to make a bigger increase to your savings, you can carry forward any unused allowance from the previous three years. But the standard allowance is reduced in some circumstances to £10,000 in 2025/26. This applies if you draw your savings before retirement or flexibly once you have retired or you are a high earner (broadly speaking earning £260,000 or more including pension contributions from your employer). This reduction applies only to the type of pensions where you build up your own savings pot (see *Defined-contributions schemes* below). If your savings increase by more than your Annual Allowance, you have to pay a tax charge that, in effect, claws back the tax relief you've had on the 'excess' savings.

The government also used to limit the amount you can save through pension schemes over your whole lifetime by setting a Lifetime Allowance. However, this allowance (which stood at £1,073,100 in 2022/23) was in effect abolished from 6 April 2023 onwards. This means you can save however much you like and whatever you draw as pension is simply taxed up to your marginal rate in the normal way that applies to any income (see Chapter 4). There is still a limit on the amount you can take out of your pensions as a tax-free lump sum and this is set at a total of £268,275 in 2024/25. If you want to take a bigger lump sum, the 'excess' is taxed as income in the normal way. Before the Lifetime

Allowance was abolished, you had to pay subtantial extra tax if you went over the limit, in effect capping the amount you could save through pension schemes. There has been speculation that the new government will reinstate the Lifetime Allowance.

The standard Annual Allowance (and the old Lifetime Allowance) is high compared with the amount most people can afford to save for retirement, so you might not need to worry about them. However, it's important to be aware that, if you do draw out some or all of your pension savings early, your Annual Allowance can fall sharply, making it harder to rebuild your savings – for more about this, see *Drawing your savings early* later in this chapter.

Workplace pension schemes

Under a system of automatic enrolment, nearly every employee will find themselves by default belonging to a pension scheme at work. Although you can opt out if you want to, it's usually a good idea to stay in the scheme as not only does your employer contribute, but you often get other benefits as well as a pension and tax-free lump sum when you retire. These could include life insurance, which pays a lump sum and/or a pension to your dependants if you die. It could also include a pension if you have to retire early because of ill health.

There are several different types of workplace scheme. You might find yourself in a company scheme set up by your employer, or in some type of group personal pension plan arranged by your employer but provided by another organization, usually an insurance company. You could be enrolled into a multi-employer scheme, which is like a company scheme but has members from many different firms, or you might be in NEST (the National Employment Savings Trust), a multi-employer scheme set up by government. The key difference when thinking about your retirement is whether the scheme promises you a certain level of pension (a defined-benefit scheme) or you are simply building up a personal pot of savings (a defined-contribution scheme). The new government has said that it will 'adopt reforms to workplace pensions'. This is set to include the way schemes invest (see Chapter 5) but might also look at widening access and other aspects.

DEFINED-BENEFIT SCHEMES

These are the Rolls-Royce of pension schemes because they promise a known proportion of your pay when you retire. They are always company schemes set up by your employer. Defined-benefit schemes used to be quite common, and are still the norm if you work in the public sector, but are becoming rare in the private sector.

How much you get is worked out from how many years you're in the scheme and your annual salary while working. You build up a pension at a certain rate – 1/60th or 1/80th is quite common – so for each year you've been a scheme member, you receive, say, 1/60th of your annual pay. For example, if you were in the scheme for 10 years and your salary was £30,000, you'd receive a £5,000 a year pension – that is, 10/60ths of £30,000.

How your salary is defined depends on the scheme rules. In the past, it typically meant your pay shortly before retiring (or at the time you left the scheme if earlier) and these are known as *final salary schemes*. These days it is more common for 'salary' to mean your average pay during all the years you've been a member of the scheme. Pay in the earlier years will have been lower because the cost of living was lower, so usually your pay from previous years is revalued in line with price inflation before the average is worked out. For this reason, such schemes are often called *career average revalued earnings (CARE) schemes*.

Once you start to draw a defined-benefit pension, typically it is increased in line with inflation but only up to a maximum amount, such as 3 or 5 per cent a year.

Defined-benefit schemes are costly for employers to run. A combination of people living longer, statutory improvements to benefits and increased regulation have made these schemes safer and more generous over time for employees, but have pushed up the costs and uncertainties for employers, to the point at which many have pulled back from this type of scheme. Typical changes are to switch from a final salary to a CARE basis, close the defined-benefit scheme to new members, stop existing members building up future defined-benefit pensions and offer some form of defined-contribution scheme to employees instead. These changes are not usually backdated, so when you reach retirement you may find you have a pension with several parts, for example a bit that's worked out on a final-salary basis, another bit on a CARE basis and some on a defined-contribution basis.

Another way that some employers have been trying to cut the costs of defined-benefit schemes is to buy out your pension rights. You may be offered an eye-watering sum that you can transfer into a defined-contribution scheme (and then perhaps cash it in – see below). However, just because an offer is big, that doesn't mean it's good value. For example, if you gave up a pension of £20,000 a year that would have increased with inflation up to a maximum of 5 per cent a year, in mid-2024 you would need around £406,000 to replace that income using an annuity. So, if the amount you're offered to give up the pension is less than £406,000, it's not a good deal.

DEFINED-CONTRIBUTION SCHEMES

All other workplace pension schemes are defined-contribution schemes. These can be company schemes set up by your employer, but are often some type of personal pension scheme – see *Pensions you arrange for yourself* later in this chapter – or multi-employer schemes, such as NEST. The money paid in by you and your employer is invested and builds up a fund that provides your income when you retire. Since April 2019, the minimum amount paid in must be 8 per cent of your salary between a lower and upper limit, with at least 3 per cent of that coming from your employer. You typically pay 4 per cent, and tax relief adds the final 1 per cent. With defined-contribution schemes, you don't know the amount of pension you'll get at retirement. This will depend on how much you and your employer pay into the fund, how well your invested contributions perform, the charges taken out of your fund by your pension provider, how much you take out as a tax-free lump sum at retirement (or cash in before then) and the terms on which you eventually convert your savings into pension (including your decisions about whether to inflation-proof your income – see Chapter 5 *Investment*).

It helps to think of defined-contribution pensions as having two stages:

1 *Accumulation.* The fund is invested, usually in stocks and shares and other investments, with the aim of growing it over the years before you retire. Most schemes offer a choice of investment funds, but have a default fund that you are invested in if you don't make an active choice. You can find information about choosing investments in Chapter 5, but broadly speaking, for savings that you will not be cashing in within the next 10 years, it usually makes sense to invest mainly in shares. For savings you do intend to cash in or use to buy an annuity, it is common to gradually shift your savings towards safer investments such as cash and bonds (a process sometimes called 'lifestyling').
2 *Decumulation.* When you retire, you can take a tax-free lump sum from your fund and use the rest to provide an income – either in the form of a lifetime annuity or through drawdown (leaving your savings invested and just cashing in amounts as you need them).

ANNUITIES

A lifetime annuity is an income you buy with part or all of your pension fund. It provides a secure income for the rest of your life, however long you live, so is best thought of as insurance against living longer than your savings would otherwise last. While the average 66 year old today can expect to survive to age 85 (man) or 87 (woman), you'd be unwise to plan your retirement on an average, since you might well be in the half of the population that lives longer – often much longer. According to the Office for National Statistics, a man aged 66 has a one in four chance of reaching age 92, and a one in ten chance of surviving to age 96. For women, there's a one in four chance of reaching age 94 and a one in ten chance of surviving to age 98.

On the other hand, many people worry that, having handed over a large chunk of their savings for an annuity, they might die within a few years and not get value from the annuity. But some types of annuity can help you guard against this. You'll find information about different types of annuity in Chapter 5.

If you are buying an annuity, it's important to shop around for the type that's most suitable for you and the best deals on the market. MoneyHelper has a free tool to help you do this (Directory, p 33).

DRAWDOWN

Don't confuse drawdown with taking cash out of your pension savings before retirement (discussed below). Drawdown lets you choose the point at which you want to start drawing some kind of retirement income. First, you take any tax-free lump sum, and what remains goes into your drawdown fund. These savings are invested, usually with quite a high proportion still in shares because your fund may have to support you for several decades. This means the value of your drawdown fund will go up and down with the stock market.

Drawdown is very flexible. You don't have to draw out anything and, if you do, you choose how much to draw out and when. You might opt to draw out sums regularly to create an income. You might draw out lump sums to cover one-off expenses. You can even cash in the whole lot! Whatever you do draw out, the whole sum counts as income for that year and is taxed in the normal way (as explained in Chapter 4). Any unused amount left in your fund on death can be left as a pension or lump sum to anyone you choose – there is more information about this in Chapter 15.

A challenge with drawdown is that you do not know how long your savings will have to last. You might want to draw out a steady income each year, rising just enough to keep pace with inflation, but there is a risk that your savings will run dry part way through retirement. To guard against this, some advisers suggest you draw off a set percentage of your savings each year, say 4 per cent. The drawback with doing that is that in years when the value of your investments falls, your income will also fall. On the other hand, if you doggedly carry on drawing the same income in pounds each year, when the market dips, you will have to sell investments at a loss and you will lose the future growth they might have produced, so your pension pot may run out sooner. The big stock market falls seen during the 2020 pandemic highlighted this dilemma and many advisers now suggest that you keep enough in cash to cover two years' spending so you don't have to cash in any of your drawdown funds when the stock market is low.

Opting for drawdown affects your Annual Allowance (described in *How much you can save* earlier in this chapter). The limit on the amount you can save in future each year through defined-contribution pension schemes is capped at £10,000.

STRIKING A BALANCE

Annuities and drawdown each have advantages and disadvantages, and many experts suggest you use both.

One strategy is to work out the minimum income you would be prepared to live on. Check whether your State Pension plus any defined-benefit pensions from work provide that minimum. If not, consider buying an annuity to top up your income to the minimum. This ensures you have secure sources of income up to that level. You could then use any remaining pension savings for drawdown.

Another strategy is to rely on drawdown during the early part of your retirement, but use part or all of the remaining drawdown fund to buy an annuity once you reach, say, age 85. The annuity then covers the remaining risk that you might continue to need an income until a very old age. This strategy is helped by the fact that annuities get cheaper as you get older (because the income they provide is expected to be paid out for a shorter period than buying the same income when you are younger).

Pensions you arrange for yourself

Pension schemes you arrange for yourself are always defined-contribution pensions, so all of the information in the last four sections applies (except there are usually no employer contributions).

Anyone can have a pension scheme, and anyone else can pay into it for you – for example, if you're caring for children or doing other unpaid work, your partner could pay into a scheme for you; and grandparents, say, could pay into a pension scheme for grandchildren even from the day they are born. But usually people arrange their own scheme in order to top up the savings they are building up through their workplace scheme or because they are self-employed.

There are several types of personal pension scheme:

- *Stakeholder pensions* must have certain features, including capped charges, low minimum contributions, flexible contributions, penalty-free transfers and a default investment fund – i.e. a fund your money will be invested in if you don't want to choose one yourself.
- *Standard personal pensions* are similar to stakeholder pensions, but they usually offer a wider range of investment funds. Personal pension charges may be similar to stakeholder pension charges or lower (sometimes much lower), but some are higher.
- A *self-invested personal pension (SIPP)* gives you an even wider choice of investments, including for example property, direct investment in stocks and shares, as well as a huge range of investment funds. The charges for SIPPs are usually higher than for other types of personal pension, so make sure you really do want the greater range of options they offer.

Stakeholder schemes and standard personal pensions are typically provided by insurance companies, while SIPPs tend to be offered by stockbrokers and investment firms, often through online platforms.

Another option if you are self-employed is to join NEST. It has been designed with relatively low charges in order to offer good-value pensions, but has only a limited range of investment choices. For more information, visit NEST (Directory, p 33) and search for 'Joining as self-employed'.

Starting your pension

A company pension scheme usually has a normal pension age which is the earliest age at which you can start to draw your full pension. With a personal pension scheme, you choose the age at which you want it to start.

You can often choose to start your pension earlier but, in that case, the amount of pension you get from a company defined-benefit scheme will be lower and stay at that lower level throughout your retirement. Similarly, with a company defined-contribution scheme or any personal pension scheme, the pension pot you've built up (and so the amount of pension it can provide) will be permanently lower if you retire early. Some company schemes pay a higher amount of pension for a few years to bridge the gap between your retiring early and your State Pension starting. The extra amount is called a 'bridging pension' and the whole arrangement is sometimes called a 'step-down pension'. It's important to understand this arrangement if it applies to you so you are not taken by surprise when your company pension falls at State Pension age.

The earliest you can normally start drawing a pension is currently age 55. This is due to rise to 57 in 2028 when State Pension age reaches 67. You can start your pension at any age if you have to retire early because of ill health. Starting your pension later may mean you get a larger pension.

Some employers have rules that prevent you continuing to work for them after starting your pension or limit the number of hours you can work – check your scheme rules to see if this applies. But there is no general rule stopping you working and drawing pensions, so you could take work elsewhere or start your own business. It is now increasingly common for people to gradually phase into retirement, combining work and pension.

Drawing your savings early

Since April 2015, with many defined-contribution schemes, provided you have reached at least age 55 (57 from 2028), you can draw out some or all of your savings before retirement to use in any way you choose. Your pension provider can tell you if it offers this option; if not, you might consider transferring your savings to another scheme that does.

These early withdrawals go by the ungainly name of 'uncrystallized funds pension lump sums' (UFPLS). 'Uncrystallized' means that you have not yet turned your pension pot into an annuity or drawdown fund, so your savings are still in that first (accumulation) stage.

A quarter of any sum you draw out in this way is tax-free, but the rest counts as taxable income for the year you make the withdrawal. This can come as a shock, especially if it tips you into a higher tax bracket, as in the real-world example following. You might pay less tax if you take several smaller lump sums spread over several years.

Tax on an UFPLS withdrawal is usually deducted automatically by the provider using the PAYE system (which is explained in Chapter 4). The system is designed to cope with regular payments rather than large one-off lump sums and can result in the wrong amount of tax being deducted. You would then need to claim a tax refund (or, less usually, have extra tax to pay) – how to do this varies with circumstances. You can find out more using the tool at GOV.UK (Directory, p 37).

REAL-WORLD EXAMPLE

John is normally a basic-rate taxpayer (paying a top rate in 2024/25 of 20 per cent), and his income is £5,000 below the threshold at which higher-rate tax starts. He decides to draw £50,000 out of his pension savings. A quarter of this (£12,500) is tax-free. The remaining £37,500 is added to his income for the year and taxed in the normal way. £5,000 uses up his remaining basic-rate band, but the rest is taxed at 40 per cent. The total tax bill on his UFPLS withdrawal is £14,000. After tax, his £50,000 withdrawal has shrunk to £36,000.

You cannot make UFPLS withdrawals from a defined-benefit scheme. However, if the scheme is run by a private-sector employer, you could transfer your pension rights out of that scheme and into a personal pension scheme that does allow early withdrawals. You should think carefully before doing this, because you will be giving up a secure promised pension that you might need in retirement. If the value of the pension rights you are transferring comes to more than £30,000, you will in any case have to take professional financial advice.

If you belong to a public-sector defined-benefit scheme, you are not allowed to transfer your pension rights to a defined-contribution scheme.

Drawing your savings early affects your Annual Allowance (described in *How much you can save* earlier in this chapter). The limit on the amount you can save in future each year through defined-contribution pension schemes is capped at £10,000.

The tax-free lump sum

As mentioned earlier, a quarter of your pension savings can be taken as a tax-free lump sum (up to a maximum sum of £268,275 in 2024/25). Tax-free money is a good thing, right? However, taking a lump sum means there is less money left in your pension pot to provide your retirement income, which may then be less than you would like. Fortunately, there are several ways in which you can maximize your pension income while still getting the benefit of the tax-free lump sum:

- **Use UFPLS withdrawals to create a stream of income.** A quarter of each withdrawal is tax-free, as described in the previous section.
- **Opt for 'phased retirement'.** This is where, each time you need an income payment, you use just part of your pension pot. You can take a quarter of that part as a tax-free lump sum and put the rest into drawdown. You don't have to take any income from the drawdown fund and could just use each tax-free sum as your 'income'.
- **Buy a purchased lifetime annuity (PLA).** You take a quarter of your whole pension pot as a tax-free lump sum and use the rest for drawdown or to buy an annuity. However, you use the tax-free lump sum to buy a PLA. This is similar to the type of annuity you buy with your pension pot, but taxed in a different way. There is more information in Chapter 5.

How safe is your pension?

Pensions seem constantly to be in the news, usually making bad headlines. Scandals are typically of two types: defined-benefit schemes breaking their pension promises, and individual savers in all types of scheme being scammed out of their money.

Although big news when it happens, most defined-benefit schemes do not fail and, where they do, there is a compensation scheme to help. The Pension Protection Fund (PPF) (Directory, p 33) may take over a scheme where the employer running it has become insolvent. Members already retired get 100 per cent of their pension; others will receive 90 per cent. PPF pensions used to be paid only up to a cap that varied with age. However, a court ruled that this broke age-discrimination legislation, so the cap has now been removed. When PPF pension payments start, pensions built up since 1997 are increased each year in line with inflation up to a maximum of 2.5 per cent a year, but any part of the pension built up during earlier years does not increase.

There is also a Fraud Compensation Fund (Directory, p 32) that may take over pensions where company scheme members lose out because of fraud or negligence. This applies to both defined-benefit and defined-contribution company schemes.

Personal pension schemes and annuities are covered by a different compensation scheme, the Financial Services Compensation Scheme (FSCS). This can help where the provider has become insolvent owing you money, provided the firm is authorized to operate. You can check a firm's authorization by consulting the Financial Services Register (Directory, p 9). Compensation is generally up to a maximum of £85,000. This limit is low relative to the amount you may have saved, but pension savings should be ring-fenced and kept separate from the provider's own finances to keep your money safe. Where you are receiving income from an annuity, the compensation is unlimited.

While pension scams have been around for decades, they have increased significantly in recent years. The Pensions Regulator (Directory, p 9) and Financial Conduct Authority (FCA) (Directory, p 8) publish guidance on their websites on how to protect yourself against being scammed. They highlight five common tactics that should set your alarm bells ringing: contact out of the blue (whether by phone, email or other means); promises of high and/or guaranteed returns; free pension reviews; access to your savings before age 55; and pressure to act quickly.

Since January 2019, it has become illegal for firms to cold call you about pensions. The only pension calls that are legitimate are from authorized firms where you have specifically given your consent to be contacted. If you are contacted in any other circumstances, treat it as a scam call and hang up.

Information, guidance and advice about private pensions

If you find it difficult to understand how your pension scheme works, you are not alone! Pensions are notoriously complicated and governments do like to keep changing the rules.

If you have a query or if you are concerned in some way about a workplace pension, you should approach whoever is responsible for the scheme in your organization. If the company is large, there may be a special person who looks after the scheme on a day-to-day basis. This could be the pensions manager or, quite often, it is someone in the human resources department. In a smaller company, the pension scheme may be looked after by the company secretary or managing director.

With a pension you've arranged for yourself, your first port of call for any queries or concern should be your pension provider. If you need more general information or you are confused by the response from your company scheme or pension provider, MoneyHelper has a wealth of information (Directory, p 9), and can provide guidance through its telephone helpline.

MoneyHelper also runs the government's Pension Wise service (Directory, p 33). This offers a free guidance appointment to discuss your options if you have a defined contribution pension, as long as you are aged 50 or over.

Guidance is not the same as advice. If you do not feel confident making pension decisions on your own, consider paying for professional financial advice (see Chapter 1).

Other help and advice

MAKING A COMPLAINT

If you are unhappy with the way a personal pension scheme has been marketed or sold to you, you should first complain to the firm involved. Authorized firms are required to have a complaints procedure that you can use. The firm should reply within eight weeks. If it doesn't, or if you're unhappy with its response, you can take your complaint to the Financial Ombudsman Service (FOS). This is an independent, free-to-use service. It can order the firm to put matters right, which may include compensation up to a maximum of £430,000 (since 1 April 2024).

In most other cases, whether your complaint concerns a workplace pension or a personal pension scheme you've arranged for yourself, you should again give the scheme provider a chance to resolve the matter first. If you don't get a reply or you are not happy with the response, you can take your complaint to the Pensions Ombudsman (Directory, p 33).

KEEPING TRACK OF YOUR PENSIONS

In addition to understanding your current pension scheme, you may also need to chase up previous schemes of which you were a member. These pots are left behind when workers move between jobs, particularly at the start of their careers. As retirement approaches, many face problems tracking down small-sized funds, or simply don't think to look for them. However, there is a free, government service, the Pension Tracing Service, which can help you trace your old pensions. You can use the service by phone, post or online (Directory, p 33).

From the schemes you are in touch with, you will normally receive a regular statement showing your possible pension when it starts. With government encouragement, the pensions industry is working on creating a 'pensions dashboard' which will let you view all your pensions in one place. This should make it easier to keep track of your pensions, spot if an old pension is missing and estimate how much income you may have in retirement. Many different organizations will offer you this dashboard service – for example, your bank, your employer, your pension providers, advice agencies or an app you download to a smartphone. Pension dashboards are now due to be available on or before 31 October 2026. To learn more, visit the Pensions Dashboards Programme (Directory, p 33).

Divorce and separation

Divorce or separation typically means that you shift from living in a shared household to living alone, and may become newly eligible to claim state benefits if your income is low – see Chapter 2.

These life events can have a big impact on your financial situation. Pension savings and pensions built up by you and your partner are a major part of those finances, so it's important to think about how they are affected and what you can do to make sure they give you the best support.

Divorce

On divorce or the dissolution of a civil partnership, the couple's assets have to be split between them. Often, the two most valuable assets will be a property if the couple have bought their home, and any private pensions each has built up. Because women still traditionally take on most of the unpaid work of caring and looking after the home, it is common for the husband to have built up the bulk of the couple's private pensions, with the original intention that they would share the income in retirement. There are three ways in which pension savings can be dealt with on divorce:

- *Offsetting.* This means one person might keep the pensions, but the other get a similarly valuable asset, such as the home.
- A *pension attachment order* (earmarking in Scotland). There is no immediate change to the pension arrangements, but it is agreed that, once the pension starts to be paid, part of it will be transferred to the former partner. Similarly, benefits might be due to be paid to you if your ex-partner dies.
- *Sharing.* Part of the pension savings are transferred to the former partner, so this part becomes their own savings and will provide their own pension in retirement.

You can agree to offsetting without involving a court, but a court order is needed for pension attachment, earmarking or pension sharing.

Offsetting and pension sharing are both commonly used and have the advantage of creating a clean break between the couple. Pension attachment orders (earmarking) are less popular. There is no clean break, and they have several other drawbacks. For example, the partner with the pension scheme might die, stop paying into the scheme or delay their retirement, all of which affect the amount of pension the other person may get. If you are due to receive part or all of any death benefits, you might not be aware if your ex-partner dies. If there is a possibility that they may have died but you have not been informed, you can check by contacting the General Register Office (Directory, p 32). The indexes to all birth, marriage and death entries in England and Wales are available from the National Archives website (Directory, p 33).

If either or both of the couple have already started to draw pensions, this income will be taken into account as part of the divorce settlement.

How to split pension savings is particularly complex, and a subject to raise with your solicitor if you are in the process of divorce proceedings. For a free and less formal discussion of your options, contact MoneyHelper (Directory, p 9).

The old state basic pension could not be shared, but for divorced people who reached State Pension age before 6 April 2016, they can use their ex-partner's NICs record to increase their own State Pension as high as the full rate. A court can order that any state additional pension be shared.

Under the new State Pension, each person builds up their own pension and there are no arrangements for sharing either State Pension or NICs. However, for many years to come, people reaching State Pension age on or after 6 April 2016 will be covered by transitional rules because they spent time in both the old and new State Pension systems. Under these rules, you might have a 'protected payment' which is an amount over and above the full new pension rate (see *How much is the new State Pension?* earlier in this chapter). A court can order that this protected payment be shared with your ex-partner on divorce. Contact the Pension Service (Directory, p 33) for help understanding which rules may apply to you and how.

Separation

If you separate without getting divorced or going through any other formal proceeding, there is usually no change to your pensions. You may, however, want to check that in the event of death, any survivor pension from a company scheme could still be paid to your separated partner if that is what you want to happen.

You might consider getting a judicial separation (where a court formally recognizes your separation and can make orders about your finances). In that case, the court can make an order for a pensions attachment order or offsetting (but not pension sharing).

Lifetime Individual Savings Accounts (LISAs)

Individual Savings Accounts (ISAs) are a tax-efficient way to save or invest for all sorts of purposes and there's information about them in Chapter 5. However, since April 2017, Lifetime ISAs (LISAs) became available specifically designed as a way for younger people to save for retirement. A LISA can be taken out by anyone aged between 18 and 40. The maximum amount you can save is £4,000 a year, but the government adds a bonus of 25 per cent to this (so a maximum government bonus of £1,000 a year). The money grows tax-free within the LISA and, from age 60 onwards, can be withdrawn tax-free and used for any purpose.

Savings in a LISA can also be drawn out early, and will be tax-free if used as a deposit to buy a first home. Otherwise, on early withdrawal, the government bonus is taken back and there is also a 5 per cent penalty charge. If you are a non-taxpayer or pay tax at no more than the basic rate (20 per cent in 2024/25), a LISA is a more tax-efficient way to save for retirement than a pension scheme. However, bear in mind that workplace pension schemes also benefit from money paid in by your employer. LISAs are offered by a range of providers, including some banks, building societies and investment firms. For a list of providers, see Which? (Directory, p 35) and search for 'Lifetime ISAs'.

CHAPTER FOUR

Tax

There is no doubt that your tax position is likely to change once you start to take retirement, and it is vital that everyone reaching retirement age should invest some time in understanding how the tax system applies to them.

The most common types of tax are income tax, National Insurance contributions and capital gains tax (CGT), all covered in this chapter, and inheritance tax (IHT), which you'll find in Chapter 15.

In general, the tax burden on households is currently increasing. This is not because rates are rising, but because most allowances and thresholds have been frozen – or in some cases cut. Freezing allowances and thresholds causes 'fiscal drag' meaning that, as your income rises with inflation, you end up in a higher tax bracket than previously even though your standard of living (after taking account of inflation) has not necessarily improved. Fiscal drag can also be a problem because you may find yourself unexpectedly having to fill in a tax return when previously you didn't.

The new Labour government has said it will not increase National Insurance, income tax rates or VAT. Other taxes might change.

Income tax – the basics

This is calculated on all (or nearly all) of your income, after deduction of the personal allowance (which most people get). The reason for saying 'nearly all' is that some income you may receive is tax-free (see below). Having deducted the personal allowance, what remains is the income on which tax may be due.

Most income counts. You will be assessed for income tax on your pensions (including your State Pension), interest you receive from most types of savings, dividends from investments, any earnings from a job (even if these are only from casual work) and profits from being self-employed, plus rent from any lodgers, should the rent you receive exceed £7,500 a year. However, there are other allowances that may reduce or eliminate the tax you pay on savings income, dividends and very small business ventures. Many state benefits are also taxable.

You may pay less income tax if you have some types of expenditure that qualify for tax relief – these are sometimes called 'outgoings'. The most common outgoings that qualify for relief are payments you make to a pension scheme and donations to charity.

Income tax is an annual tax. The tax year runs from 6 April to the following 5 April, so the amount of tax in any one year is calculated on the income you receive (or are deemed to have received) between those dates.

Personal allowance

You don't pay tax on every single penny of your money. Most people are allowed to retain a certain amount before income tax becomes applicable. This is known as your personal allowance. It does not matter where the income comes from, whether from earnings, an investment, a pension or another source. The personal allowance is given automatically; you do not have to claim it.

The personal allowance for 2024/25 is £12,570 and is frozen at this level until April 2028 (unless the new government decides to change this).

Not everyone gets the personal allowance. For people with income of more than £100,000, their personal allowance is reduced: £1 of allowance is lost for every £2 by which their income exceeds £100,000. This means that in 2024/25, someone earning £125,140 or more does not get any personal allowance.

Rates of income tax

What's left of your income after subtracting your personal allowance is divided into slices, called tax bands, and different rates of tax apply to each band. Scotland has different tax bands and rates from the rest of the UK. Wales also has the power to set its own Welsh income tax rates, but in 2024/25 has chosen to set these at the same level as the rates for England

and Northern Ireland. The four different rates of income tax for 2024/25 for the UK apart from Scotland are:

1   The 0% savings rate, which applies to the first £5,000 of any taxable savings income. However, if an individual's taxable non-savings income exceeds the savings rate limit, then the 0% rate for savings will not be available for savings income.
2   The 20% basic rate for taxable income up to £37,700 (frozen until April 2028).
3   The 40% higher rate, which is levied on all taxable income from £37,701 up to £125,140.
4   The top rate of 45% on income in excess of £125,140.

Different tax rates apply to dividend income, and these are described later in the chapter.

Scottish income tax

Scotland has the power to set its own tax bands and rates of tax for all types of income, except savings income and dividends – for these, the UK rates described later in this chapter apply. Scotland must also have the same personal allowance as the rest of the UK. Scottish income tax applies if your only or main home is in Scotland. Your tax is still collected by HMRC on behalf of the Scottish tax authority, Revenue Scotland.

Scotland charges less tax than the rest of the UK on lower incomes, but more on higher incomes. In 2024/25, it does this through a system of six tax bands:

1   a 19% starter rate on the first £2,306 (in excess of your personal allowance) of income from pensions, earnings, rents and so on;
2   a 20% basic rate on taxable income from £2,307 to £13,991;
3   a 21% intermediate rate on taxable income from £13,992 to £31,092;
4   a 42% higher rate on taxable income from £31,093 to £62,430;
5   a 45% advanced rate (new from 2024/25) on taxable income from £62,431 to £125,140;
6   a 48% top rate on taxable income over £125,140.

Welsh income tax

Since April 2019, Wales can set its own Welsh income tax rate for all types of income, except savings income and dividends – for these, the UK rates described later in this chapter apply. Wales must also have the same personal allowance as the rest of the UK. If you live in Wales, you count as a Welsh taxpayer (even if you work over the border in England or elsewhere).

The way Welsh income tax works is that the normal UK rates are reduced by 10 per cent – so the UK basic rate becomes 10 per cent instead of 20 per cent, the higher rate becomes 30 per cent instead of 40 per cent, and the additional rate becomes 35 per cent instead of 45 per cent. The Welsh Assembly can then add a Welsh income tax rate on top of these reduced UK rates. For 2024/25, the Welsh rate has been set at 10 per cent for all the tax bands. This means you pay the same total tax rate as taxpayers in the rest of the UK except Scotland. Your tax is still collected by HMRC, and the Welsh part is passed to the Welsh Revenue Authority.

Other allowances

In addition to your personal allowance, there are some other tax allowances that can reduce the amount of tax you have to pay. Tax relief is given in different ways, depending on the allowance.

BLIND PERSON'S ALLOWANCE

Registered blind people can claim an allowance of £3,070 in 2024/25. This reduces your tax bill by being deducted from your taxable income before tax is worked out (in the same way as the personal allowance).

If both husband and wife are registered as blind, they can each claim the allowance. If you think you would be eligible, you should contact the HMRC helpline, 0300 200 3301, with relevant details of your situation (Directory, p 25).

MARRIAGE ALLOWANCE

Marriage allowance is not really an extra allowance; rather, it is the ability to transfer some of your personal allowance to your partner, if you are married or in a civil partnership. To be eligible, neither you nor your partner must be paying tax at more than the basic rate (or no more than the intermediate rate in Scotland). The most common situation where the transfer is worthwhile is if your income is too low to use your full personal allowance, but your partner is taxed on a bigger income.

The amount you can transfer is one-tenth of your personal allowance, so a fixed amount of £1,260 in 2024/25. The way your partner then gets tax relief is different from the personal allowance. Tax relief is worked out as 20 per cent of the £1,260 marriage allowance, which comes to £252. This amount is deducted from your partner's tax bill, but cannot reduce the bill to less than zero.

You have to claim Marriage Allowance, and should normally do this online GOV.UK (Directory, p 37). The person with the lowest income should make the claim. If you cannot claim online, phone the HMRC general enquiries helpline on 0300 200 3300.

If you or your partner were born before 6 April 1935, consider claiming Married Couple's Allowance instead as this is more generous.

MARRIED COUPLE'S ALLOWANCE

This is an extra allowance for older couples where one or both of them were born before 6 April 1935. In 2024/25, the full allowance is £11,080. Tax relief is 10 per cent of this – £1,108 – and given as a reduction in your tax bill. But the allowance cannot reduce your tax bill to less than zero.

However, that's not the end of the story. The amount of Married Couple's Allowance you can get also depends on your income. In 2024/25, if your income is more than £37,000, the Married Couple's Allowance is reduced by £1 for every £2 of 'excess income'. But the Married Couple's Allowance is only ever reduced to a minimum amount of £4,280 (2024/25). That means the tax relief you get will be somewhere between £428 and £1,108, assuming your original tax bill is at least that much. To work out what you might get, there's a calculator at GOV.UK (Directory, p 37).

Since the amount varies with your income, you are probably asking: whose income? Mine or my partner's? For marriages before 5 December 2005, Married Couple's Allowance is given initially to the husband to set against his income. For marriages and civil partnerships on or after that date, it goes to whichever of you has the higher income. But, in either case, you can arrange to transfer the whole allowance to the other person, agree to split it equally between you, or transfer any unused part.

Claim Married Couple's Allowance through your tax return or by calling the HMRC general helpline, 0300 200 3300.

Tax relief on 'outgoings'

Separate from any personal allowances, you can obtain tax relief on the following:

- a donation to charity under the Gift Aid scheme or through a payroll giving scheme at work;

- contributions to workplace pension schemes and personal pensions that you arrange yourself;
- some maintenance payments, if you are divorced or separated and you or your partner were born before 6 April 1935;
- for some older borrowers only, mortgage interest on a loan taken out to provide you with extra income.

DONATIONS TO CHARITY

You can get tax relief on a donation to charity if you make a Gift Aid declaration. Usually the charity provides you with a form to fill in to do this. Donating this way means that the charity can claim a top-up from HMRC equal to 25 per cent of whatever you give. For example, if you give £8, the charity gets £10 once the HMRC top-up is added on. The top-up the government gives to the charity is equivalent to giving you tax relief at the basic rate (20 per cent in 2024/25) on your donation.

If you are a higher-rate or additional-rate taxpayer, you can claim extra tax relief. To do this, you need to fill in a tax return or ask HMRC to adjust your tax code (see below for information about this). Beware of using Gift Aid if you are a non-taxpayer or pay very little tax. If you do not already pay at least as much tax as the top-up, HMRC can ask you to pay the difference.

Some employers run payroll giving schemes that let you make donations to charity direct from your pay. Your employer deducts the donations from your pay before working out how much tax to collect (through the PAYE system described later in this chapter). This means you automatically get tax relief up to your highest rate, and there is no need to fill in a tax return.

PENSION CONTRIBUTIONS

The tax rules surrounding pension contributions are quite complex, and you can read about them in Chapter 3.

MAINTENANCE PAYMENTS

In general, maintenance payments you receive are not taxable, and you cannot claim tax relief on any maintenance payments you make to a partner following separation, divorce or the dissolution of a civil partnership. An exception has been made in cases where one (or both) of the divorced or separated partners was born before 6 April 1935. Those paying maintenance are still able to claim tax relief, but only at a rate of 10 per cent and only on payments up to £4,280 (2024/25). This gives maximum tax relief of £428, which you get as a reduction in your tax bill. (However, your tax bill cannot be reduced to less than zero.)

TAX RELIEF ON MORTGAGE INTEREST

Mortgage interest relief was abolished on 6 April 2000. The only purpose for which relief is still available is in respect of loans secured on an older person's home to purchase a life annuity (a home income scheme). However, to qualify, the loan must have been taken out (or at least processed and confirmed in writing) by 9 March 1999. Borrowers in this situation can continue to benefit from the relief for the duration of their loan. The relief applies to interest on only the first £30,000 of the loan, and is given at a rate of 10 per cent. You get the relief by making reduced payments to your lender, who then claims the relief back from HMRC.

Tax-free income

Some income you may receive is entirely free of tax. It is important to know what income is non-taxable and can be ignored for tax purposes. If you receive any of the following, you can forget about the tax aspect altogether (for a full list see the Low Incomes Tax Reform Group in the Directory, p 37).

- Some state benefits, including for example: Attendance Allowance, Bereavement Support Payment, Council Tax Reduction (Support), Housing Benefit, Pension Credit, Personal Independence Payment, Universal Credit, £10 Christmas bonus for pensioners and Winter Fuel Payments.
- Child Benefit, unless you or your partner has income over £60,000 – see *Caring for children or adults* in Chapter 3.
- Some types of saving, such as: National Savings & Investments (NS&I) Premium Bond prizes and Savings Certificates interest; income from Individual Savings Accounts (ISAs); interest and bonuses from Save As You Earn (SAYE) schemes.
- Interest and dividends covered by your Personal Savings Allowance and Dividend Allowance, respectively. See *Income tax on savings and investments* later in this chapter.
- Up to a quarter of savings you draw out of pension schemes either before or at retirement subject to an upper limit (see Chapter 3).

- Winnings on the National Lottery and other forms of betting.
- Rental income of up to £7,500 a year from letting out rooms in your home (called Rent-a-Room Relief).
- Up to £1,000 a year of income from using your home (called Property Allowance). This could cover, for example, renting out your home for short periods through an internet platform or renting out your drive as a parking space. You cannot combine this with Rent-a-Room Relief.
- Up to £1,000 a year of income from trading if you are self-employed (called Trading Allowance). This could cover, say, selling things you make or own at craft fairs or online. You claim the allowance instead of expenses. There is more information about the Trading Allowance in Chapter 9.
- Income received from certain insurance policies (mortgage payment protection, permanent health insurance, creditor insurance for loans and utility bills, various approved long-term care policies) if the recipient is sick, disabled or unemployed at the time the benefits become payable.
- Up to £30,000 of compensation for being made redundant.
- Maintenance payments following separation, divorce or dissolution of a civil partnership.

There are some other forms of money you may get that do not count as income. These include, for example, loans you receive and gifts from some-body (see *Inheritance tax (IHT)* in Chapter 15 for how tax works if you are the giver). Similarly, if you sell something for a profit, that does not count as income, but you might have to pay CGT on the profit (see *Capital gains tax* later in this chapter).

Some types of insurance can be used as investments. The return you get may be tax-free in your hands, although this is because the insurance company has already paid tax on this money and you cannot reclaim what the company has paid.

Income tax on savings and investments

Savings

Savings income means interest from bank and building society accounts, National Savings & Investments (NS&I) products, credit union accounts, peer-to-peer lending, government bonds (gilts), corporate bonds and investment funds that invest in similar assets. In general, savings income is taxable. However, there are several reasons why in fact you might not have to pay any tax on it.

First, some types of savings income is specifically tax-free (see the list above). In particular, each year you can put up to a certain amount (frozen at £20,000 in 2024/25) into ISAs. If you don't use your full annual ISA allowance, you cannot carry it forward – so use it or lose it! There are several different types of ISA: cash ISAs, which take the form of bank, building society or NS&I accounts; stocks and shares ISAs, through which you can invest in shares, gilts, corporate bonds and investment funds; and Innovative Finance ISAs, through which you can invest in peer-to-peer lending and other forms of crowdfunding. The most popular type of ISA is the cash ISA, accounting for three-quarters of the ISAs taken out each year, according to HMRC.

The previous government consulted on introducing a new type of ISA, the UK ISA, from some future date. The aim is to promote investment in UK-focused assets and the intention was that you will be able to invest up to £5,000 on top of the normal ISA allowance. It is rumoured that the new government will not take this plan forward.

There are also some special types of ISA aimed mainly at younger people to help them save for a home or retirement, and Junior ISAs for children (with their own separate annual limit frozen at £9,000 in 2024/25).

If your income including taxable savings income is no more than £ 17,570 in 2024/25, you might benefit from the savings-rate band. As explained above, you have a personal allowance (£12,570 in 2024/25), and the first tax band after that is the savings-rate band (£5,000 in 2024/25 with a 0 per cent tax rate but only on savings income). The personal allowance and savings-rate band are set first against any income you have from sources like pensions, earnings and rental income. Whatever is left is next set against any savings income (and any left after that against dividend income). This is most easily understood by looking at a couple of case studies.

REAL-WORLD EXAMPLE

In 2024/25, Adrian's income is made up of £9,000 pension, £3,000 earnings and £6,000 of interest from savings. His personal allowance (£12,570) is set against the pension, the earnings and £570 of the interest. The savings-rate band is then set against £5,000 of the remaining interest. So at least £5,570 of the interest from his savings is tax-free. (And, in fact, the remaining £430 is also tax-free, as we will see shortly.)

REAL-WORLD EXAMPLE

In 2024/25, Gemma has income as follows: £16,000 pension and £6,000 of interest from savings. Her personal allowance (£12,570) is set against the pension. That leaves £3,430 of pension which falls into the savings-rate band, but because it is not savings income, it is taxed at the normal basic rate (20 per cent in 2024/25). But there is £1,570 of the savings-rate band left to set against part of the interest she gets, so that £1,570 of interest will be tax-free. (And, in fact, another £1,000 of the interest will also be tax-free, as we will see shortly.)

Finally, since 2016/17, basic-rate taxpayers and higher-rate taxpayers have a Personal Savings Allowance (PSA). The allowance is £1,000 for basic-rate taxpayers and £500 for higher-rate taxpayers. Additional-rate taxpayers don't get any PSA. This allowance is set against the first chunk of savings income that would otherwise be taxed at your top rate. In the case studies above, both Adrian and Gemma are basic-rate taxpayers. The last £430 of Adrian's income is savings income that falls into the basic-rate band, but he pays no tax on it because he can set his PSA against that interest. In Gemma's case, she has £6,000 of interest. The first £1,570 is covered by her savings-rate band; another £1,000 is tax-free because it's covered by her PSA; that leaves just £3,430 of the interest in the basic-rate band to be taxed at the normal 20 per cent rate.

If a substantial part of your income comes from savings, you could have up to £18,570 of tax-free income by combining your personal allowance, the savings-rate band and your PSA.

Savings income is paid to you without any tax deducted (in other words, this income is paid 'gross'). Because of the PSA, in the past, most savers had no tax to pay. However, recent high interest rates mean that you might now be over the PSA limit. In that case, you will need to declare the interest, usually by completing a tax return, so that you pay the right amount of tax.

Investments

'Investments' usually means assets whose value can go up and down: mainly shares and bonds quoted on the stock exchange. For tax purposes, income from bonds counts as savings income and is taxed as described above. This section describes the tax treatment of income from shares – called 'dividends' – and investment funds that invest in them.

In some circumstances, dividend income may be tax-free. This is most common where you have invested through an ISA. You can invest up to

£20,000 in ISAs in 2024/25 as outlined in *Savings* earlier in this chapter. The following rules apply to taxable dividend income:

- There is no tax on dividends covered by your personal allowance.
- The first £500 (2024/25) of dividends that fall into the basic-rate, higher-rate or additional-rate bands are tax-free because they are covered by your Dividend Allowance. This allowance has been cut from £2,000 and then £1,000 over the last two years, so you might now find you have tax to pay even though you did not in previous years.
- Remaining dividends that fall into the basic-rate band are taxed at a rate of 8.75% in 2024/25.
- Remaining dividends that fall into the higher-rate band are taxed at a rate of 33.75% in 2024/25.
- Remaining dividends that fall into the additional-rate band are taxed at a rate of 39.35% in 2024/25.

Dividends are paid without any tax deducted. If you have tax to pay, you will normally have to fill in a tax return.

Paying and reclaiming income tax

Nobody wants to pay more tax than they have to. However, underpaying tax can be equally problematic because you may face a sudden bill for back taxes later on that could be hard to manage. Therefore, it's important to understand how tax is collected and check that you're paying the right amount. Tax is collected in two main ways: through Pay As You Earn (PAYE) and Self Assessment.

Pay As You Earn (PAYE)

Income tax on earnings and private pensions is collected through the PAYE system. This means your employer or pension provider acts as tax collector. They deduct the tax you owe from your pay or pension before you get it, and hand the tax direct to HMRC. PAYE does not simply collect the tax due on those particular earnings or that particular pension. The system is designed so that it can collect all the tax you owe on your income from all sources and also collect or refund tax relating to earlier tax years. In particular, PAYE on a private pension may be used to collect tax due on your State Pension (since State Pensions are taxable, but paid gross).

REAL-WORLD EXAMPLE

In 2024/25, Masud gets a State Pension of £9,000 and a private pension of £7,000, giving him a total income of £16,000. The first £12,570 is covered by his personal allowance and so is tax-free. Basic-rate tax at 20 per cent is due on the remaining £3,430, which comes to £686. The whole £686 tax is deducted through PAYE from his private pension. This means he receives £9,000 pension from the state and £6,314 from his pension provider.

Your employer or pension provider knows how much tax to deduct because each year HMRC provides them and you with a coding notice, detailing how much tax-free pay or pension you are entitled to, and a tax code that tells your employer or pension provider what tax rates to apply. If you have both a job and a pension or more than one job or pension, you will have a separate tax code for each. Usually your personal allowance is set against whichever source of PAYE income seems to be your main one. Your tax code is made up of a number and one or two letters. The number is your tax-free pay or pension divided by 10, and the letter says something about your tax circumstances – for example, if you just get the full personal allowance of £12,570, your code will be 1257L. An M in your code means you get Marriage Allowance and an N that you've given Marriage Allowance to your partner. An S means you pay Scottish income tax, a C that you pay Welsh income tax, and so on. HMRC do sometimes make mistakes, so it's important to check your code and tell HMRC if it's wrong. The HMRC website has a tool to help you check that you have been given the correct tax code: GOV.UK (Directory, p 37). This tool also lets you inform HMRC if your code is wrong. You will need to register to create an account in order to use this tool. If you cannot use the online tool, contact HMRC.

Income tax is an annual tax, based on your income for the whole year. If you change job part way through the year, or you stop work and start a pension, your old employer will give you a P45 form which details the income you've had so far. You hand this to your new employer or pension provider so that they can seamlessly deduct the correct amount of tax from your new income source. Sometimes the system is not quite so seamless, in which case you may be put on a 'Month 1' (or similar weekly) basis, sometimes called an 'emergency tax code'. This means you pay tax as if what you receive this month is the same as what you get every month of the tax year, regardless of whether the amount was/will be more or less in previous or subsequent months. Once your correct code is issued, you'll get a refund or have to pay extra normally through PAYE. This emergency tax code may in particular apply if you take a lump sum out of your pension savings before retirement (an UFPLS, as described in Chapter 3), so make sure to check the tax deducted and claim a refund if necessary.

You might not have a P45 or you might be starting a pension. In those cases, you will be asked to complete a 'Starter checklist' (also called a 'New starter form'). It will ask you to select one of three options: A (first job and no other sources of income), B (you're changing job or coming off benefits but have no pensions) or C (you have another job and/or one or more pensions). For most people transitioning to retirement, the correct option will be C. It's important to tick the correct option, otherwise your PAYE code is likely to be incorrect.

HMRC cross-checks the income on which you pay tax and, if it thinks you have under- or over-paid tax through PAYE, you may get a P800 form. This shows the income HMRC thinks you have, and you should check this carefully. If HMRC reckons you have paid too little tax and the amount is under £3,000, this can be collected through an adjustment to your PAYE code. If the tax owed is £3,000 or more, you'll normally be expected to pay it in a single lump sum. If you have paid too much tax, you will get a refund either by cheque or by claiming through your online account.

Self Assessment

If you have non-PAYE income, such as profits from self-employment or rental income, or you have made a capital gain (see later in this chapter), you will usually have to fill in a tax return each year and pay tax through a system called Self Assessment.

However, since 2016/17, HMRC has also been using a system of Simple Assessment which aims to reduce the number of people who have to complete a tax return. Under Simple Assessment, you may receive a letter from HMRC detailing the income it thinks you have and the tax you owe. If the details are wrong, you have 60 days to get in touch with HMRC to ask them to put it right. Once the Simple Assessment is finalized, the amount due has to be paid by a set date, normally 31 January after the tax year to which the assessment applies.

TAX RETURNS

Tax returns normally have to be submitted by a set 'filing date', which is 31 October following the end of the tax year if you use a paper tax return or 31 January if you submit online (as most people do these days). There is an automatic £100 fine if you miss the January deadline (even if you don't owe any tax). If you are not already completing a tax return each year and have some untaxed income or gains, you must let HMRC know within six months of the end of the tax year (so by 5 October 2025 for income or gains received in the 2024/25 tax year). HMRC will then arrange for you to receive a tax return (or notice to file online) and you may be given a bit longer than the normal deadline to do this.

If you fill in a tax return, you will need to supply details of all your income and any taxable capital gains, giving details of any tax already paid for example through PAYE. So the tax return asks you about, for example, your earnings from any jobs, profits from self-employment, rental income, foreign income (say, from investments or property abroad), bank and building society interest, dividends, pension income and tax-deductible outgoings such as charitable gifts and pension contributions. There is also a section if you receive income from trusts or the estate of someone who has died, and a capital gains section. And, if you spend some or all of your time abroad, you will need to complete a section to establish in which country (or countries) you are resident and domiciled for tax purposes. HMRC may have already pre-filled some of your income where it has information (for example from the PAYE system), but it's still your responsibility to check that the figures are correct.

If you want to file your tax return online, you can use commercial software if you want to, but HMRC provides its own free online service, which is what most people use. You need to register in advance and activate your account using a code sent to you by post, so allow enough time for this.

KEEPING RECORDS

HMRC advises that taxpayers are obliged to keep the records on which the information in their tax return is based for 12 months after the filing date (normally 22 months after the end of the tax year to which they relate). However, if you are self-employed or a partner in a business, you need to keep these records for five years after the filing date. You can be fined up to £3,000 if you cannot produce your records.

CALCULATING AND PAYING THE TAX

For the 2024/25 tax year, Self Assessment tax (due for example on self-employment profits or rental income) is due in instalments on 31 January 2025 and 31 July 2025, with a final balancing charge or refund on 31 January 2026; tax on a capital gain is paid in a single lump sum by the deadline of 31 January 2026. But if you owe less than £3,000 tax and have a source of PAYE income, you can ask for the tax to be deducted from that income through PAYE.

If you send in a paper tax return, HMRC will send you a calculation of the tax you owe, based on the information in your return. If you file online, the software will calculate your tax bill, but will not usually take into account any instalments you have already paid for the year.

If you make a gain from selling property, rather than waiting until you send in a tax return, you must declare the gain and pay the tax due within 60 days of the sale completing. For more information see the GOV.UK page 'Reporting and paying Capital Gains Tax'.

MAKING TAX DIGITAL (MTD)

Making Tax Digital (MTD) is a 10-year government strategy to automate the tax system. For those who need to complete a tax return, the system can be complex and onerous. The aim of MTD is to make paying tax through Self Assessment as easy as PAYE and to reduce Self Assessment errors and fraud (which are estimated to cost billions every year in lost tax).

MTD requires you to keep digital records and use software that sends information quarterly to HMRC, using secure digital channels. Tax due can then be calculated more or less continuously using this real-time information and the government is requiring quarterly tax reporting compared with annual reporting under the current Self Assessment system. MTD already applies to VAT (see Chapter 9) and (following various delays), from April 2026, will apply to income tax paid by businesses and landlords with incomes over £50,000 a year and from April 2027 for those with income over £30,000. You can voluntarily sign up to MTD before then (Directory, p 37).

SORTING OUT PROBLEMS

As the 'self' in the name suggests, under Self Assessment, it's your responsibility to declare all your taxable income correctly and pay the right amount of tax. Even if HMRC calculates your tax bill for you, it's still your responsibility to make sure the calculation is correct. You might think that Self

Assessment opens the way for people to forget some of their income, either by accident or design. However, HMRC may check what you're doing and can impose hefty fines if you are found to have negligently or deliberately under-declared your income or gains.

If you make a mistake on your tax return, you have a year to correct it without too much fuss – in the case of an online return, just go back online to make the changes and then refile your return. For the tax return covering the 2024/25 tax year, this means you can make corrections up to 31 January 2027. If you filed a paper return, you'll need to contact HMRC.

If, say, you find you have failed to claim a tax relief or allowance in the past, you can go back up to four years to put matters right. For example, providing you claim by 5 April 2025, you can go back to the 2020/21 tax year to claim an allowance or relief and get a refund of the tax you paid. You need to write to HMRC to do this.

If you pay tax late, you will be charged interest (in addition to any fines). You normally get (tax-free) interest on tax refunds, though the rate of interest is currently low. In May 2024, interest was charged on tax paid late at 7.75 per cent a year, but paid on refunds at just 4.25 per cent a year.

An independent Adjudicator's Office can examine taxpayers' complaints about their dealings with HMRC and, if considered valid, determine what action would be fair. Complaints appropriate to the Adjudicator are mainly limited to the way HMRC has handled someone's tax affairs, for example excessive delay, errors, discourtesy or how discretion has been exercised. In deciding fair treatment, the Adjudicator has power to recommend the waiving of a payment or even the award of compensation if, as a result of error by HMRC, the complainant had incurred professional fees or other expenses. Before approaching the Adjudicator, taxpayers must have tried to resolve the matter first with HMRC.

Getting a tax refund

When you retire, you may be due for a tax rebate. If you are, this would normally be paid automatically, especially if you are getting a pension from your last employer. The matter could conceivably be overlooked, either if you are due to get a pension from an earlier employer (instead of from your last employer) or if you will be receiving only a State Pension and not a company pension in addition.

In either case, you should ask your employer for a P45 form. Then either send it – care of your earlier employer – to the pension fund trustees or, in the event of your receiving only a State Pension, to the tax office together with details of your age and the date you retired. Ask your employer for the address of the tax office to which you should write.

A note of caution: of course everyone likes a tax rebate and HMRC processes tens of thousands per year after checking Self Assessment returns. But however welcome a cash payment may seem, don't believe any email promising a refund. These are 'phishing' scams, designed to get your financial details. HMRC says it never sends notifications of a tax rebate by email, and never asks you to disclose personal or payment information by email. For more advice see GOV.UK (Directory, p 37).

National Insurance contributions (NICs)

Getting older has some benefits and one is that, once you reach State Pension age, you no longer pay National Insurance contributions (NICs) even if you carry on working. There are different classes of National Insurance: Class 1 is paid by employees; self-employed people pay Class 4 (and used to pay Class 2). If you are the owner-director of your own company, you are technically an employee and pay Class 1 contributions.

If you work for an employer, once you reach your State Pension birthday, you need to show your employer proof of your age – usually your birth certificate or passport, if you have one. However, if you do not want your employer to see your documents, you can ask HMRC to provide you with a letter confirming that you've reached State Pension age. You might have a 'certificate of age exemption' issued some time ago. HMRC no longer issues these, but, if you have one, you can show that to your employer as proof. Class 1 contributions stop as soon as you reach State Pension age. If you've paid any NICs since then, you can get a refund provided the error is put right before the end of the tax year.

If you're self-employed, Class 4 contributions continue a bit longer, and you stop paying them from 6 April following the tax year in which you reached State Pension age.

If you're under State Pension age, you can find details about National Insurance contributions for the self-employed in Chapter 9. For employees, these are the rules:

• You pay Class 1 contributions. These are a percentage of your earnings split into two bands with different rates applying to each.

- In 2024/25, they are 8% on earnings above £12,570 a year falling to 2% on earnings above £50,270. The thresholds are frozen at these levels until April 2028 (unless the new government changes this).

Capital gains tax

You may have to pay CGT if you make a profit (called a 'taxable gain') on the sale or other disposal (for example, gift) of a capital asset – for example, stocks and shares, jewellery, any property that is not your main home (and, in some cases, part of the profit from selling your main home) and other items of value. CGT applies only to the actual gain you make, so if you buy shares to the value of £100,000 and sell them later for £125,000, the tax office will be interested only in the £25,000 profit you have made.

Not all your gains are taxable. Some types of gain are always tax-free (see the next section). In working out your gain, you may be able to deduct various expenses, such as buying and selling costs, and the cost of changes that enhance the value of the asset (but not maintenance costs). You can deduct losses you have made in the same tax year, as well as losses carried forward from earlier years. Then, the first slice of otherwise taxable gains is tax-free, because you have an annual exempt amount of £3,000 in 2024/25. This is a large reduction from the previous levels of £12,300 and then £6,000 in the previous two years. If you are still left with a taxable gain, CGT is charged at the following rates:

- 18% and 24% (previously 28%) in the case of residential property;
- 10% and 20% in other cases (for example, shares and other investments).

Now comes the complicated bit! To work out which of the rates applies, you add the taxable gain to your taxable income. Any part of the gain that falls into the basic-rate income tax band is taxed at the lower rate; anything more is taxed at the higher rate.

REAL-WORLD EXAMPLE

Arif inherited a house when his father died. The value of the house at that time was £200,000. The value had risen by the time Arif sold the home. He had never lived there, and, after deducting various expenses and his annual exempt amount, he had a taxable gain of £10,000. His income that year used up all of his basic-rate income tax band except the last £1,000. This means that when the gain was added to his income, £1,000 of the gain fell into the basic-rate band and was taxed at 18 per cent. The remaining £9,000 of gain was taxed at 24 per cent. Therefore, his CGT bill was £2,340, leaving him with a net gain after tax of £7,660.

Free of CGT

The following assets are not subject to CGT and do not count towards the gains that may be taxed:

- your only or main home (but see below);
- your car;
- wasting assets, meaning those with an expected life of 50 years or less (such as a caravan or boat);
- personal belongings up to the value of £6,000 each (sets of things count as one asset);
- British money, which includes gold sovereigns from 1837 onwards, and foreign currency for your personal use abroad;
- gains on some investments, including, for example: assets held in an ISA, UK government stocks (gilts), most corporate bonds, life insurance policies (in most cases) and terminal bonuses from SAYE contracts;
- building society mortgage cashbacks;
- betting and lottery winnings, including Premium Bond wins;
- gains on the disposal of qualifying shares in a Venture Capital Trust (VCT) or within the Enterprise Investment Scheme (EIS), provided these have been held for the necessary holding period.

Some types of transaction (regardless of the assets involved) are also free of CGT. These include:

- gifts to registered charities and community amateur sports clubs;
- gifts between husbands and wives or civil partners (but be aware that any gain or loss does not disappear, but is taken over by the recipient and may be taxed when they eventually sell or give it away);
- gains made during your lifetime on whatever you leave at death.

Your home

Any gain you make when you sell your only or main home is usually exempt from CGT. This exemption is called 'private residence relief' or PRR.

However, there are certain 'ifs and buts' that could be important. If you convert part of your home into an office or into self-contained accommodation on which you charge rent, that part of your home may be separately assessed and CGT may be due when you sell.

There may also be a CGT bill on part of the gain if you do not live in your home for prolonged periods. Some periods of absence are usually still exempt – for example, if you have to live away because of work – and living somewhere else during the first year of ownership is ignored for CGT if you are doing the place up. The last nine months of ownership is also always free of CGT regardless of whether you still live in the home or not. A longer 36-month period applies for people moving into a care home.

If you let out part or all of your home, in general CGT applies to that part of any gain you make when you dispose of the home. However, if you let just part of your home and provided you are living in the rest of the home, tax may be reduced if you are eligible for 'letting relief'. The amount of letting relief is the lowest of: the value of PRR you are getting on the rest of the home; the amount of the gain associated with the letting; or £40,000.

CGT normally does not apply if you simply take in one lodger who is treated as family, in the sense of sharing your kitchen or bathroom.

If you leave your home to someone else who later decides to sell it, then he or she may be liable for CGT when the property is sold, but only on the gain since the date of death. (But see Chapter 15 for the inheritance tax rules.)

If you own two or more homes, only one of them at a time can count as your main residence and so be exempt from CGT. Each time the number of homes you have changes, you have a two-year window in which you can nominate which home is your main home. Having made the nomination, you can switch it to a different home at any time. Husbands and wives, and civil partners, can only have one main home between them, but unmarried partners can each have a different main home.

Information and advice about tax

The main source of information about UK taxes is GOV.UK. It has general guides to most aspects of the taxes discussed in this chapter, and also forms and helpsheets that accompany the Self Assessment tax return (Directory, p 37). If you need to check the detailed tax rules, HMRC publishes the manuals which its own tax inspectors use (Directory, p 37). You can also check the letter of tax law at legislation.gov.uk. HMRC has a variety of helplines to help with all aspects of tax (GOV.UK, Directory, pp 36–37).

There are also some well-informed non-government guides to tax, such as the Low Incomes Tax Reform Group's site (Directory, p 37). If you are looking for an offline source, try *The Daily Telegraph Tax Guide*, updated yearly by Kogan Page.

Many people have straightforward tax affairs and can manage them for themselves. However, in some situations, you may want the help of a professional (contact information for the following and other professionals/organizations is available in the online directory that accompanies this book):

- If you run a business, you might employ an accountant to help you draw up your accounts and complete your tax returns.
- If you have complex tax affairs, want advice on saving tax or are in a dispute with HMRC about the amount of tax you owe, you might want to consult a tax adviser, such as a member of the Chartered Institute of Taxation (CIOT).
- If you want advice about IHT, estate planning or setting up a trust, consider a member of the Society of Trust and Estate Practitioners (STEP).
- If you need tax advice but cannot afford the fees that professionals normally charge, you may be eligible for free help from TaxAid (for tax problems you've been unable to resolve with HMRC, only if your income is £20,000 a year or less), or Tax Help for Older People (if you are 60 or older and have income of less than £20,000 a year).

There are also firms that offer to fill in your tax return for you. They do not all have formal qualifications, so you might want to consider a member of the Association of Tax Technicians (ATT).

There are various online calculators that can help you estimate how much tax and National Insurance you may have to pay on your salary. These include (Directory, pp 37–38):

- **GOV.UK**
- **MoneySavingExpert**

Check Which? (Directory, p 38) to calculate the tax implications when drawing a lump sum from your pension savings, as well as calculators for tax on dividends and National Insurance.

CHAPTER FIVE

Investment

Whether you have a lot to invest or only a little, deciding on the right investment strategy for you depends on your goals and other factors. If you are approaching retirement, a key concern may be how to invest your pension pot for an income that is robust even when inflation is high. At the same time, you might want to be reassured that your investments are helping to tackle environmental and social challenges, such as climate change, or at least avoiding support for firms that use child labour, manufacture arms or are involved in other practices that you feel strongly about.

General investment strategy

Investments differ in their aims, their tax treatment and the amount of risk involved. Since no one can predict the future accurately, the aim for most people is to acquire a balanced portfolio, which typically means diversifying your saving and wealth across a mix of investments from the four main 'asset classes':

1 *Cash investments* are savings accounts with banks, building societies and National Savings & Investments (NS&I), and similar investments. Many offer easy access to your money. They are lower risk and so the potential returns are much less than other types of investment. Your money is generally secure, but you risk losing value due to tax and inflation.

2   *Bonds* are, effectively, an IOU from the government or big companies. When you buy one, you are lending money that earns an agreed fixed rate of interest. UK government bonds (gilts) are backed by the state and are assumed to be as good as guaranteed, whereas the status of other countries' government bonds varies and corporate bonds carry greater risk but offer the possibility of improved returns. Another way of investing in loans to companies is peer-to-peer lending.

3   *Investing in property* either directly as a buy-to-let investor or indirectly through investment funds that hold mainly commercial property and/or shares in property companies. Property carries more risk than the previous two asset classes, but can be a relatively stable source of income. Property prices go down as well as up, and it can take longer to sell property, so you need to be prepared for delays in getting your money back.

4   *Equities (shares)* basically means backing the companies that drive economic growth. You can do this by buying shares in individual companies. This asset class typically exposes you to a higher risk of losing some (or even all) of your investment but higher returns and more chance of staying ahead of inflation.

With all the asset classes, you can invest direct or through professionally managed investment funds. There are a variety of funds available, each with different objectives and each carrying different levels of risk and reward.

The precise mix of asset classes that is right for you depends on your life stage, circumstances and personal views about investing. In general, when you are young, experts recommend that you have all or the vast majority of your long-term investments in equities. In the past, the standard advice was to gradually shift towards lower-risk investments, such as bonds and shares, during the last 10 years before your intended retirement. (An often-quoted rule of thumb was to subtract your age from 100 and that's the proportion of your portfolio to have in equities – for example, at age 60, have 40 per cent in equities.) However, that strategy was based on the idea of buying an annuity when you retire and, if that's not your plan, it may be appropriate to have substantial equity investments even after retirement.

Source of money to invest

If you are looking at your investment options, you will need first to work out what money you have available. Possible sources include:

- *Your pension savings.* As explained in Chapter 3, many people these days have defined-contribution pension schemes (where you build up your own personal pot of savings) and, during your working years, you may want to get involved in how these savings are invested. On reaching retirement, many people are looking at drawdown as a way to provide retirement income. This means leaving your pension savings invested and so requires you to make choices about how to invest them. You can also draw cash lump sums out of your pension scheme before, at or during retirement. That's fine if you are planning to spend the money or give it away. However, with the exception of your tax-free lump sum at retirement, it's generally a bad idea to withdraw money from a pension scheme simply to save or invest it elsewhere, where it's likely to be taxed more heavily and/or be less likely to keep pace with inflation.

- *Individual Savings Accounts (ISAs)* are a way of investing tax-efficiently. There are different types and, although cash ISAs are the most popular, others let you invest in a range of investments of your choice.
- *Insurance policies* designed mainly for investment rather than life cover. These are normally free of tax in your hands (though tax will have been paid by the insurer). Many let you choose how you want to invest your money, from a range of investment funds.
- *Profits on your home*, if you sell it and move to smaller, less expensive accommodation. Provided this is your main home, there is no capital gains tax (CGT) to pay so you may have a substantial sum to invest.
- *Redundancy money*, golden handshake or other farewell gift from your employer. You are allowed £30,000 redundancy money free of tax and you may receive other taxable sums too, such as pay in lieu of notice and a lump sum for holiday you are owed (see Chapter 2).
- *Sale of SAYE* and other employee shares. The tax rules vary according to the type of scheme, the date the options were acquired and how long the shares were held before disposal. You can check the rules at GOV.UK (Directory, p 37).
- *Saving out of your income* may mean drip-feeding quite small amounts into your savings accounts or investments, but small sums quickly build up and regular saving removes trying to guess the 'best' time to invest. There are even apps these days that will automatically sweep excess money in your bank account to a savings or investment account; other apps round up amounts you spend with the extra few pence going into a savings account.

Your goal

Some saving and investment goals are fairly universal. For example, everyone's first saving priority must be to build up and maintain a 'rainy day' fund (also called an emergency fund) to cover unexpected expenses or dips in income. It needs to be held in cash accounts that you can access easily. If you are still working, ideally you should aim for at least three months' outgoings. This ensures that if your earnings stop, for example because of illness or redundancy, you can still cope financially until your situation improves or you can adapt to your new circumstances. If you're already retired, provided you have a secure income, you might be able to manage with a smaller emergency fund. However, if you are relying on drawdown for essential income, you might be wise to have enough cash savings to cover two or even three years' outgoings, so you can ride out dips in the stock market.

Another universal goal is having a secure income in retirement, but how you tackle this goal depends on your life stage. If you're of working age, your goal is to build up (accumulate) the funds you need. It's important that your planning ahead takes inflation into account both by setting your goal in terms of the buying power you'll need in retirement (see Chapter 2) and choosing investments that are likely to grow at least as fast as inflation. If you have reached retirement, your aim is to draw on (decumulate) your savings in a sustainable way that ensures you can maintain your living standards. This means choosing strategies or investments that will help you to increase your income over time as prices rise. This is not as daunting as it sounds. While inflation has been very high in recent years, it has now fallen back and the average over a long period of time is typically lower and likely to be closer to the government's target of 2 per cent a year.

Other goals vary substantially from one individual to another, for example saving to buy a home, for a holiday, to leave an inheritance. For a goal to be workable, you need to think about:

- *Scale.* How much will you need? This determines how much you must save or how much you need to draw from existing savings.
- *Timescale.* When will you need to draw on your savings, or how long must they last?
- *Degree of flexibility.* Does it matter if you miss your goal? By how much?

The choice of savings and investments for achieving your goal depends crucially on the amount of risk you are willing and able to take, the degree to which the tax system may help you build up or maintain the sums you need, and how much of your return is lost in charges.

Understand risk

In an ideal world you would be able to invest your money securely and achieve amazing returns. In the real world, those opportunities do not exist. If a deal sounds too good to be true, it really is. It will be a scam or have hidden charges or both. Don't be fooled. If you want a safe home for your money, the return will be low. If you want a higher return, you will have to take on some risk. And, for very high returns, the risk will also be very high (as, for example, buyers of cryptocurrencies have found).

The asset classes in broad order of increasing risk are: cash, gilts, corporate bonds and peer-to-peer lending, property and shares. The key to managing risk is diversification (spreading your money across different investments). So, don't invest in one company, one industry, one country or one asset class. Spread your money across a range. A convenient way to do this is to use investment funds, which are ready-made portfolios. You can manage risk further, by mixing and matching different funds.

There are three dimensions to consider when thinking about risk: comfort, need and capacity. The first is the level of risk you feel comfortable taking. In general, there is no point taking on so much risk that you have sleepless nights. However, you must balance that against the level and type of risk that you *need* to take in order to achieve your goal. For example, cash savings may feel safe, but they grow slowly and lose value as prices rise. So, to protect yourself against inflation, you may need to take on some degree of risk. Third, you should consider your capacity for loss. This means not taking risks with money that you really cannot afford to lose. For example, if you need a given minimum level of income to get by in retirement, it makes sense to secure that using low-risk investments like annuities rather than a higher-risk strategy such as drawdown. However, drawdown would be fine to provide any income over and above your minimum needs.

Look out for tax and charges

Your money has to work harder for you if part of your return is lost in taxes and charges. Chapter 4 explains the tax treatment of savings and investments, but you should always choose your savings and investments primarily on the basis of your goals and circumstances, not tax.

Charges also eat into the returns you make. In the case of savings, there are usually no explicit charges – they are simply reflected in the interest rate on offer. Use price comparison websites (Directory, p 32) to find the best returns, or check the tables published in the personal finance sections of newspapers. In general, expect to get a higher return if you have to lock up your money for a while (notice accounts and term bonds). Take note if the return includes a 'teaser rate' (payable for the first few months only), and be prepared to switch to a different account once the teaser rate ends.

If you invest direct in bonds and shares, you will have dealing charges to pay. For many people, it's more convenient and economical to invest through investment funds. However, these come with a range of fees and charges. Look for the 'ongoing charges' figure which bundles together the main charges into a single figure. Charges are typically expressed as a percentage per year of the amount you have invested. There are two points to note: the level of annual charges may sound low, but because they are taken year after year they have a substantial impact on the final value of your investment. For example, charges of 1 per cent a year would reduce the value of your investments by a sixth after 20 years and by a quarter after 30 years. Second, charges are deducted regardless of whether your investment has grown or not, so the fund managers get paid even if your investments earn you nothing or have fallen in value. So always check what charges you will pay and, if they are high, make sure you are satisfied that the extra charges are justified by the superior or extra service you expect to receive.

Sustainable and ethical investing

It has long been possible to choose investments and funds that match your ethical values. Typically, this has been through 'negative screening' (avoiding investment in, say, the arms industry, gambling, firms that exploit child labour, and so on) or 'positive screening' (seeking out investments in, say, green energy and firms supporting good employment practices). Some investment funds are specifically designed to comply with Sharia law and, because of the ethical stance this provides, can be an attractive choice for any investor, not just those of the Islamic faith.

However, the escalating climate emergency has given increased impetus to what has now become known as Environmental, Social and Governance (ESG) investing, especially for environmental sustainability. A survey by professional services firm PwC found that three-quarters of investors now feel sustainability is important but they want better information.

A major problem is inconsistency in the way ESG credentials are measured, with the risk of 'greenwashing' (where businesses and investments claim to be environmentally responsible but in reality are not). In the UK, European Union and some other countries, firms are required to publish reports disclosing their environmental impact and on a more consistent basis. Workplace pension schemes in the UK must explain how they take ESG matters into account when making investment decisions. When it comes to UK investment products, the regulator has introduced new rules effective from December 2024 on disclosure and labelling of funds so that it should become easier to direct your money into environmentally beneficial investments.

Meanwhile, the government has started to issue 'green gilts' and similarly some companies are issuing 'green bonds'. The money you invest through these is used for projects that tackle climate change.

To promote economic growth more generally, the previous government introduced policies aimed at encouraging those company pension schemes that work on a defined-contribution basis to invest in 'patient capital'. This means investing in assets that are designed to produce returns over the long term but cannot readily be cashed in over the short to medium run. They cover, for example, investment in infrastructure including green technologies. If you belong to this type of pension scheme, you'll see that the information you get includes details about the scheme's investments in these 'illiquid assets'. The requirement does not affect schemes' overriding duty to invest for the benefit of members. The new Labour government has pledged to review workplace pensions with a view to their investing more in UK industry.

More information

The sections which follow give details of the main different types of savings and investment available. Here, in addition, are some organizations that are well worth checking out and have information on savings and investments (website details can be found in the Directory, p 34–35):

- Fund information: **Trustnet** and **Morningstar**
- **Moneyfactscompare**
- **MoneyHelper**
- **MoneySavingExpert**
- **MoneySuperMarket**
- **This is MONEY**
- **UK Sustainable Investment and Finance Association (UKSIF)**
- **Which?**

Annuities

Annuities are financial products from insurance companies that give you an income in exchange for a lump sum. The income may be for a fixed period (a temporary annuity) or for life (lifetime annuity). The lump sum you buy it with may be your pension savings (in which case, you buy a pension annuity) or from any other source (in which case you buy a 'purchased life annuity') – the distinction matters because the two types of annuity are taxed in different ways.

Pension annuities

In the past, the most popular way to convert the money saved up in a pension pot into income was to buy a lifetime annuity. It promises to pay a guaranteed income for life, no matter how long you live, in return for you handing over part or all of your pension savings. This type of annuity is best thought of as a type of insurance, because it protects you against living longer than your savings would otherwise last. The money is paid to you by the annuity provider (insurer) and can be paid monthly, quarterly or annually. Income tax on pension annuities is worked out in the same way as tax on earnings and usually collected through PAYE (see Chapter 4).

You choose at the outset what type of annuity you want to buy and from which provider. Once you've made the purchase, you are locked into whatever deal you have struck. There are several factors that determine the amount of income you'll get from a lifetime annuity:

1 **Interest rates**. Annuity rates go up and down with the interest rates on UK government bonds. From 2008 to 2021, interest rates were low and annuities were perceived by many as being poor value and so fell out of favour. Since 2022, interest rates have increased markedly and so the income offered by annuities has risen substantially too. As a result, annuity sales have soared.

2 **Life expectancy**. When you buy an annuity, you are basically put in a pool with lots of other people of the same age as you. The average life expectancy of people in the pool determines the level of annuity income you are all offered. If life expectancy generally is rising, the amount of annual income you're offered will fall because it is expected to be paid out for longer. Recently, it looks as though life expectancy increases have slowed, which may help to stabilize the income offered.

3   **Your personal life expectancy.** The older you are when you buy an annuity, the higher the income you get, because your remaining life is expected to be shorter than when younger. You can also get a higher-than-average annuity income if your health is poor, you smoke or you are affected by other factors that tend to reduce your life expectancy.

4   **The type of annuity you choose.** A standard annuity offers a level of income that is the same year after year. Disadvantages are that the income stops when you die, even if you die soon after purchase, and that inflation reduces the buying power of the income. There are all sorts of different types of annuity that aim to overcome these disadvantages and offer other options too. The more special features you add to an annuity, the lower the starting income tends to be.

Be aware that some pension schemes promise to pay annuities at a rate that was set some time ago – these are called 'guaranteed annuity rates' (GARs). Often, these rates were set when the general level of interest rates was much higher, and so the GARs offer a more generous income than you can normally get today. Your pension scheme provider may offer to buy out your GAR for a cash sum (to be transferred to another pension scheme or possibly, if you are aged 55 or over, to be paid out). Think carefully before accepting such a deal as you will be giving up a valuable secure retirement income. If your GAR is worth £30,000 or more, you will be obliged to get professional financial advice before making a decision.

You don't have to use your whole pension pot to buy an annuity. For example, you might use part to buy an annuity to top up your retirement income to the minimum secure income you want and then put the rest into drawdown. You could use part of your savings to buy an annuity now and another tranche to buy another annuity later on. You don't have to buy a lifetime annuity: you could buy a temporary annuity that provides an income for a set number of years, and then shop around later on to buy a further annuity if you want to.

Purchased lifetime annuities

Purchased lifetime annuities (PLAs) are similar to the type of lifetime annuity you buy with your pension pot, except they tend to offer slightly worse value and are taxed in a different way.

You buy a PLA with any lump sum that is not a pension pot – but could be the tax-free lump sum you've taken from a pension pot (see Chapter 3). Part of every income payment you get is treated for tax as if it were a return of a bit of your original lump sum and is tax-free; only the remaining part of each payment you receive is treated as income and is taxable in the same way as interest (see Chapter 4). The size of the tax-free part depends on how long you are expected to live (the longer your life expectancy, the lower the tax-free part). The insurance company will tell you how much taxable interest you are getting and will normally deduct the tax due.

Types of annuities

Whether you are considering a pension annuity or a purchased life annuity, there is a whole range of annuities you can buy.

CONVENTIONAL/LEVEL ANNUITIES

You will receive a fixed income for life. This is the simplest and most straightforward annuity available. According to the Association of British Insurers, 82 per cent of annuities sold are of this type because they know what their income will be for the rest of their life, no matter how long they live. However, to some extent, this certainty is an illusion, because inflation will over the years reduce the amount that this level income can buy.

ESCALATING ANNUITIES

This is where income grows each year either by a set amount or in line with inflation. If you want your annuity to partially or fully increase with the cost of living, this could be the type to choose.

However, the starting income will be a lot lower and, with few providers offering inflation-linked annuities, they are not necessarily good value for money. An alternative strategy would be to choose a conventional annuity but save part of it for use later on in maintaining your standard of living.

INVESTMENT-LINKED ANNUITIES

The amount you get from this type of annuity is dependent on the performance of stock market investments. These annuities expose your pension to the ups and downs of the stock market. There is the possibility of rising retirement income: you are taking the risk that you may get less in the hope you will get more. If you are comfortable with this risk, you might want to consider drawdown instead.

ENHANCED/IMPAIRED-LIFE ANNUITIES

This type of annuity means more income for smokers or those with poor health. They offer extra if your life is likely to be shorter than average. Some 40 per cent of people should consider buying an enhanced annuity as it could make a huge difference to their income. You can qualify on grounds such as blood pressure, high cholesterol or being overweight.

ANNUITY WITH GUARANTEE

A reason why people are reluctant to buy an annuity is the fear of dying soon after and so receiving too few payments to recoup the outlay. Annuities with guarantee address this problem by paying out for a set number of years (often 5 or 10), even if you die. Such guarantees reduce the level of income you get, but not dramatically unless you are fairly elderly. If you die within the guarantee period, your nominee will receive the balance of the guarantee as income. An annuity with guarantee is not a good way of providing for someone who is financially dependent on you (or co-dependent because you share bills), because they may survive much longer than the remaining guarantee period – consider a joint-life annuity instead.

CAPITAL-PROTECTED ANNUITY

This type of annuity is similar to an annuity with guarantee, except that it pays out a lump sum to your nominee if you die during the early years. A capital-protected annuity guarantees to pay out as much as you originally paid for the annuity. If you die before your payments equal the full amount, the balance is paid to your nominee. With pension annuities, if you were under 75 at the time of death, the payment (up to a limit – see Chapter 15) is normally tax-free. If older, your nominee pays income tax on the lump sum at their normal rate.

JOINT-LIFE ANNUITIES

These annuities continue to pay out after one partner dies. They are particularly suitable for couples (married or not), and especially if one partner has no pension of their own. But they come at a cost: you will receive a lower income level. Joint-life annuities pay out as long as one of a couple is living, and you have a choice of percentages for the survivor's pension, such as 100 per cent, 50 per cent or two-thirds, which are commonly offered.

FLEXIBLE ANNUITIES

These are annuities where the income you receive changes in a pre-defined way or alters if specified events occur. They are sometimes described by the shape that the income would make if plotted against time on a graph. For example, a U-shaped annuity starts with a relatively high income to support active early retirement, declines in the years when perhaps you stay home more and kicks up again in the later years when you might need care. Other variable annuities might pay an income that is normally level, but increases if you develop care needs. Although flexible annuities became a possibility in the UK from 2015 onwards, to date they have not really taken off.

DRAWDOWN AND OTHER ALTERNATIVES TO ANNUITIES

The main alternative to buying an annuity is to put your pension pot into a drawdown fund where it remains invested and you can flexibly draw out income and lump sums as and when you want to.

Because insurance companies make sure they can keep on paying the income an annuity promises by investing in relatively low-risk investments, there is little point investing your drawdown fund in those same types of investment, or, worse still, cash – you'll simply get the similar low-risk, low-return income that an annuity would provide, but without the guarantee that your income will continue for life. For drawdown to produce a superior income, the fund needs to be invested in higher-returning, but higher-risk, investments such as equities. This gives the best chance of generating a higher income over the long term that can keep pace with inflation even after paying the charges associated with drawdown funds. However, the value of equities can go down as well as up, so you need to be prepared for an income that, while hopefully on a rising trend, may nevertheless need to go down in some years.

From time to time, so-called 'third-way' products come onto the market. These work in a variety of ways but basically aim to offer the best of both worlds: a secure income (like an annuity) but higher (by linking to the stock market like drawdown). The charges for these products are often high, and you should question whether you really need them since you can usually create your own DIY third way by using part of your pension pot to buy an annuity and putting the rest into drawdown.

How to obtain an annuity or drawdown

In general, you should shop around to see which providers offer the best annuity rates. The MoneyHelper comparison tool is a good place to start

(Directory, p 33). However, you are strongly recommended to get advice from a financial adviser specializing in annuities and drawdown. They can help you decide on a suitable strategy for you and, if annuities are part of that strategy, which type to choose and whether you may be eligible for the higher income that comes with an enhanced or impaired-life annuity. Bear in mind that your pension pot is a juicy target for scammers, so never take advice from strangers who contact you out of the blue or anyone who offers you a deal that sounds too good to be true. See Chapter 1 for how to find an adviser.

National Savings & Investments (NS&I)

NS&I is one of the biggest savings institutions in the country, tasked with raising money for the government. Normally, it deliberately does not try to out-compete banks and building societies and its products are ultra-safe because they are backed by the government, so normally you will not get the highest return on your savings. For many people, NS&I is attractive because the government guarantee is unlimited (compared with the maximum £85,000 per person per institution with bank and building society savings accounts), and it offers some unique products such as Premium Bonds and Green Savings Bonds where the money raised is used for environmental projects. A relatively new NS&I offering is British Savings Bonds, launched in 2024. These are fixed-term bonds offering a guaranteed income or growth and with the rather vague promise to invest your money 'back into supporting the UK'.

In the past, NS&I also offered index-linked certificates, where your savings grew with inflation. Although these have not been available to new savers for many years, existing savers have been able to roll over their old certificates into replacement index-linked ones. This strategy has paid off during recent periods of high inflation and underlines why it makes sense to diversify your savings and investments.

Most types of investment offered by NS&I are broadly similar to those provided by banks and other financial bodies. Full details of all their products and how to invest are listed on their website (Directory, p 35).

Bank and building society accounts

Banks, building societies and credit unions offer a range of accounts and savings products. As with NS&I (mentioned above), what distinguishes all these products is that the amount you originally invest is generally secure (no capital risk) but vulnerable to inflation and the return you get is in the form of interest, which can either be rolled up in the account or, depending on the product, paid out. Unlike NS&I products, if your bank, building society or credit union went bust, your savings would be protected only up to a maximum of £85,000 (see *Investor protection* later in this chapter for more about this), so you might want to spread your money across several institutions if you have a large amount of savings.

Broadly speaking, there are two types of products on offer: transaction accounts and savings accounts.

Transaction accounts

Transaction accounts are the ones you use for managing your money day to day, typically a current account, and usually pay no interest.

There is a huge difference between being in credit and dipping into the red. Charges on current account overdrafts can be high. Some accounts come with a small free overdraft facility which can be a useful buffer. If you are worried about going accidentally overdrawn, you could consider a basic bank account, which has most of the features of a current account except you cannot go overdrawn. All the big banks offer basic bank accounts, though they tend not to publicize this, so ask if you are interested in banking this way. If you have a smartphone, there are also apps either from your own bank or separate app providers that you can set up to send you alerts if the balance in your account dips below a pre-set level. There are also apps that let you automatically transfer a short-term loan from a separate provider into your bank account if you're about to go overdrawn, which can be cheaper than a traditional overdraft.

Savings accounts

Banks and building societies also offer a wide range of savings accounts. These differ in a variety of ways: whether you operate the account online, by phone or post, or can visit physical branches; whether your money is readily accessible or locked in for a while (in which case you should expect a higher return); whether the interest you get is variable or fixed; whether the interest is taxable or tax-free; the minimum you have to save, whether as a lump sum or regular amount; and how the return is paid to you, as income or a lump sum.

Here are some of the different types of savings accounts available.

INSTANT-ACCESS SAVINGS ACCOUNT

This attracts a relatively low rate of interest, but it is both easy to set up and very flexible, as you can add small or large savings when you like and can usually withdraw your money without any notice. It is a good home for an emergency fund or if you are saving short term for, say, a holiday.

FIXED-TERM SAVINGS ACCOUNT

You deposit your money for an agreed period of time, which can vary from a few months to over a year. In return for this commitment, you will normally be paid a superior rate of interest. There is a minimum investment: roughly £1,500 to £10,000. If you need to withdraw your money before the end of the agreed term, there are usually hefty penalties.

ISA SAVINGS

The advantage of a cash ISA is that your interest up to any amount will be tax-free and, as far as anyone can tell, that will continue to be the case for as long as your account continues to be an ISA. (This contrasts with relying on your Personal Savings Allowance to make your interest tax-free, since the allowance might not cover all your interest and could be reduced in future years.) You can use up to the full amount of your annual ISA allowance (£20,000 in 2024/25) to invest in a cash ISA. While ISAs generally can be thought of as a tax wrapper that you fill up with investments of your choice, cash ISAs are invariably a single account that comes ready wrapped as an ISA. So, if you are interested in taking out a cash ISA, you must search for accounts with the word 'ISA' in their name.

You used to be limited to taking out an ISA with just one provider each year, but that restriction has been lifted since April 2024. Now, you can start multiple ISAs in the same year, as long as the providers involved agree to accept your savings. Once you have an ISA, you can transfer it to another provider if you want to. A word of warning though: do not cash in the ISA with a view to reinvesting with the new provider – that way you lose the tax-free ISA status. Instead, tell the new provider you want to make a transfer, and they will deal directly with your old provider to make the transfer and retain the tax-free status. But be aware that not all ISA providers accept transfers.

More information

Interest rates vary considerably and change over time, so you should regularly check whether you are still getting a good deal and be prepared to switch if necessary. There are a host of price comparison websites that let you compare the deals on offer, and the personal finance sections of news-papers publish a selection of deals from these services. It's best to use at least a couple of sites rather than rely on just one, for example (for websites, see Directory, p 32):

- **Moneyfactscompare**
- **MoneySavingExpert**
- **MoneySuperMarket**
- **Which?**

If you are interested in digital apps that help you compare, switch and/or manage your savings, explore the list of regulated providers on the Open Banking site (Directory, p 35). (Open Banking is the technology that enables secure sharing of your financial information.)

Fixed-interest securities

'Fixed-interest securities' (also called fixed-income securities or bonds) is a generic name for loans that investors make to a government, local authority, company or other organization. The loans are used by government to fund its spending programmes, by companies to finance investment, and so on. However, instead of the investor waiting until that organization eventually pays the loan back, you can sell the loan on the stock market, and similarly buy existing loans there too. For as long as you are the owner of the bond, you usually receive regular interest payments.

The return from investing in fixed-interest securities comes in two parts: the interest you get, and any gain or loss you make on selling the bond or when it is repaid (called 'redemption'). If you hold the bond until redemption, you know exactly what return you will get (since the interest and repayment amount are both fixed). But if you intend to sell earlier, you don't know what return you'll get because that depends on the future stock market price. There is an inverse relationship between a bond's price and the general level of interest rates in the economy, so if future interest rates are expected to fall, the stock-market price of bonds will tend to rise.

Credit risk is the risk that the issuer of the bond will not make all the promised payments of interest and pay the redemption value. Credit risk is one of the main determinants of the price of a bond: the higher the risk of the issuer defaulting, the bigger the return the investor needs in order to be persuaded to take on the risk. In general, UK government bonds (called gilts) are considered very low risk (because governments can as a last resort use tax or monetary policies in order to keep up the loan repayments or buy back the bonds). Therefore, the return on gilts is lower than the return from the corporate bonds of a well-established company which itself is lower than the return from bonds of a new-venture company. Specialist credit-rating agencies assess the risk of default and give bonds a rating, the highest of which is AAA (triple-A).

As well as conventional government bonds, you can also invest in index-linked gilts. With these, the interest and redemption value increase in line with inflation.

A type of corporate bond that has been popular with private investors in the past is permanent interest-bearing shares. These are a form of fixed-interest investment previously offered by some building societies as a means of raising share capital and still available to purchase on the stock market. They pay regular, fixed sums of interest. However, unlike most bonds, as the name suggests, PIBS are 'permanent', in other words, they have no redemption date. This means that the only way to get your money back is to sell them on the stock market or to accept whatever offer is made if the issuer decides to buy back the PIBS. Moreover, the market in PIBS is not particularly active, so you might struggle to sell at a good price.

Interest from bonds is taxable as savings income, but any gains from gilts and most corporate bonds are free of CGT (see Chapter 4). However, even the interest is tax-free if you invest through a pension scheme or a stocks and shares ISA. Whatever you invest in the latter uses part (or even all) of your annual ISA allowance (£20,000 in 2024/25).

More information

For comprehensive information about gilts, visit the government's Debt Management Office (DMO) website (Directory, p 35). To get started, search on 'Publications' for its useful guide for private investors. The Building Societies Association has a handy guide to PIBS (Directory, p 34).

Corporate bonds are often bought and sold in quantities that exceed private investors' means, but 'retail bonds' are corporate bonds tailored specifically for the private investor market. Information on what's available and current prices can be found on the London Stock Exchange website (Directory, p 35).

You can buy and sell bonds through a stockbroker, and the London Stock Exchange has a searchable register you can use to find a broker (Directory, p 35). If you want to invest through an ISA, choose a broker that offers this option. You will only be able to hold bonds directly through a pension scheme if you have a Self-Invested Pension Plan (SIPP), and many brokers offer this arrangement. Alternatively, for gilts, the DMO provides a dealing service for private investors (Directory, p 35). A stockbroker can offer advice if you want it, while the DMO provides just an 'execution-only' service (carrying out your dealing instructions but no advice). With both, you pay dealing charges, and the DMO service may be cheaper. Alternatively, invest through an investment fund.

Peer-to-peer lending

Traditionally, savers have deposited their money with banks, which lend the money to individuals and firms who want to borrow. Now savers can lend direct to borrowers without the bank as a middleman by going through platforms (websites with the appropriate information and tools). This is called peer-to-peer lending.

Peer-to-peer platforms do not have the branch networks and infrastructure of banks and building societies, so can operate at low cost and typically charge fees to borrowers. While the details of each platform vary, as an investor, you normally spread your money across loans to a wide range of borrowers for a set term and, in return, receive interest. You can often choose the level of risk you want to take and receive a higher return for making riskier loans.

Marketing for peer-to-peer lending often targets savers who would traditionally have used bank and building society accounts, questioning why you would leave your money languishing at low interest rates when you can get much higher returns from peer-to-peer lending. But make no mistake: peer-to-peer lending is not the same as putting your money in a savings account. You are lending to individuals and businesses that may default on their loans, so this is more like investing in corporate bonds. However, unlike corporate bonds, there is no stock market for peer-to-peer lending, and you might struggle to find an investor willing to take over your loans if you want your money back early and/or have to pay a fee to the platform. Be aware too that peer-to-peer loans do not count as deposits for regulatory purposes and so the deposit-protection scheme that protects up to £85,000 of bank and building society savings does not apply to peer-to-peer lending. Some peer-to-peer platforms have set up their own compensation schemes, but these have yet to be fully tested. The pandemic highlighted the risks with an increase in defaults, and widespread suspension of new loans and of withdrawals for investors. In the aftermath, some platforms no longer accept loans from retail investors; another prominent platform has converted to a bank and so no longer offers peer-to-peer lending at all. Stricter regulations since 2019 had already caused some platforms to stop accepting loans from private investors.

The interest you earn from peer-to-peer loans is taxable and taxed in the same way as savings income (see Chapter 4). If you make a loss because a borrower defaults, you can deduct the loss from other peer-to-peer loan interest you get before working out the tax due. (You cannot set losses off against any other type of income.) However, where the platform offers this route, you can invest in peer-to-peer lending through an Innovative Finance ISA in which case your interest will be tax-free. Whatever you invest this way uses part of your annual ISA allowance (£20,000 in 2024/25).

More information

To investigate peer-to-peer lending opportunities, see (Directory, p 36):

- **MoneySuperMarket.**

Always check that any peer-to-peer firm you are considering is authorized by the FCA by checking the Financial Services Register (Directory, p 9). For details about the taxation of peer-to-peer loans, visit GOV.UK (Directory, p 37).

Equities

Companies need money when they first start up, and often later on to fund new investment. You have already seen that one way they do this is to issue corporate bonds. Another way is to issue equities (shares). Unlike corporate bonds, shares do not (usually) offer you a fixed return. Instead, shareholders may receive a share of the profits the company makes, through the payment of dividends, and may make a gain – or loss – if they can sell the shares for more than they paid.

Existing shares in public companies can be bought and sold by investors through a stock market. The main stock markets in the UK are the London Stock Exchange where well-established companies trade and the Alternative Investment Market (AIM) for newer and smaller companies. When you buy shares, you in effect become an owner of a small part of the business, and shareholders can usually have a say in how the company is run by voting at its annual general meetings.

Equities are risky – you may lose some or even all of your money and dividends are not guaranteed. However, shares tend to give higher returns over the long run (10 years or more) than either cash or bonds. It's easy to see why: when experts talk about economic growth, they are really talking about the collective output of all the firms in the country. So investing in shares means you are investing in the growth of the economy. Providing you will not need your money back soon or at short notice and so can sit out any short-term dips in the stock market, shares are likely to be the backbone of your investment portfolio.

That said, share prices can be artificially inflated and subsequently depressed by, for example, the Bank of England's monetary policy. And booming share prices for firms in 'hot' sectors like artificial intelligence may turn out to be bubbles that burst. Moreover, some firms reliant on fossil fuels that thrive today may slump if they do not adapt to policies to tackle climate change. So equity investing is not straightforward.

Chapter 4 explains how dividend income from shares is taxed and how you may need to pay CGT if you make substantial gains from shares. However, private investors do not pay tax if their dividends fall within their Dividend Allowance (£500 in 2024/25) and their gains are less than their annual CGT exemption (£3,000 in 2024/25). Note that both these allowances have been cut sharply over the last two years, so, while you might have escaped tax on your shares in the past, you might find you have to pay tax now. However, income and gains from equities will be tax-free if you hold them through a pension scheme or stocks and shares ISA.

For most people, the best way to invest in shares is through an investment fund – see the next section.

More information

Information about share prices is published daily in some newspapers, including the *Financial Times*, and is available online, for example, on stockbrokers' websites and the London Stock Exchange (Directory, p 35). Another useful source is Yahoo Finance (Directory, p 35).

You can buy and sell shares through a stockbroker, and the London Stock Exchange has a searchable register you can use to find a broker (Directory, p 35). Brokers offer three levels of service:

- *execution-only*, where they just carry out your buying and selling instructions;
- *advisory*, where they provide reports and recommendations as well as carrying out your dealing instructions;
- *discretionary management*, where the broker makes the buying and selling decisions and runs a portfolio for you that is suitable given your goals and circumstances.

The more input you have from the broker, the more expensive the service. Thus, execution-only is the cheapest option. These days, dealing is normally done through an online platform, though there are still some high-street brokers and banks that offer stockbroking through their dwindling branches or by phone. You may be charged commission on each trade, and you can expect to pay about £10 to £12 per trade and/or a regular platform fee, say £25 a quarter. Stamp duty is charged on purchases (but not sales) of existing shares (but not new shares), normally at a rate of 0.5 per cent of the size of the transaction. If the value of your purchase or sale is more than £10,000, you will have to pay a 'PTM levy'. This funds the work of the Panel on Takeover and Mergers (PTM) which supervises and regulates deals between companies that affect shareholders.

If you want to invest through an ISA, make sure the broker you choose offers this option. You will only be able to hold shares directly through a pension scheme if you have a SIPP, and many brokers offer this arrangement.

To learn more about investing in shares and other stock market investments, a good read is *How the Stock Market Works* by Michael Becket of *The Telegraph*, published by Kogan Page.

Investment funds

Investment funds are ready-made portfolios of shares, bonds and/or other investments. There are literally thousands of funds to choose from with a huge diversity of investment aims and risk-return profiles. While this can be confusing, once you find your way around, mixing and matching different funds offers an abundance of ways to tailor your asset allocation to your particular needs and circumstances. There are many different categories of investment fund but, broadly, you can invest in:

- **The money market.** This corresponds to the cash asset class, but you are investing at wholesale money market rates that tend to be higher than the returns you can get from bank and building society accounts. Although high interest rates have raised returns in this sector, what's important is whether your returns are beating inflation.
- **Government and corporate bonds.** Some funds specialize in gilts, others UK corporate bonds, and yet others the bonds of overseas governments and companies. These funds are often useful for investors seeking income. However, the rise in interest rates since 2021 made gilt markets unusually volatile.
- **Equities.** This includes funds investing in UK equities, global equities or the shares of companies in particular countries or regions, such as Europe, Asia or the United States. Regardless of region, some funds focus on well-established companies, others on smaller ones. Some funds specifically aim to produce a steady income, while others focus mainly on capital growth.
- **Property.** These funds either invest directly in property – usually commercial premises, such as office blocks, shopping centres, care homes and student accommodation – or they invest in the shares of developers and other property firms. Because property generates rental incomes, these funds can be particularly useful for income investors. However, high interest rates (pushing up costs where property purchase has been funded by borrowing) and the rise in home-working (reducing demand for office space) have created a tough climate for commercial property.
- **Mixed investment.** The best portfolio for you will often require a mix of asset classes. Some funds offer this mix ready-made, with a choice of the proportion of the fund invested in equities up to, say, 35, 60 or 85 per cent. Some funds achieve the mix by directly holding assets from the different classes. However, others are 'funds of funds', in other words a single fund that invests in a selection of other funds. A point to watch out for with funds of funds is that you have two layers of charges, which can make them expensive.
- **Absolute return funds.** These aim to achieve a positive return after charges in all market conditions. However, there is no guarantee, and these funds do not have a particularly good track record.
- **Specialist.** There are also a whole host of funds investing in assets, such as gold, other commodities, the oil sector, fintech, healthcare, and so on.

Investment funds can be structured in a variety of different ways: unit trusts and open-ended investment companies, investment trusts, exchange traded funds, life insurance funds and pension funds. What they have in common is that your money is pooled with that of lots of other investors, and professional managers select the investments in the fund.

The main advantages of investing through an investment fund are:

- **Affordability and risk management:** unless you have a lot to invest, it would be hard for you to spread your money across as many different shares, bonds or other investments as a fund can. With an investment fund, investing as little as £500 as a lump sum or £50 a month can give you a diversified portfolio that targets the right level of risk for you.
- **Convenience:** with a fund, you are not involved in the administration of making trades, gathering dividends and looking after each investment in your portfolio. This is an especially welcome advantage if you want to invest in assets in another country where the systems involved may be very different from those in the UK. In addition, someone else makes decisions about which investments to buy and sell and when, saving you the time and effort of acquiring skills and researching this for yourself.

The downside of using an investment fund is that there are a variety of middlemen involved who all have to be paid, including for example the fund managers, the custodians responsible for the safe-keeping of assets and the dealers who carry out the fund's buying and selling instructions. The higher the charges, the less of the return on the underlying assets is left for you. The precise range and nature of charges vary depending on how the fund is structured, but a key figure to look for is 'ongoing charges' which bundles together the main charges into a single figure that you can use to compare the costs of one fund with another.

A large part of the ongoing charges figure is the annual management charge (AMC) which pays the professionals who run the fund. The AMC will be higher for a fund that uses 'active management', meaning that the fund managers are trying to 'beat the market' by picking stocks and the timing of deals that they think will do well. This contrasts with passive investment, which simply aims to replicate the market return. (Passive funds tend to have 'tracker' or 'index' in their name, or refer directly to the index they track, such as the FTSE 100.) Research by Morningstar in 2021 found that 80 per cent of active funds had ongoing charges between 0.5 and 2 per cent, while 90 per cent of passive funds charged less than 0.5 per cent.

Paying higher charges could be worthwhile if active funds consistently deliver superior returns. But there have been numerous studies over the decades that suggest this is not the case. Research by the UK's financial regulator in 2016 estimated that over a 20-year investment term a passive investor would be £14,439 better off than a typical active-fund investor.

However, the firms that dominate stock market indices include oil and gas companies, so if you're interested in environmentally sustainable investing, you might find appropriate active funds suit you better than funds that track the market. Alternatively, there are now passive funds that track specially constructed indices of low-carbon businesses' equities and/or bonds.

More information

Before you invest, you should be given or directed to a Key Investor Information Document (KIID) or Key Facts Document, which sets out the aims, charges and risks of the investment fund, and broadly where your money will be invested. The KIID is set out in a standardized way that will help you compare one fund with another. Funds also usually publish their own factsheet with further information. You can obtain these documents either direct from the fund manager or from the broker or other intermediary through which you invest.

You can find a lot of information and data about investment funds on the websites of the two main trade bodies for the sector:

- The **Investment Association** (Directory, p 35): the trade body representing unit trusts, open-ended-investment-companies (OEICs), insurance funds and, since 2019, eligible exchange traded funds (ETFs). These are all types of investment fund (called 'open-ended') where the price you pay closely reflects the value of the underlying assets in the fund.
- The **Association of Investment Companies (AIC)** (Directory, p 34): the trade body representing investment trusts, venture capital trusts and similar funds. These are all types of investment fund (called 'closed-ended') that you buy and sell on a stock market and the price you pay may be at a discount or premium to the value of the assets in the fund.

Other useful websites for general information, news and data about investment funds include:

- **MoneyWeek** (Directory, p 32)
- **Morningstar** (Directory, p 35)

- **This is MONEY** (Directory, p 35)
- **Trustnet** (Directory, p 35)

There are a variety of ways to invest. Some funds are available only if you are using a financial adviser. With others, you can contact the fund managers direct. If you have a pension plan or investment-type life insurance, the provider gives you access to the available funds. However, a common way to buy investment funds is through online investment platforms, often called 'fund supermarkets'. Traditionally, you would access an investment platform through a computer, but increasingly you can use smartphone apps. Some well-known investment platforms and apps, which can be found in the Directory, pp 35–36, are:

- **AJ Bell**
- **Fidelity**
- **Hargreaves Lansdown**
- **Interactive Investor**
- **iWeb**
- **Nutmeg**
- **True Potential Investor**
- **Wealthify**

To find a stockbroker, use the London Stock Exchange searchable register (Directory, p 35).

Investment-type life insurance

Life assurance can provide you with two main benefits: it can provide your successors with money when you die and/or it can be used as a savings plan to provide you with a lump sum (or income) on a fixed date or when you decide to cash in the policy. There are three basic types of life assurance: term policies, endowment policies and whole-life policies.

Term policies involve making regular payments for an agreed period, for example until such time as your children have completed their education, or the seven years until the risk of a tax bill on a lifetime gift (potentially exempt transfer, see Chapter 15) has expired. If you die during this period, your family will be paid the agreed sum in full. If you die after the end of the term (when you have stopped making payments), your family will receive nothing. So term insurance is not used for investment.

Endowment policies also promise to pay out on death within a fixed period of time, but unlike term policies, endowment policies also pay out a cash sum if you survive to the end of the term. This makes endowment policies expensive if all you need is life cover, but a possible basis for a savings plan or lump-sum investment bond. As a savings plan, you sign a contract to pay regular premiums over a number of years and in exchange receive a lump sum on a specific date. Most endowment policies are written for periods varying from 10 to 25 years. There are penalties if, having paid for a number of years, you decide that you no longer wish to continue. As an investment bond, you pay in a lump sum which can either be left to grow or can be used to provide a regular income.

Whole-life policies are designed to run for the whole of your remaining life and to pay out on your death whenever that occurs. Assuming you keep the policy going, it will definitely pay out one day, and so it builds up a cash-in value. That cash-in value makes whole-life policies suitable as a basis for investment.

Both whole-life policies and endowment policies offer three basic options: without profits, with profits or unit-linked:

- *Without profits.* This is sometimes known as 'guaranteed sum assured'. What it means is that the insurance company guarantees you a specific fixed sum (provided of course you meet the various terms and conditions). You know in advance the exact amount your successors will get. This type of policy is expensive because of the guarantee.
- *With profits.* You are assured a relatively low guaranteed fixed sum plus an addition, based on the profits that the insurance company has made (in part from investing the payments made by you and other policyholders). By definition, the profits element is not known in advance. This is the type of policy that in the past was popularly combined with an interest-only mortgage to form an 'endowment mortgage'. However, in recent times the widespread failure of the endowment policies to produce enough to pay off the mortgage in full means that endowment mortgages are less common these days.
- *Unit-linked.* The premiums you pay are invested in one or more investment funds. These may be the insurance company's own funds or a selection of unit trusts and OEICs. The value of your policy depends on the performance of the investments in the funds.

Charges can be high and the taxation of life policies is complex – see the HMRC Helpsheet *HS320 Gains on UK life insurance policies* from GOV.

UK. Be aware that, although the return on investments held through a life policy may be tax-free in your hands, the insurer has usually already paid tax that you cannot reclaim.

More information

To invest through a life insurance policy, either contact insurance companies direct or arrange through a financial adviser.

Investor protection

There are stringent rules on businesses offering investment services, overseen by a regulatory body, the FCA. This is charged by Parliament with responsibility for ensuring that firms are 'fit and proper' to operate in the investment field and for monitoring their activities on an ongoing basis. Investment businesses (including firms giving financial advice) are not at liberty to operate without authorization or exemption from the FCA. Operating without such authorization (or exemption) is a criminal offence. You can check whether a firm is authorized and for which types of business by looking them up in the Financial Services Register (Directory, p 9). If the firm is not authorized or you have any doubts, do not do business with it.

Authorized firms must comply with the FCA's high-level principles and detailed conduct of business rules. The principles embed a 'Consumer Duty' that requires firms 'to act to deliver good outcomes for retail customers'. These outcomes should be: products and services that are fit for purpose and offer fair value; timely, understandable information to help you make decisions; and support that meets customers' needs. Unsolicited visits and telephone calls to sell investments are for the most part banned. Where you do take up a product, you typically have a cooling-off period (typically 7 or 14 days) within which to change your mind. Firms must also have a proper complaints procedure, with provision for customers to receive fair redress, where appropriate.

Complaints and compensation

If you have a complaint against an authorized firm, in the first instance you should take it up with the firm concerned. You may be able to resolve the matter at this level, since all authorized firms are obliged to have a proper complaints-handling procedure.

If you have gone through the firm's complaints procedure, or if after eight weeks you are still dissatisfied, you can approach the Financial Ombudsman Service (FOS) (Directory, p 9), which will investigate the matter on your behalf and, if it finds your complaint is justified, may require the firm to pay compensation; depending on your losses, this could be up to £430,000 in 2024/25. If you disagree with the Ombudsman's decision, you still have the right to go to court should you wish to do so.

The Financial Services Compensation Scheme (FSCS) (Directory, p 9) is the compensation fund of last resort for customers of authorized financial services firms. If a firm becomes insolvent or ceases trading, the FSCS may be able to pay compensation to its customers. The amount of compensation varies depending on the type of product involved: up to £85,000 per person per institution in the case of bank, building society and credit union accounts; up to £85,000 in the case of investments; and up to 100 per cent without limit in the case of life insurance products (including annuities).

However, be aware that these complaints and compensation arrangements protect you if you have been unfairly or dishonestly treated by a firm. They do not provide protection against investment risk. Unless you were misled or badly advised to take on a risky investment, the ups and downs of bonds, shares, investment funds and similar investments are just an inherent part of those assets.

Scams

According to the trade body, UK Finance, consumers lost £1.17 billion to fraudsters in 2023 – a huge sum, although slightly less than in the previous year. According to the FCA, the most common investment scams involve shares, bonds, foreign exchange and cryptocurrencies. In the past many scams started with a cold call, but these days email, websites or social media are even more common ways for scammers to try to get your money.

To stay safe, as a minimum, the FCA recommends that you do not respond to any contact out of the blue; check the firm against the Financial Services Register (Directory, p 9) and against the FCA warning list of known scams (Directory, p 9); and get professional advice before handing over any money. For more information about what to do if you are contacted by a scammer or lose money this way, see Chapter 1.

CHAPTER SIX

Your home

Over the years, surveys have consistently shown that many people consider owning property as part of their plan for financing retirement. The home is seen as a valuable asset that provides a kind of super-emergency fund. However, this begs the question of how the home will be converted into cash if the need arises – for example to provide extra income or pay for care. Moreover, your home is not just an investment, it is a place to live. So other considerations as you age are how well your home still meets your needs. For some people, the right option may be to move to a smaller property that releases cash or is easier to manage. For others the answer may be to stay put and adapt their present home or consider equity release (for example, as a way to cope with the rising cost of living).

Whether you move or stay, there are also many ways that you can organize and manage your home to make it a more financially viable, safer and more comfortable place to live in later life.

Staying put

Since moving house is said to be one of the most stressful things in life, it makes sense to consider whether there are ways of adapting your existing home to provide what you want.

Extending and improving your home

There are all kinds of ways to improve your property and maximize its potential: from relatively simple cosmetic updates (such as redecorating) to more complicated work including adding a new kitchen or a downstairs bathroom. Before embarking on any improvements, it is sensible to work out which ones will be most suitable and add value to your property or improve your living standards. Large-scale projects such as loft conversions and extensions inevitably involve some financial investment. But the total cost of improving your home may be lower than the cost of moving, once fees and stamp duty are taken into account. Building an extra room, often through a loft conversion, is popular as it can add an extra bedroom and possibly even a bathroom. Other favourites are a kitchen makeover, refreshed or extra bathrooms and, increasingly, energy efficiency measures, such as new windows and solar panels. Whatever you decide, stick to the rules. Any new work must comply with building regulations (GOV.UK: Directory, p 20). You may need planning permission (GOV.UK: Directory, p 20) and, under the Party Wall Act (GOV.UK: Directory, p 20), where appropriate you must also notify your neighbours.

A few judicious home improvements carried out now could make the world of difference in terms of comfort and practicality. Stairs need not be a problem, even when you are very much older, thanks to the many types of stair lifts now available. Even so, a few basic facilities installed on the ground floor could save your legs in years to come. Similarly, gardens can be redesigned to suit changing requirements. Areas that now take hours to weed could be turned into extra lawn or a patio. Decking is also a popular option, but can be slippery and high maintenance, so choose the materials carefully.

Options if you have a leasehold property

There are two ways of owning your home: freehold or leasehold. With freehold, you own your home indefinitely and it's up to you what improvements or other changes you want to make to it and even the extent to which you keep your property in good repair. With leasehold, you own the property for a set period of time – when first created, leases are typically anything from 99 years to 999 years, though you may have bought from a previous leaseholder and so have a shorter period left. When the lease ends, the property reverts to the freeholder and, in the meantime, you pay an annual sum in ground rent to the freeholder. You and the freeholder have joint responsibility for the property. The freeholder may organize regular mainte-nance, but require you to pay an annual service charge to cover the costs. If major work is required, the freeholder may ask you for a lump sum towards the cost. You may also have to pay a permission fee if you want to make changes, such as rewiring or adding a conservatory.

Long leases are rare in Scotland, but in England and Wales, most flats are leasehold. Historically, houses have been freehold, but in recent years new-build homes have been sold on a leasehold basis and with scandalously high and escalating ground rents. As a result, new legislation was passed affect-ing properties in England and Wales. Since 30 June 2022, ground rent on most new leases must be zero, and the same has applied to new leases on retirement properties since 1 April 2023. Further legislation to cap ground rents for existing leaseholders was unfortunately abandoned when Parliament scrambled to finish its business once last year's General Election was announced. However, other measures did pass, including: a ban on the sale of new leasehold houses other than in exceptional circumstances; making it easier for leaseholders to buy their freehold; making the standard lease extension 990 years (up from 90 for flats and 50 for houses); removing the two-year ownership requirement before being eligible to buy a lease extension; making service charges more transparent and easier to challenge when unreasonable. The new government's manifesto promises to go further, with the aim of ending leasehold altogether and also ending unfair mainte-nance costs.

Many people do not necessarily want to buy the freehold or extend the lease but do want protection from a landlord. Among other rights, where leaseholders believe that their service charges are unreasonable they can get free, independent advice from the government-funded Leasehold Advisory Service (Directory, p 18) and, if necessary, ask a tribunal, rather than a court, to determine what charge is reasonable. This includes work that has been proposed but not yet started. Also, where there are serious problems with the management of a building, tenants can ask the tribunal to appoint a new manager. Further information is available at GOV.UK (Directory, p 18). For information about leasehold rights in Northern Ireland, see Directory (p 18).

Another useful source of information and help for leaseholders is the Federation of Private Residents' Associations Ltd (FPRA) (Directory, p 18), which is the national not-for-profit organization for private residents and residents' associations.

Moving to a new home

If you do decide to move, it may make sense to do this sooner rather than leaving it to the point where you feel forced to move (say, due to health reasons). With time to spare, you will have a far greater choice of properties and are less likely to indulge in panic buying. Beware of taking on commitments such as a huge garden. While this might be a great source of enjoyment when you are in your 60s, it could prove a burden as you become older. If you are thinking of moving out of the neighbourhood, there are other factors to be taken into account such as access to shops and social activities, proximity to friends and relatives, availability of public transport and even health and social support services. While these may not seem particularly important now, they could become so in the future.

The question of downsizing is something that affects many over-60s. While a smaller house may be easier and cheaper to run, make sure that it is not so small that you are going to feel cramped. Remember that, when you and your partner are both at home, you may need more room to avoid getting on top of each other. Also, if your family lives in another part of the country, you may wish to have them and your grandchildren to stay. For advice on adapting to a smaller home, contact APDO UK (the Association of Professional Declutterers and Organisers) (Directory, p 16). And, if it's decluttering that is putting you off moving, you might consider hiring a storage unit so that you can move now and sort through your possessions at a more leisurely pace later on.

You should also consider the area you are moving to. Even if you think you know an area well, check it out properly before coming to a final decision. If possible, take a self-catering let for a few weeks, preferably out of season when rents are low and the weather is bad. A good idea is to limit your daily spending to your likely retirement income rather than splurge as most of us do on holiday. Do your research, for example visit Property Detective (Directory, p 17). To check out local crime rates, see the police website (Directory, p 17).

This is even more pertinent if you are thinking of moving abroad; see Chapter 7.

Counting the cost

Moving house can be an expensive exercise. It is estimated that the cost is between 5 and 10 per cent of the value of a new home, once you have totted up extras such as stamp duty, valuation fees, legal fees, estate agent's commission and removal charges. If you are moving to release some of your housing wealth, you are probably a cash buyer and so will not need a mortgage, but do not be tempted to skimp on areas that a mortgage lender would have insisted on, such as a valuation and buildings insurance.

For a free, anonymous-to-use calculator that can give you a ball-park figure for tax, legal and other costs of moving, see the Moving Cost Calculator at House Move Pro (Directory, p 17) or Reallymoving (Directory, p 17).

SDLT AND ITS EQUIVALENTS

Stamp Duty Land Tax (SDLT) is a tax on the purchase (but not sale) of a property in England and Northern Ireland. There are equivalent taxes in Scotland (Land and Buildings Transaction Tax, LBTT) and Wales (Land Transaction Tax, LTT). What you pay for the property is divided into slices, and a different SDLT rate applies to each slice. Assuming this is your only home, since 23 September 2022 normally the first slice up to £250,000 (due to fall back to £125,000 from 31 March 2025) is tax-free; the next £675,000 at 5 per cent, the next £575,000 at 10 per cent and anything over that at 12 per cent. (There are special rates for first-time buyers – see GOV.UK (Directory, p 17) for details.)

If you already own another residential property, an extra 3 per cent SDLT is added to the above rates. So the first slice of £250,000 is taxed at 3 per cent, the next £675,000 at 8 per cent, and so on. This would apply, for example, if you bought your new home before selling your old one. However, you can claim a refund of the extra 3 per cent SDLT, provided you sell the additional home within 36 months. Claim back the SDLT by post or online GOV.UK (Directory, p 16).

You don't have to do the sums yourself. There is a stamp duty calculator at GOV.UK (Directory, p 17). For Scottish LBTT, see Directory (p 18). For Welsh LTT, see Directory (p 18).

REAL-WORLD EXAMPLE

Marloes decided to sell her four-bedroom house and buy a bungalow closer to where her son lives. There was no immediate buyer for her house, but she went ahead and bought the bungalow on 6 October 2024 for £320,000, using money from her pension fund and other savings. This meant she had to pay an extra 3 per cent SDLT. The tax bill worked out as (3% × £250,000) + (8% × £70,000), or £13,100 in total. As long as she sells her old house by 5 October 2027, she will be able to claim back £9,600 of the SDLT (3% × £320,000).

SURVEY OR VALUATION FEE

A lender will require you to have a valuation report (cost from £150 to £1,500 but free with some mortgages) but this does not tell you about the condition of the property you are buying. For that, you need a survey. The cheapest (around £250) is a condition report but it is superficial and may not alert you to flaws that cause you trouble and expense later. Many people opt for a Homebuyer's Report (cost about £450) which is more detailed. If you are buying an older property or one in a poor state of repair, it is worth getting a full structural survey (£600 or more). To find a surveyor, visit the Royal Institution of Chartered Surveyors (RICS) website (Directory, p 17).

If you are buying a newly built house, there are a number of safeguards against defects. Look for a National House Building Council (NHBC) warranty or its equivalent. The NHBC operates a 10-year 'Buildmark' residential warranty and insurance scheme under which the builder is responsible for putting right defects during the first two years. If a problem becomes apparent after more than two years, the homeowner should contact NHBC (Directory, p 17), as the Buildmark covers a range of structural aspects as well as double glazing, plastering and staircases.

LEGAL COSTS

As both a seller and a buyer, you will in effect have two sets of legal fees though you will normally appoint the same solicitor or conveyancer to handle both transactions. Expect to pay £1,250 upwards (including VAT at 20 per cent). In addition to the legal expert's own fees, there will also be the cost of local searches they carry out, for example, to check whether the property you are buying will be affected by any planning applications or unusual obligations, such as contributing to the maintenance of a local church (in which case, your solicitor will probably advise you to take out chancel repair liability insurance). These could all add another £400 to £700.

Most properties in England and Wales are these days recorded on the HM Land Registry, with just 14 per cent of land now unregistered. Similar registers apply in Scotland and Northern Ireland. Your solicitor or conveyancer will search the register to check that you and the other seller are the rightful owners and to check out anything unusual in the deeds of the home you are buying, such as covenants that restrict how you use the property, who is responsible for boundaries, and so on. However, you can also carry out searches of the relevant land registry (England and Wales, Scotland or Northern Ireland) yourself if you want to – see the Directory (p 17).

ESTATE AGENTS

Using an estate agent is free if you are a buyer, but you pay if you are a seller. The agent is acting on behalf of the seller (not prospective buyers) and should be aiming to get the best price consistent with achieving a sale. However, estate agents also have the normal obligations of any business to treat its customers honestly and fairly whether you are a buyer or a seller. What's more, the 1993 Property Misdescriptions Act prohibits estate agents and property developers from making misleading or inflated claims about a property, site or related matter.

Anyone can set up as an estate agent, so you might want to choose one that is a member of the National Association of Estate Agents (NAEA) Propertymark scheme. Propertymark requires its members to observe professional standards, such as having relevant qualifications, insurance and a complaints procedure if things go wrong. You can find a Propertymark member by looking out for the logo or visiting its website (Directory, p 17).

All estate agents by law must belong to one of the two approved complaints bodies: the Property Ombudsman service (Directory, p 17) or the Property Redress Scheme (Directory, p 17). You must have complained first to the estate agent involved and allowed up to eight weeks for a response.

Cost varies from around 1 to 3 per cent of the sale price plus VAT at 20 per cent. However, a few estate agents charge a flat fee of, say, £900 to £1,400 including VAT. As a buyer, finding your dream house may take a while. Websites are often a good place to start, so try Rightmove, Zoopla and OnTheMarket (Directory, pp 17–18).

ENERGY PERFORMANCE CERTIFICATE (EPC)

As a seller in any part of the UK, you will need to have an Energy Performance Certificate (EPC) that rates your property's energy use and suggests ways to make energy-saving improvements. As a buyer, you will want to inspect the EPC for the new home you are considering as it will give you a clue to potential running costs and any potential outlay required to make the property more energy efficient.

The EPC rating is on an A–G scale (like the EU energy label used on fridges and other white goods); the closer to 'A', the more energy efficient the home is. The average UK home has a 'D' rating, and the Energy Saving Trust suggests you think carefully before choosing any home with an 'F' or 'G' rating. For its size it will be expensive to heat, and your carbon footprint will also be larger. EPCs are valid for 10 years. You do not need an EPC for a listed property.

EPCs are produced by accredited Domestic Energy Assessors and cost from £35 to £100, depending on the size of the property. Your estate agent can arrange an EPC for you, but you will usually pay less if you arrange it yourself. To find an assessor in Scotland, use the online directory of domestic energy assessors (Scotland) (Directory, p 7). For the rest of the UK, see domestic energy assessors (Directory, p 7).

BRIDGING LOANS

With a home to sell, many older buyers do not need a mortgage. However, it's not always possible to align the timing of your sale and purchase. Tempting as it may be to buy before you sell, unless you have the money available to finance the cost of two homes – including the extra stamp duty involved as explained above – you need to do your sums very carefully indeed. Bridging loans are a way of getting over the problem, but can be a very expensive option. As an alternative to bridging loans, some of the major institutional estate agents operate chain-breaking schemes and may offer to buy your property at a discount (some 10 or 12 per cent less than the market price).

Bridging loans are available from mortgage lenders and also specialist firms (which may be tied to a single lender or able to search the market more widely). Check any firm you deal with against the Financial Services Register (Directory, p 9).

REMOVALS

Whether you are moving to the next street or halfway across the world, using a reputable firm of removers and shippers will remove many of the headaches. A full packing service is something you might consider, as it saves much anxiety and a lot of your time. Costs vary depending on the type and size of furniture, the distance over which it is being moved and other factors, including insurance and seasonal troughs and peaks. It pays to shop around and get at least three quotes from different removal firms. Remember, however, that the cheapest quote is not necessarily the best. Find out exactly what you are paying for and whether the price includes packing and insurance.

The British Association of Removers (BAR) (Directory, p 16) promotes excellence in the removals industry for approved firms, all of whom work to a rigorous code of practice.

Homes that are different

Not everyone wants to live in a conventional home, and some people get to a stage where they welcome some extra support. However, be aware that the alternatives to a conventional freehold home often involve extra costs and/or less security, so make sure you understand what you are getting into before you make the leap.

Retirement housing and sheltered accommodation

The terms 'retirement housing' and 'sheltered accommodation' cover a wide variety of housing, and while you may not wish to move into this type of accommodation just now, if the idea interests you in the long term it is worth planning ahead, as there are often very long waiting lists. See Chapter 14 for more detail.

Caravan or park home

Many retired people consider living in a caravan or park home. These can be kept either in a relative's garden or on an established site, possibly at the seaside or in the country. If you want to live in a caravan on land you own or other private land, you should contact your local authority for information about any planning permission or site licensing requirements that may apply. If, on the other hand, you want to keep it on an established site, there is a varied choice.

As anyone who has holidayed in a caravan will know, these are not always the small affairs that you hitch to the tow bar of your car. Many caravans are spacious and, while capable of being moved, are largely static, being permanently sited on a dedicated holiday or residential park. Park homes are similar in that they are technically classified as mobile homes, but are larger, more substantial prefabricated bungalows. Whether you are looking at a caravan or a park home, if this is to be your only or main home, you need to be aware of your rights and the range of issues that you need to check out. The information given here applies to England in particular, but the rules are very similar in the rest of the UK.

When you choose to live in a park home (or caravan), you typically buy the home but rent the land (called the pitch) on which it stands from the owner of the site where the park home is situated. If you want this to be your permanent home, it is essential that you check a number of facts about the site. First, does the site owner have planning permission and a licence to use the land as a caravan or park home site? Does the licence allow residential use rather than just holiday use and, if both, is the home you are interested in located in the residential part of the site? Is the permission indefinite or time-limited? If time-limited, your right to remain on the land will also expire, so it's essential that you choose a site with indefinite permission.

Provided the site is licensed for residential use and can have mobile homes on it all year round, you are likely to have a 'protected agreement' which means that the law gives you certain rights. This includes security of tenure, the right to give your home to another family member or to leave it in your will, and the right to sell your home. The site owner has obligations to maintain the pitch and provide the infrastructure of the park (pathways, lighting, pipework, and so on), but also has rights which include a commission equal to 10 per cent of the sale price if you sell your home to someone else. Governments in England, Wales and Scotland have looked at changing or phasing out the commission, but a 2022 study for the government suggested this could cause 40 per cent of sites to become loss-making and no change has been made.

You will be entering into a contract with the site owner, so you need to check the terms and conditions carefully. There may be restrictions on who can live on the site – for example, over-50s only, no children and only some types of pets. Importantly, you need to check the rent for the pitch – called the pitch fee – and how it can be reviewed, plus any other charges and the arrangements for services, such as gas, electricity, water and sewerage. Commonly, pitch fees are increased annually in line with inflation and often the site owner contracts with the providers of services and resells to you the energy, water, and so on, but may not charge more than they paid (plus VAT).

Park homes are becoming an increasingly mainstream form of housing, and you can search for them on exactly the same sites as you would when looking to buy any other home, such as Rightmove, Zoopla and OnTheMarket (Directory, pp 17–18). You buy either from the site owner or from an existing park homeowner. Park homes, while usually cheaper than a conventional home of similar size, are nevertheless often surprisingly expensive given that you are not acquiring the land on which they stand. Technically, you don't need a solicitor, but you will be spending a substantial sum and are strongly recommended to get legal advice (from a lawyer you choose, not one recommended by the site owner) and also to have a survey of the home done before you buy.

For more information about your rights when buying and living in a park home, you can find the websites for park homes in England, Wales, Scotland and Northern Ireland in the Directory (p 18).

For advice about buying and owning a park home, contact the Leasehold Advisory Service (LEASE) (Directory, p 18).

Self-build

Up to 1 in 10 new homes (around 12,000) completed each year in the UK are self-build homes. This is much lower than some other countries – for example 80 per cent of new homes in Austria. With typical cost savings estimated at between 25 and 40 per cent, the number of people wanting to self-build has been high and growing. As a result, the government introduced a statutory 'right-to-build' in England from October 2016. (There is no equivalent legislation in the rest of the UK.) Under this right, people can register their interest in self-building with the local authority where they want to build, and the local authority has a duty to consider granting planning permissions for suitably serviced self-build plots to meet local demand. You can find your local register on your local council's website and useful information about them through the National Custom & Self Build Association (NaCSBA) website (Directory, p 17).

Some lenders offer self-build mortgages to finance the purchase of land plus construction costs. However, as with any mortgage, it is essential to make sure that you are not in danger of over-committing yourself. The Building Societies Association publishes a useful guide on mortgages for *Self and custom build* (Directory, p 16).

Here are some other useful websites:

- **BuildStore** (Directory, p 16): advice on self-build, renovation, plots of land for sale, buying building materials and seeing how others build their own home, including a UK map of land for sale, plot search and calculator for working out your self-build costs.
- **Centre for Alternative Technology** (Directory, p 16): the Centre for Alternative Technology provides a free information and advice service on sustainable living and environmentally responsible building.
- **Homebuilding & Renovating** (Directory, p 17): self-build and renovation website, featuring house plans, building costs, house design, land for sale,

exhibitions and all the information you will need, including a self-build cost calculator.

- **Self Build Portal** (Directory, p 17): website from NaCSBA with comprehensive information and guidance on all aspects, including an interactive guide to help you decide whether your project is feasible, links to local authority registers and a diary of shows, workshops and other events for people interested in custom or self-build.

How green is your home?

Between 2021 and 2023, domestic energy bills increased from an average of around £1,000 a year to around £2,500 – and would have risen by even more without government schemes to cap the increase. Although global wholesale energy prices then eased and UK investment in sustainable energy sources is increasing, the expert consensus is that household energy bills are unlikely to revert to pre-2021 levels any time soon. This has made everyone look at ways to save energy, and simultaneously raised awareness of what greener lifestyles may entail if we are to tackle climate change. The previous UK government had already committed to reach zero net carbon emissions by 2050, and reinforced that by committing to get three-quarters of the way to that target by 2035. UK households account for about a quarter of the UK's greenhouse gas emissions (which drive global warming) and half of that comes from energy use in our homes. So, the UK will not meet its targets unless we make changes to the amount and type of energy we use, especially for heating our homes. The good news is that changes can cut our energy bills and some are free and easy to implement. But other changes require an upfront financial outlay, though there are some government grants that might help. Moreover, because the options and technology are still developing, knowing what changes to make can be confusing. So, let's take a look at the position as it stands now.

Some quick wins

There are lots of small ways to save on your annual energy bills and reduce your carbon footprint at the same time. Here are some suggestions from Energy Saving Trust:

- do one less dishwasher run per week: £12
- don't leave appliances on standby: on average saves £45

- insulate your hot-water tank: saves £40
- draught-proof doors and windows: saves £80
- turn off lights when no one's in the room: saves £7
- cut your time in the shower by four minutes a day: saves up to £55
- don't overfill your kettle: saves £29
- avoid the tumble dryer: saves £50
- do one less wash a week and switch to 30-degree cycles: saves £24

Turning down your heating thermostat by one degree Celsius can save a massive £105 a year. However, don't turn your heating so low that you jeopardize your health. Public Health England recommends a minimum home daytime temperature in winter of 18 degrees Celsius, or slightly higher for people aged over 65 or with a health condition.

Help with the cost of green improvements

Since 1 April 2022, if you live in England or Wales, you may be eligible for a government grant with the cost of replacing an existing fossil-fuel heating system (gas, oil or electric) with an air-source heat pump, a ground-source heat pump or, in some cases, a biomass boiler under the government's Boiler Upgrade Scheme (Directory, p 7). The grant is given as a £7,500 discount on the price you pay your installer. You will need to use an MSC-certified installer (Directory, p 7). Your home must have an Energy Performance Certificate (Directory, p 16) and be appropriately insulated. The number of grants available is small compared with the expected volume of demand for heat pumps, but the government sees the grants as a way of pump-priming the market and expects the price of heat pumps to fall as they become more mainstream. There is a lot of misunderstanding about whether air source heat pumps can work efficiently during the winter. However, these pumps have been used for decades in Scandinavian countries and are easily suitable for the British climate.

Until March 2019, the government actively encouraged homes to fit solar panels through a system of feed-in tariffs that paid households for selling their excess electricity to the national grid. Government-backed incentives have gone, but the price of solar panels has dropped dramatically and, under a replacement scheme (Smart Export Guarantee), commercial energy companies are obliged to strike deals with households to buy their excess energy.

The availability of other help with your energy bills and energy-saving home improvements varies across the nations and council regions of the UK. To find out what is available in your area, if you live in England or Wales, you will need to contact your local authority (Directory, p 7). If you are in Scotland, visit the Home Energy Scotland website (Directory, p 7). For Northern Ireland, contact the Northern Ireland Energy Advice Line (Directory p 7).

Here are some other websites (see Directory, p 7) that give advice and information on help with the costs of installation:

- **Energy Saving Trust**
- **Free Insulation**
- **Get Insulation Grants**
- **GOV.UK**: Find a grant
- **Home Heating Guide**

Insulation

One of the best ways of reducing utility bills is to get your house properly insulated (and you must do this to be eligible for the Boiler Upgrade Scheme). Heat escapes from a building in four main ways according to the Energy Saving Trust: through the roof, walls, floor and loose-fitting doors and windows. Insulation can not only cut heat loss dramatically, but will usually more than pay for itself within four or five years. Main types of insulation to consider are:

- *Loft insulation*: up to 25 per cent of your heat escapes through the loft. You may be able to lay insulation yourself. To find a specialist contractor, use the National Insulation Association (NIA) website (Directory, p 7). Be aware that loft insulation scams are rife, so do not respond to cold calls, texts or doorstep callers who tell you your existing insulation is now illegal or dangerous or offer you free inspections or spray insulation. Only do business with genuine firms with whom you have initiated the contact.
- *Doors and windows*: which account for about 20 per cent of heat loss, half of which can be saved with double glazing. Triple glazing is even more efficient but costs about 20 per cent more. Installation must be done by a FENSA-registered installer; see the Glass and Glazing Federation website (Directory, p 7). For a cheaper fix, consider draught-proofing strips.
- *Walls*: around a third of heat escapes this way. If you have cavity walls, consider injecting insulation between them. Cost could be around £200 for each two-storey wall but savings on your energy bills mean you should get your money back within five years. Solid wall insulation is considerably more expensive. This is work for specialist contractors, for example those registered with: British Board of Agrément (Directory, p 7); Cavity Insulation Guarantee Agency (CIGA) (Directory, p 7); Insulated Render &

Cladding Association Ltd (Directory, p 7); and National Insulation Association (NIA) (Directory, p 7).

- *Floors*: up to 15 per cent of heat loss can be saved by filling gaps in floorboards and skirting. Cork tiles, carpeting and underlay also help. See Energy Saving Trust (Directory, p 7).

Greening your electricity usage

According to National Grid, in 2023, 41 per cent of the electricity the UK uses came from renewable sources. You cannot physically change the make-up of the electricity delivered into your home because power generated from all the different sources goes into the national grid and you get what the grid delivers. However, by choosing a different provider or a 'green tariff', you can direct your money towards supporting green energy production.

Providers can supply you with green energy in different ways. For example, a provider may invest directly in its own wind farms or may buy some or all of their energy from other firms that generate green energy. Providers should tell you how their green deals work. Some green tariffs are time sensitive, so more of your usage is matched to green energy in off-peak periods than when demand is high. That means you would increase your contribution to sustainability by, for example, running your washing machine at off-peak times. For now, green providers and green tariffs tend to be a bit more expensive than ordinary energy bills.

A more direct way to switch to green electricity would be to generate your own by installing solar panels. Usually, this involves panels on your roof, which can face any way except north. The panels generate electricity even on cloudy days, but more when it's sunny. You can either sell your surplus electricity to the major energy providers (who are obliged by legislation to buy it) or you can install a battery to store your surplus for your own later use.

Ecoexperts, which is an advice and comparison website (Directory, p 7), advise that usually homes need 6 to 14 panels with the total cost ranging from around £4,200 to £10,000. However, the average household then cuts its electricity bills by around two-thirds. Ecoexperts reckon that the break-even point (when your annual savings have recouped the initial outlay) is 14.6 years, with pure savings for the remaining 10 or so years of the panels' life. They also suggest that installing solar panels increases the value of your home by around 4 per cent.

Green heating and hot water

As well as meeting your general electricity needs, you can use solar energy to heat water. There are two ways of doing this. One is to install a dedicated solar water heating system, which uses the sun to heat water in tubes that is then collected in a tank. This system costs from £3,000 to £6,000 according to the Centre for Alternative Technology (Directory, p 7) – and is suitable mainly for households with fairly high hot-water needs. The second way is simply to use some of the electricity created by solar panels (see previous section) to run an immersion heater. Either way, you'll need enough space to install a hot-water tank if you don't already have one.

When it comes to heating the rooms in your home, you could use solar panels to drive electric heating but you'd then need more panels, which might not be feasible depending on the size of your roof.

According to the government's 2021 Census, three-quarters of homes in England and Wales currently rely on gas boilers for their heating and hot water. Currently, the focus is on replacing them with electric heat pumps and the GOV.UK website has a heat pump check service (Directory, p 7) to help you decide whether this would be a suitable option for you. There are two types of pump: ground-source and air-source. They work like fridges in reverse by heating up a refrigerant turning it from liquid to gas.

With a ground-source heat pump, a series of pipes is buried in your garden which collect heat from underground. So, this is suitable only if you have a sufficiently large garden (and don't mind it being dug up). The more common option, an air-source heat pump, takes heat from the air (and works even down to air temperatures as low as –15 degrees Celsius). You'll need enough exterior wall space to house the extraction unit, which could be next to your garden or on a large balcony.

With both ground- and air-source heat pumps, the extracted heat is cranked up to a higher level by passing it through a compressor. The output tends to be around 40 degrees Celsius (compared with 60 degrees Celsius for a gas boiler) and so rather than giving instant heat, heat pumps more gradually heat the air space in a room and are run more continuously to maintain that level of heating. They work well with underfloor heating because of the large area from which the heat emanates. However, they can be used with radiators too, although you might want to replace your existing radiators with ones that have a larger surface area. If you want to heat water too, you'll need space for a hot-water tank (although a thermal battery could be an option if you don't have space for a tank).

Heat pumps are more expensive to buy and install than gas boilers. Depending on the size and type of your home, an air-source heat pump could cost between £5,250 and £9,500, while a ground-source heat pump would be £12,000 to £19,000 (before any government grants). You might have additional costs on top of that for a water tank or thermal storage battery (£775 to £3,000) and radiator changes (£125 to £225 per radiator). You might also have the cost of improving your home's insulation (see above) although this will be worth doing anyway to reduce your energy bills and use energy more efficiently.

Running a heat pump uses electricity, so that part of your bills will rise, but you will no longer have a gas bill (or heating-oil bill if that's your current system). Heat pumps reduce your carbon emissions by around two-thirds (more if you are on a green tariff for your electricity). They are more efficient than older boilers or other electrical heating, so overall your heating bills are likely to be less unless you already have an energy-efficient gas or oil boiler.

You might be wondering how noisy an air-source heat pump would be. Experts advise that they run at about 40 to 60 decibels at a distance of one metre, which is similar to an air-conditioning unit or dishwasher. For this reason, it's best to locate an air-source heat pump as far from neighbours as you can and away from windows.

Hydrogen boilers are also suggested as a potential method of home-heating in the future. This sounds appealing because superficially it seems relatively simple: just replace current natural gas boilers with hydrogen boilers. However, this possibility is still years away and the consumer body Which? has warned that the so-called 'hydrogen-ready' boilers currently being marketed are designed to run on a blend of 80 per cent natural gas and 20 per cent hydrogen, not 100 per cent hydrogen and that a full switch to hydrogen would involve changing gas pipes as well as boilers. Moreover, the challenges of cost-effectively creating and storing large volumes of 'green hydrogen' (as opposed to making hydrogen from fossil fuels) are still to be solved. So, heating your home with hydrogen is not something you can bank on just yet.

Help with fuel bills

If you are getting means-tested benefits, you will usually automatically get the Winter Fuel Payment (or Scottish equivalent) if you are over State Pension age, and regardless of age, Cold Weather Payment during a cold spell – see Chapter 2.

The largest energy providers have an Energy Company Obligation (ECO) to provide help with energy-saving home improvements if you are claiming means-tested or disability benefits, or if you live in social housing with an EPC rating of E or above. While the range of possible improvements is wide, the focus is mainly on cavity wall and loft insulation. The improvements might be free or you might be required to contribute towards the cost. To find out if you are eligible, contact your energy supplier.

If you're getting the Guarantee Credit part of Pension Credit (see Chapter 2) and your energy provider is part of the Warm Home Discount Scheme (Directory, p 7), you may qualify automatically for a one-off discount on your electricity bill for the winter months. If you don't qualify automatically, but your income is low, contact your supplier to see if you can be included in the scheme. If you live in a park home, there is a form you can complete; in order to be sent details contact https://charisgrants.com/partners/park-homes/.

Improvement, repair and adaptations

If your house needs structural repairs, a wise first step would be to contact RICS (Directory, p 17) to help you find a reputable chartered surveyor.

You may qualify for help with the cost of improvements and repairs from your local authority. Alternatively, you might qualify for help from the government with the interest payments on a mortgage to pay for them, if you are getting state benefits because your income is low – see Chapter 2.

Local authority assistance

Local authorities have discretion to help with renovations, repairs and adaptations to the home, or to help someone move to more suitable accommodation if that is a better solution. Any assistance given must be in accordance with the authority's published policy, which will set out the conditions for eligibility – for example, having income and/or savings below a specified limit. For further information contact the environmental health or housing department of your local authority. In addition, local authorities operate schemes aimed specifically at helping people with disabilities.

DISABLED FACILITIES GRANT (DFG)

Available in England, Wales and Northern Ireland, a grant from your council can help towards the costs of adapting your home to enable you to live there, should you become disabled. It can cover a wide range of improvements, including, for example, adaptations to make the accommodation safe for a disabled occupant, work to facilitate access either to the property itself or to the main rooms, the provision of suitable bathroom or kitchen facilities, the adaptation of heating or lighting controls, or improvement of the heating system. Provided the applicant is eligible, up to £30,000 may be available in England for all the above (local authorities may use their discretionary powers to provide additional assistance), £25,000 in Northern Ireland and up to £36,000 in Wales.

As with most other grants, there is a means test. The local authority will want to check that the proposed work is reasonable and practicable according to the age and condition of the property, and the local social services department will need to be satisfied that the work is necessary and appropriate to meet the individual's needs. The grant can be applied for either by the disabled person or by a joint owner or joint tenant or landlord on his or her behalf. For further information, contact the environmental health or housing department of your local council. See GOV.UK (Directory, p 2). If you live in Scotland, visit the Scottish Government website (Directory, p 5) for guidance on equipment that you either buy yourself or might be able to get from the NHS or your local authority.

Do not start work until approval has been given to your grant application, as you will not be eligible for a grant once work has started.

OTHER HELP FOR DISABLED PEOPLE

Your local authority may be able to help with the provision of certain special facilities such as a stair lift, telephone installation or a ramp to replace steps. Apply to your local social services department and, if you encounter any difficulties, ask for further help from your local disability group or Age UK group.

Many local Age UK branches operate a handyperson service, providing someone who can undertake small jobs around the home, such as putting up shelves, fitting a smoke alarm or grab rails, installing window locks or energy-efficient light bulbs, and so on. Call the Age UK Advice Line on 0800 678 1602 or visit the website to see if this is available in your area (Directory, p 3). To find other tradespeople, here are some useful contacts (Directory, pp 3–5):

- **APHC Ltd** (Association of Plumbing and Heating Contractors Ltd) maintains a national register of licensed members and can put you in touch with a reputable local engineer.
- The **Chartered Institute of Plumbing and Heating Engineering** can provide a list of professional plumbers.
- The **Federation of Master Builders**: lists of members are available from regional offices.
- The **Guild of Master Craftsmen** can supply names of all types of specialist craftspeople including, for example, carpenters, joiners, ceramic workers and restorers.
- **RICS** will nominate qualified surveyors in your area, who can be recognized by the initials MRICS or FRICS after their name.
- The **Royal Institute of British Architects (RIBA)** has a free Clients Service which, however small your building project, will recommend up to three suitable architects.
- The **Scottish and Northern Ireland Plumbing Employers' Federation** is the national trade association for all types of firms involved in plumbing and domestic heating in Scotland and Northern Ireland.

Home improvement agencies

Home improvement agencies (sometimes known as 'staying put' or 'care and repair' agencies) work with older or disabled people to help them remain in their own homes by providing advice and assistance on repairs, improvements and adaptations. They also advise on the availability of funding and welfare benefits, obtain prices, recommend reliable builders and inspect the completed job. Website details for the below are in the Directory, pp 19–20:

- **Care & Repair Cymru** is the organization to contact if you are in Wales.
- **Care and Repair Scotland**.
- **Foundations** is the national body for home improvement agencies in England.
- **Housing Advice NI** is the contact for Northern Ireland.
- Information on home improvement agencies and care and repair in the UK can also be found by contacting **EAC** (Elderly Accommodation Counsel) which helps older and elderly people with their housing, support and care needs.

- If you are a veteran, the **Royal British Legion** runs a service that can help with home improvements.

Safety in the home

The vast majority of accidents are caused by carelessness or by obvious danger spots in the home that for the most part could very easily be put right. Here are a few suggestions for you to make your home safer.

Steps and stairs should be well lit, with light switches at both the top and the bottom. Frayed carpet is notoriously easy to trip on. On staircases especially, defective carpet should be repaired or replaced as soon as possible. All stairs should have a handrail to provide extra support – on both sides if the stairs are very steep. It is also a good idea to have a white line painted on the edge of steps that are difficult to see – for instance in the garden or leading up to the front door. It may be stating the obvious to say that climbing on chairs and tables is dangerous – and yet we all do it. You should keep proper steps, preferably with a handrail, to do high jobs in the house such as hanging curtains or reaching cupboards.

Floors can be another danger zone. Rugs and mats can slip on polished floors and should always be laid on some form of non-slip backing material. Stockinged feet are slippery on all but carpeted floors. Spilt water or talcum powder on tiled or linoleum floors can cause accidents.

The *bathroom* is particularly hazardous for falls. Sensible precautionary measures include using a suction-type bathmat and putting handrails on the bath or alongside the shower. For older people who have difficulty getting in and out of the bath, a bath seat can be helpful. Soap on a rope is safer in a shower, as it is less likely to slither out of your hands and make the floor slippery. Make sure that all medicines are clearly labelled. Safely dispose of any prescribed drugs left over from a previous illness.

The *kitchen* is another place where it is important to be careful. Spills should be wiped up immediately to avoid slips. Any items you use regularly should be kept easily within reach. If you are having trouble preparing meals or doing the cleaning, your local social services can assist you with advice on helpful equipment. Living made easy (Directory, p 5) has guidance on aids to help with all sorts of tasks.

Falls are a great risk for older people. Two-thirds of people who fracture a hip in later life regain enough mobility to return home – but a third don't. So it pays to try to prevent such accidents. If you have a fall, stay calm. If you're unhurt, look for something firm to hold on to and get slowly to your feet again – then sit down and rest. If you are injured, try to get comfortable, stay warm and shift position every half hour or so until help arrives.

Fires can all too easily start in the home. If you have an open fire, you should always use a fireguard and sparkguard at night. The chimney should be regularly swept at least once a year, maybe more if you have a wood-burning stove. Never place a clothes horse near an open fire or heater, and be careful of flammable objects that could fall from the mantelpiece. Upholstered furniture is a particular fire hazard, especially when polyurethane foam has been used in its manufacture. If buying new furniture, make sure that it carries a fire-safety label, indicating that it is resistant to smouldering cigarettes and is match-resistant.

Portable heaters should be kept away from furniture and curtains and positioned where you cannot trip over them. Paraffin heaters should be handled particularly carefully and should never be filled while alight. Avoid leaving paraffin where it will be exposed to heat, including sunlight. If possible, it should be kept in a metal container outside the house. Never dry clothes near a portable heater or open fire.

Gas appliances should be serviced regularly by a Gas Safe Register registered installer (Directory, p 4). You should also ensure that there is adequate ventilation when using heaters. Never block up air vents: carbon monoxide fumes can kill. *If you smell gas or notice anything you suspect could be dangerous, stop using the appliance immediately, turn off your gas supply at the mains if you can, open the doors and windows and call the National Gas 24-hour emergency line free: 0800 111 999.*

More than one in three fires in the home are caused by accidents with *cookers*. Chip pans are a particular hazard: only fill the pan one-third full with oil and always dry the chips before putting them in the fat or, better still, use oven-ready chips that you just pop into the oven to cook. Pan handles should be turned away from the heat and positioned so you cannot knock them off the stove. If you are called to the door or telephone, always take the pan off the ring and turn off the heat before you leave the kitchen.

Cigarettes left smouldering in an ashtray could be dangerous if the ashtray is full. Smoking in bed is a potential killer.

Faulty electric wiring is another frequent cause of fires, as are overloaded power points. The wiring in your home should be checked every five years and you should avoid using too many appliances off a single plug. It is a good idea to get into the habit of taking the plug out of the wall socket when you have finished using an appliance, whether TV or toaster.

All electrical equipment should be regularly checked for wear and tear, and frayed or damaged flexes immediately replaced. Wherever possible, have electric sockets moved to waist height to avoid unnecessary bending whenever you want to turn on the switch. In particular, *electric blankets* should be routinely checked in accordance with the manufacturer's instructions. It is dangerous to use both a hot water bottle and electric blanket – and never use an under blanket as an over blanket or vice versa.

Electrical appliances are a common feature of labour-saving *gardening* but can be dangerous unless treated with respect. They should never be used when it is raining. Moreover, gardeners should always wear rubber-soled shoes or boots, and avoid floppy clothing that could get caught in the equipment.

As a general precaution, keep *fire extinguishers* readily accessible. Make sure they are regularly maintained and in good working order. Make sure you install a smoke alarm on each floor of your home and test them monthly. Whether mains wired or battery operated, there is an industry consensus that smoke alarms should be replaced every 10 years. The following have useful information (Directory, pp 3–5):

- **Age UK** (information and advice)
- **Fire kills campaign**
- **Independent Living**
- **Living made easy**
- **SaferHouses**

Home security

Most burglaries are opportunist crimes – so don't be an easy target. The most vulnerable access points are doors and windows. Simple precautions such as fitting adequate locks and bolts can do much to deter the average burglar. Doors should have secure bolts or a five-lever mortice lock strengthened by metal plates on both sides, a door chain and a spy hole in the front door. Additionally, you might consider outside lights (ideally with a sensor) to illuminate night-time visitors, an entry-phone system or a 'smart' doorbell linked to your phone so you can identify callers before you open the door.

Windows should also be properly secured with key-operated locks. Draw your curtains at night so potential intruders cannot see in. Louvre windows are especially vulnerable because the slats can easily be removed. A solution is to glue them in place with an epoxy resin and to fit a special louvre lock. An agile thief can get through any space larger than a human head, so even small windows such as skylights need properly fitted locks. Both double glazing and Venetian blinds act as a further deterrent. If you are particularly worried, you could also have bars fitted to the windows or install old-fashioned internal shutters that can be closed at night. Alternatively, many DIY shops sell decorative wrought-iron security grilles.

Increasingly these days you can fit smart devices, not just for doorbells, but also to control lighting and other aspects of your home (such as automated blinds), making it appear that your home is occupied. These devices have been taking off very fast and are seen as a challenge to traditional burglar alarms (see below), particularly because smart devices can be self-installed and they cost less.

Another obvious security safeguard is to ensure that your home is securely locked, both front and back doors, whenever you go out, even for five minutes. If you lose your keys, you should change the locks without delay. Insist that official callers such as meter readers show their identity cards before you allow them inside. If in doubt about unexpected callers, keep them out. Gas, electric and water companies can give meter readers and engineers a password so you know they are genuine. If you install a smart meter, this will automatically relay readings to your supplier, reducing the number of uninvited callers visiting your home. If a stranger knocks on your door asking for help, sadly the request might not be genuine so take sensible precautions – for example, engage the door chain or close the door while you make an emergency phone call on their behalf.

If you are going away, even for only a couple of days, remember to cancel the milk and the newspapers. You might also like to take advantage of the Royal Mail's Keepsafe service (Directory, p 5), which will store your mail while you are away and so avoid it piling up and alerting potential burglars to your absence. There is a charge for the service, which starts at £20 for up to 10 days. However, bear in mind that these days mail is delivered by a wide range of companies, and Royal Mail will only hold on to mail sent through their own service.

Finally, if you are not using smart devices to control your lights and other home appliances, consider a time switch (cost around £10) that will turn the lights on and off when you are away.

Further useful information is supplied by:

- **Age UK** provide a booklet *Staying safe: Stay safe at home, out and about and when you're online* (Directory, p 3).
- **Master Locksmiths Association** (Directory, p 5).
- **Police UK** has guidance on ways to make your home more secure (Directory, p 5).
- **Trading Standards** can be contacted if you have problems or disagreements with suppliers of goods or services – from overcharging to faulty goods, from dodgy workmanship to reporting unscrupulous traders ('cowboys') or scams. To find your local trading standards office, see Directory (p 5).
- **TrustMark** is a scheme that finds reliable, trustworthy tradesmen (Directory, p 5).
- **Victim Support** is a support and witness service for those affected by crime (Directory, p 41).

Burglar alarms and safes

More elaborate precautions such as a burglar alarm are among the best ways of protecting your home. Although alarms are expensive – installation starts from around £200 to £300 and, if you are linked to a monitoring service, there are ongoing charges – they could be worth every penny. In the event of a break-in, you can summon help or ask the police to do what they can if you are away.

Many insurance companies will recommend suitable contractors to install burglar alarm equipment and some arrange discounts for their policyholders with manufacturers of security devices. The National Security Inspectorate website (Directory, p 5) lists approved contractors in your locality and will also investigate technical complaints. If you are going away, it is a good idea to inform your neighbours so that if your alarm goes off they will know something is wrong and give them a key so that they can turn off and reset the alarm should the need arise.

If you keep valuables or money in the house, think about buying a concealed wall or floor safe.

Personal safety

Older people who live on their own can feel particularly at risk, especially when out and about. However, crime statistics show that older people are far less likely to be attacked than younger people. A number of personal alarms are now available that are highly effective and can generally give you peace of mind. A sensible precaution is to carry a 'screamer alarm', sometimes known as a 'personal attack button'. These are readily available in department stores, electrical shops and from alarm companies.

A smartphone or traditional landline can also increase your sense of security. Some families come to an arrangement whereby they ring their older relatives at regular times to check that all is well. With a smartphone, you can set a family locator app so that family members or friends can remotely check where you are. You can also set up your smartphone with emergency information, including a contact person and details of any health condition you have or drugs you need, to help the emergency services if you are involved in an incident.

Many councils run community alarm schemes. For a small fee you get a panic button, usually on a pendant or wristband, so you can contact an emergency operator if you have a fall or are taken ill at home, or suspect a break-in. The operator phones a friend, relative or the emergency services. Age UK has been running its alarm scheme for 30 years, but try your council first.

Be aware that the landline phone system is changing. Since September 2023 it is no longer possible to order a traditional landline and from the end of 2025 the analogue phone system is due to be switched off. Sometime before then, your provider will be in touch to equip your home instead with a router to support a digital phone. There should be no charge and you should not need to have your own broadband subscription but, if your home phone is very old, you might need to buy a new handset. However, this switch to digital is controversial and one provider (BT) is delaying the switch-over for those customers who: use a pendant healthcare alarm, are aged over 70, use only landline, have no mobile signal or have disclosed additional needs. This is to allow time to resolve various problems. Unlike current landlines (which have their own electricity supply), digital phones will run off your home's mains supply and so will not work during a power cut, which makes it advisable to have a mobile phone as a back-up. If you don't have a mobile or there's no mobile reception in your area, your provider should organize an alternative way for you to make emergency calls during a power cut. This might include providing you with a hybrid phone that can make mobile calls or a long-life battery as back-up. If you use a community alarm scheme, burglar alarm or other device that relies on the current phone network, check with the equipment supplier to see if it will be compatible with the new digital phone system. For more information, see the Ofgem website (Directory, p 5).

Home insurance

There are two types of home insurance that you need to consider: buildings insurance, which covers the structure of your home, and contents insurance, which covers your possessions inside it. You can take out separate policies for each or combine them in a single policy which may be cheaper and can be simpler if you need to make a claim that affects both (for example, due to a break-in, fire or flood). Another important extra feature of home insurance is 'public liability cover'. This is designed to meet claims against you as a homeowner, tenant or landlord – for example if a visitor tripped and was injured in your home (contents insurance) or if a tile fell from your roof and damaged a neighbour's car (buildings insurance) – and you are found liable for the damage or injury.

If you rent your home, your landlord is responsible for insuring the building. If you own your home and still have a mortgage, your lender will insist that you have buildings insurance, though normally you choose the insurer and arrange the policy. Once your mortgage is paid off, it's up to you whether you have buildings cover, but you'd be very unwise to skimp on this cover. Similarly, it makes sense to cover your possessions even though it's not compulsory to have contents insurance.

A brief word about flooding: with climate change, the number of homes affected by flooding has been rising and households who had already been flooded or were at the highest risk were finding their insurance premiums soaring to unaffordable levels or even being refused cover altogether. To tackle this problem, since 2016, a scheme called Flood Re has been set up. Broadly, it allows for average home insurance premiums to be a bit higher so that insurance can be offered to homes at highest risk at a more affordable price (albeit still high). The scheme is set to last for 25 years, after which insurers are expected to revert to pricing each household's insurance on their own particular risk. You can find out about the flood risk of different homes through the GOV.UK website (Directory, p 4). The Association of British Insurers (Directory, p 21) has information on various aspects of household insurance and loss prevention.

Buildings insurance

The amount you need to insure for is the full rebuilding cost of your home in the thankfully unlikely but extreme event of it being totally destroyed, for example by fire. This is not the same as the market value of your home (what someone is willing to pay to buy it). While the rebuilding value is often less than the market value, it can be higher. This can seem perplexing since, even if the home were destroyed, you would usually still have the land on which it stands. However, full rebuilding costs include the cost of clearing the site and rebuilding in similar materials and to similar standards which may be more expensive than current building norms, with the aid of architects and surveyors who all charge fees. If you don't insure for the full value, any claim you make (even small claims for, say, a window or broken bathroom fitting) will be scaled back proportionately.

For guidance on the rebuilding cost of your home, you can use the Building Cost Information Service (Directory, p 21), which includes a calculator for residential rebuilding costs. Once you have an insurance policy, the rebuilding cost you have declared is normally automatically increased each year in line with inflation, but it's a good idea to use the calculator to recheck from time to time that the insured value is still in line with the rebuilding cost. In particular, do check that you are adequately covered for any home improvements you may have added, such as a new kitchen or garage.

Contents insurance

Make sure you have the right level of cover. If you insure for more than your belongings are worth, you are wasting money. However, if you insure for less (underinsure) you risk having any claim scaled back proportionately. Once you stop work, you may need to review the value of your home contents. You may have new items you have bought with a retirement lump sum.

With existing possessions, you should assess the replacement cost and make sure you have a 'new for old' or 'replacement as new' policy. Most insurance companies offer an automatic inflation-proofing option for both building and contents policies. You should not forget to cancel items on your contents policy that you no longer possess. You must also add new valuables that have been bought or received as presents.

Where antiques and jewellery are concerned, simple inflation-proofing may not be enough. Values can rise and fall disproportionately to inflation, and depend on current market trends. For a professional valuation, contact the BADA (British Antique Dealers' Association) or LAPADA (Association of Art & Antiques Dealers) (Directory, p 21). Either of these organizations can advise on the name of a specialist. Photographs of particularly valuable items can help in the assessment of premiums and settlement of claims, as well as give the police a greater chance of recovering them in the case of theft – do include something like a coin or ruler in the photo to show the scale of the item. Property marking, for example with an ultraviolet marker, is another useful ploy to help the police trace stolen possessions.

Finding and buying insurance

To get a good deal, it is important to shop around each year and be prepared to switch to a new provider. Price comparison websites (see Chapter 2) and brokers can help you do this.

To find an insurance broker in your area, use the online directory of the British Insurance Brokers' Association (Directory, p 21).

Insurance brokers do not necessarily cover the whole market and may be selecting your policy from a panel of insurers, and the broker will receive commission from the provider of the policy you take out. An advantage of using a broker is that they will also help you if you need to make a claim. Using a broker is also a good route if you are a non-standard customer – for example, you live in a thatched property or you will spend significant periods of time away from home.

Some insurance companies offer home and contents policies for older people (age 50 and over). These policies are not necessarily cheaper than the deals you can get elsewhere, so do get some mainstream quotes too, but the following websites (Directory, p 21) will give you more information on some of the policies aimed at older people:

- **Age UK**
- **LV**
- **Saga**

Apart from shopping around, there are some other ways to keep down the cost of insurance. One is to agree to a voluntary excess, which means the first part of any claim that you make you will bear the cost of yourself. The higher the excess, the lower your premium. It is standard these days that you build up a no-claims discount with every year that you have home insurance and do not make a claim. The flip side of this discount is that, if you do claim, your premium at renewal is likely to rise sharply. This may mean that it's simply not worth making modest claims at all. Alternatively, you could pay extra to protect your no-claims discount, which means that you can make one or two claims without your premium increasing as a result.

Raising money on your home – equity release

Many homeowners find that when they reach later life they have wealth tied up in their home, but fewer savings or less income than they would like – a classic case of asset-rich but income-poor. If you are in this situation, you could consider using your home as a source of extra cash. The most obvious way to raise money from your home would be to sell it and buy somewhere cheaper (often referred to as 'downsizing'). If you don't want to move, or can't, another option is equity release – releasing wealth from your home while continuing to live there. It is important to check before taking such a step that it is the right choice for you, both now and in the future.

There are two types of equity release scheme: a lifetime mortgage and a home reversion plan. Both are designed to run until you die or move out, for example if you move permanently into a care home. You can have a scheme just for yourself, or for you and your partner. In the latter case, the plan runs until you both no longer need the home. To use equity release, you need either to own your home outright or, if you do still have a mortgage, part of the equity you release will be used to pay this off.

With a lifetime mortgage, you borrow against the value of your home. Interest is charged but typically this is added to the amount you owe. Because the next round of interest is charged on both the original loan and the rolled-up interest, the amount you owe grows at quite a pace. For example, with an interest rate of 6.5 per cent (a broad average of rates available in mid-2024), after 11 years you'd owe double the amount you originally borrowed. So, you borrow only a portion of your home's value to allow room for the added interest. It's important to choose a lifetime mortgage that has a fixed interest rate, so you know exactly where you stand, and a no-negative-equity guarantee which means the maximum you'll ever owe is the market value of your home. However, there are lots of variations these days; for example, you can opt to pay part or all of the interest during your lifetime and, with a drawdown loan, you just draw out part of the maximum loan you've arranged as and when you need money, paying interest only on the sum drawn out so far.

With a home reversion scheme, you sell part or all of your home but retain the right to live in it rent-free. To allow for the rent being waived, the amount you get from the sale is only a portion of the home's market value. Most people opt for a lifetime mortgage rather than a reversion scheme.

If equity release does look suitable for you, consider the type of scheme and features that will suit you best. Make sure you understand how the scheme works, what your options will be if your circumstances change (for example, you want to move home) and your obligations to keep your home in a good state of repair and to have buildings insurance.

In addition to financial advice, you will also need the advice of a valuer – this is especially important in the case of a home reversion scheme – and a solicitor. It is important that these experts are acting for you and not the equity release provider. Do consider talking over your plans with your children, as equity release will reduce the amount they may eventually inherit.

For more information about equity release generally and members who subscribe to the Equity Release Council code of practice, see page 8 of the Directory. Make sure any firm you deal with is authorized and on the Financial Services Register (Directory, p 9).

Using your home to earn money

Rather than move, many people whose home has become too large are tempted by the idea of taking in tenants.

There are three broad choices: taking in paying guests or lodgers; letting part or all of your home as self-contained accommodation; and other schemes, such as renting your drive as a parking space. In the first two cases, for your own protection it is essential to have a written agreement and to take up bank references, unless the let is a strictly temporary one where the money is paid in advance. Otherwise, rent should be collected monthly or quarterly, and you should arrange a hefty deposit to cover any damage. An important point to be aware of is that there are strict rules concerning the treatment of deposits, with the risk of large fines for landlords and agents who fail to abide by them. You are also required to check that your tenants (but not B&B guests) have the right to be in the UK, by copying their passport or other immigration documents, and you can be fined if you fail to do this. If you are renting your home or buying with a mortgage, you should get permission from your landlord or mortgage lender before going ahead. Also check with your home insurer as your premium may need to increase (or sometimes fall).

Paying guests or lodgers

This is the most informal arrangement, and will normally be either a casual holiday-type bed-and-breakfast let or a lodger who might be with you for a couple of years. In either case, the visitor will be sharing part of your home, the accommodation will be fully furnished and you may be providing at least one full meal a day and possibly also basic cleaning services. To encourage people to let out rooms in these ways, the government allows you to earn up to £7,500 (£3,750 if letting jointly) a year free of tax under the Rent-a-Room Relief scheme (Directory, p 18). If your rental income comes to more, you can either just pay tax on the income above the tax-free amount or you can work out tax on the profit (rather than income) you make by deducting allowable expenses from the rental income.

There are few legal formalities involved in these types of lettings, and rent is entirely a matter for friendly agreement. As a resident owner you are also in a very strong position if you want your lodger to leave. Lodging arrangements can easily be ended, as your lodger has no legal rights to stay after the agreed period.

In the case of a lodger or B&B accommodation for no more than six people at a time, your home continues to be subject to council tax. However, if you offer B&B on a larger scale, you will have to pay business rates. There is a useful guide at GOV.UK (Directory, p 18). Having a lodger means you lose any single-occupant council tax discount.

Having more than one lodger or using your home as a B&B means that part of any gain you make if you sell your home could be liable to capital gains tax – see Chapter 4 for more information.

Letting part or all of your home

You could convert a basement or part of your house into a self-contained flat and let this either furnished or unfurnished. Alternatively, you might let out the whole of your home if you will be living elsewhere for a time. In England and Wales, this is usually done by creating an assured shorthold tenancy, typically for a fixed term of 6 or 12 months, but alternatively as a rolling monthly contract. The rent you charge is set for the fixed term, but can be increased at renewal. Your tenant agrees to pay the rent for the full fixed term unless you have a break clause written into the agreement. The let can automatically cease at the end of that fixed period, or you and the tenant may agree to renew for a further term or move on to a rolling contract. Most tenancies end when your tenant decides to move. However, you can give your tenants notice to quit. At present this is usually done using a 'Section 21' notice, under which you give your tenants at least two months to leave and you don't have to give any reason – a so-called 'no-fault eviction'. This was due to change once a new Renters (Reform) Act had been passed, but the legislation stalled once the General Election was announced. Even if no-fault evictions are abolished in future, it seems likely you will still be able to evict tenants if you are going to sell the property, need it back for yourself or a family member to live in, or the tenants are being antisocial or repeatedly failing to pay the rent.

In Scotland, for new lettings since 1 December 2017, tenancy agreements already give tenants more security of tenure and more predictable rents. For information, see Scottish Government (private renting) (Directory, p 19).

As a landlord, you are responsible for ensuring the property is safe. This includes, for example, making sure that electrical and gas appliances are checked regularly, and that there are smoke alarms on each level of the property and escape routes in the event of fire. Before you can advertise the property, you must get an Energy Performance Certificate (see earlier in this chapter) so that your tenants have an idea of what their energy bills might be like. Rental properties in England and Wales must have a minimum EPC rating of E – plans to increase this to C were scrapped by the Conservative government. Both you and the tenants will want to inspect the property and have an inventory before they move in, and you will typically ask for a deposit. When the tenants move out, you can take money from the deposit to cover the cost if there is any damage caused by the tenants. In the meantime, you must keep your tenant's money safe by lodging it in a government-backed deposit protection scheme. For more information on your responsibilities, for England and Wales, Northern Ireland and Scotland, see the Directory, pp 18–19.

When you come to sell your property, if you have made a profit, there may be capital gains tax to pay on the share of the profit that represents the part of the property that was let out and/or the proportion of time for which it was let – see Chapter 4.

Other schemes

If you think a little extra cash might be useful, depending on where you live (such as near a festival site or theme park), you could turn your garden into a 'micro campsite' and earn, say, £40 per night. Campspace (Directory, p 18) aims to create a community of like-minded garden hosts and campers who will offer and use the temporary micro campsites in preference to overcrowded and under-plumbed festival ones. The only proviso is that fresh water should be available. Whether you want a queue of muddy festival goers outside your bathroom in the morning is a matter for you to decide. Similarly, if you live near a station, airport or business area and have a large or unused driveway, you can rent it out as a parking space to commuters and travellers, through sites like Park On My Drive, Your Parking Space and ParkLet (see Directory, pp 18–19).

Should you have extra space in your house and don't mind renting out a room, or you want to rent out your home for a week or two while you are away, by signing up to certain websites you can reach potential guests from all round the world. Try Gumtree, Airbnb, Wimdu, SpareRoom or Roomgo (Directory, pp 18–19). Alternatively, you can make extra money out of the empty space in your house by renting out your cellar, loft or garage as storage space: see Stashbee and ParkLet (Directory, pp 18–19).

You can offer your home for film and advertisement locations if you can cope with a lot of disruption. But it pays good money, and film producers need other types of homes besides stately ones. Look at LocationsHub and Location Works (Directory, p 18).

Since April 2017, you can earn up to £1,000 of income from using your property completely tax-free. It could cover all the ideas in this section and also rental income from a lodger – though you cannot claim this £1,000 allowance as well as Rent-a-Room Relief, so you are probably better off claiming the latter. If your property income comes to more than £1,000, you can either pay tax on the excess or pay tax instead on your profit (income less allowable expenses). There's more information at GOV.UK (tax-free allowances on property and trading income): Directory, p 37.

Council tax and help with housing costs

If your income and savings are low, you may be entitled to state help with your mortgage or rent – you can find details in Chapter 2.

Other useful sources of information and advice about help with housing costs include Citizens Advice and Shelter (Directory, pp 18–19).

Paying council tax

Council tax is based on the value of the dwelling in which you live (the property element) and also consists of a personal element – with discounts and exemptions applying to certain groups of people.

THE PROPERTY ELEMENT

Most domestic properties are liable for council tax, including rented property, mobile homes and houseboats. The value of the property is assessed according to a banding system, with eight different bands (A to H). The banding of each property is determined by the government's Valuation Office Agency. Small extensions or other improvements do not affect the valuation until the property changes hands.

Notification of the band is shown on the bill when it is sent out in March. If you think there has been a misunderstanding about the valuation (or your liability to pay the full amount), you may have the right of appeal.

LIABILITY

Not everyone pays council tax. The bill is normally sent to the resident owner or joint owners of the property or, in the case of rented accommodation, to the tenant or joint tenants. Married couples and people with a shared legal interest in the property are jointly liable for the bill, unless they are students or severely mentally impaired.

THE PERSONAL ELEMENT

The valuation of each dwelling assumes that two adults will be resident. The charge does not increase if there are more adults. However, if, as in many homes, there is a single adult, you can claim to have your council tax bill reduced by 25 per cent. Certain people are disregarded when determining the number of residents in a household. There are also a number of other special discounts or exemptions, for example:

- People who are severely mentally impaired are disregarded or, if they are the sole occupant of the dwelling, qualify for an exemption.
- Disabled people whose homes require adaptation may have their bill reduced to a lower band.
- People on a low income may qualify for a reduction in their council tax – see Chapter 2, *Council Tax Reduction or Support.*
- Disabled people on higher-rate Attendance Allowance need not count a full-time carer as an additional resident and therefore may continue to qualify for the 25 per cent single (adult) householder discount. Exceptions are spouses or partners and parents of a disabled child under 18 who would normally be living with the disabled person, and whose presence therefore would not be adding to the council tax.

DISCOUNTS AND EXEMPTIONS APPLYING TO PROPERTY

Certain property is exempt from council tax, including:

- Property that has been unoccupied and unfurnished for less than six months.
- The home of a deceased person; the exemption lasts until six months after the grant of probate.
- A home that is empty because the occupier is absent in order to care for someone else.
- The home of a person who is or would be exempt from council tax because of moving to a residential home, hospital care or similar.
- Empty properties in need of major repairs or undergoing structural alteration can be exempt from council tax for an initial period of six months, but this can be extended for a further six months. After 12 months, the standard 50 (or possibly full 100) per cent charge for empty properties will apply.
- Granny flats that are part of another private domestic dwelling may be exempt, but this depends on access and other conditions. To check, contact your local Valuation Office Agency (Directory, p 19).

BUSINESS-CUM-DOMESTIC PROPERTY

Business-cum-domestic property is rated according to usage, with the business section assessed for business rates and the domestic section for council tax. For example, where there is a flat over a shop, the value of the shop will not be included in the valuation for council tax. Likewise, a room in a house used for business purposes will be subject to business rates and not to council tax. However, if you are an employee who works from home, or you run a small business from home, using, say, a bedroom as a home office or selling goods from your home by post is unlikely to incur business rates. For more information, see GOV.UK (business rates) (Directory, p 37).

APPEALS

If you become the new person responsible for paying the council tax (e.g. because you have recently moved or because someone else paid the tax before) on a property that you feel has been wrongly banded, you have six months to appeal and can request that the valuation be reconsidered. Otherwise, there are only three other circumstances in which you can appeal:

- if there has been a material increase or reduction in the property's value;
- if you start, or stop, using part of the property for business or the balance between domestic and business use changes;
- if either of the latter two apply and the listing officer has altered the council tax list without giving you a chance to put your side across.

If you have grounds for appeal, you should take up the matter with the Valuation Office. If the matter is not resolved, you can then appeal to an independent valuation tribunal. For advice and further information, contact your local Citizens Advice.

CHAPTER SEVEN

Retiring abroad

M any dream of retiring to sun, scenery and a relaxed pace of life. But there are many examples of people who retired abroad in the expectation of being able to afford a higher standard of living and who returned home a few years later, thoroughly disillusioned.

As with other important decisions, this is where it is essential to research your options thoroughly. It is crucial to investigate property prices, as well as the cost of healthcare. While these and other risks, such as how exchange rates may affect your pension income, are perhaps obvious, a vital question that is often overlooked is the tax effects of living overseas. If the country is English-speaking, no new language skills will be needed, while elsewhere, learning a new language will be a pleasure for some but a challenge for others. There may be additional purchases – new car and insuring it, new furniture and kitchen appliances – to factor in, and there will be the costs of making a new will to take account of possessions abroad and local inheritance laws.

Moreover, while you may have fallen in love with your chosen country, it may not be so ready to welcome you. You will need to check that you meet a country's immigration conditions and, since Brexit (the UK leaving the EU), this applies to European countries too, including popular retirement destinations such as France and Spain.

There are many websites offering advice and information on retiring abroad, which can be found in the Directory, p 34:

- **BuyAssociation**
- **Expat Focus**: provides essential information and advice for a successful move abroad
- **Expatica**: detailed information on moving to, and living in, a wide range of countries
- **GoodMigrations**: to find international removals firms, but also has informative guides to the whole process
- **GOV.UK**
- **RetirementExpert**

The impact of Brexit

The UK completely left the EU on 1 January 2021. Your opportunities and rights to live in an EU country depend on whether your move was before or after that date. In either case, you can check the rules that apply by reading the relevant *Living in* guide available from the UK government at GOV.UK (Directory, p 34).

Already retired in the EU

A Withdrawal Agreement protects the rights of UK nationals already living in the EU before 1 January 2021. In that case, you continue to have mostly the same rights as you did before, for example to remain indefinitely and receive healthcare on the same basis as local people. However, some areas to watch out for include:

- You have been required to formally apply for residence status or register as a resident. You should carry your proof of residence as well as your passport when travelling to ensure you can return to your EU home.
- You may need to register to receive healthcare.
- You may need to exchange your UK driving licence for a local one.
- Some countries have different rules from nationals for non-EU citizens buying or renting property, which could affect you if you want to move home.

Thinking about retiring to the EU

Now the UK is no longer part of the EU, 'freedom of movement' within the EU no longer applies to Britons. So, if you want to retire to an EU country, you will need to check what conditions of entry apply.

Typically, you must apply for a visa and this process includes being able to show you have the financial means to support yourself and any family members who will be living with you. For example, in the first half of 2024, for Spain, you would need an annual income of at least €28,800 (£24,517 at the mid-2024 exchange rate) for yourself and €7,200 (£6,129) for each dependant – so €36,000 (£30,646) for a couple. This is substantially more than the UK State Pension, so you will need significant private income as well. The income threshold for France is based on the French minimum wage which in mid-2024 was €16,800 (£14,303) a year after tax. Strictly, this is per person but in the past the French Embassy in London has said that a couple may qualify with less than double that amount.

Unlike EU citizens, you will not normally be eligible to use the public health system, so to qualify for a visa you will also need to show that you have sufficient private health insurance (see *Healthcare overseas* below).

Healthcare overseas

UK nationals who have retired to another EU country before 1 January 2021 continue to be entitled to the same state healthcare as other residents of that country if they receive any sort of pension from that country. If they do not have a local pension, they can apply for a form S1 (formerly E106, E109 and E121), which will entitle them to state healthcare in that country on the same basis as for local people. You can download this form from the European Union website (Directory, p 34) – search for 'Living abroad' and navigate to 'Your health insurance cover'. Be aware that this does not necessarily mean your healthcare will be completely free, because even locals also often have to contribute something towards the cost of each treatment.

For UK nationals retiring to EU countries from 1 January 2021 onwards, you will need to satisfy the entry requirements for the country you are hoping to live in. You will not normally be eligible for residents' healthcare and so will have to show that you have private health insurance to fully cover any treatment you may need. The same applies if you are looking at countries other than those of the EU.

The cost of private insurance will vary depending, for example, on the country you will be living in and your age. For example, according to the Expatica wesbite, a 65 year old moving to Spain might pay around €150 (£128) a month for cover in 2024 – though cost will vary with your personal health situation. Bear in mind that private insurance typically will not cover pre-existing health conditions and many insurers set an upper age limit (for example, 75), so there is no guarantee that you will be able to satisfy visa requirements. For more information on health insurance works, see Chapter 12.

Buying property abroad

The cost of property varies across different countries. For example, France tends to be relatively expensive compared with, say, Spain or Portugal. As with any property search, the best approach is to visit the locations and view potential homes in person.

Don't forget that there are a number of additional costs, besides the purchase price, which can sometimes get overlooked: legal expenses, notary fees, transaction tax (equivalent to stamp duty), registration fees and local taxes, costs of a solicitor and surveyor, to name a few. Removal costs from the UK to the new country can be quite heavy too.

So, if you decide to retire overseas, be careful. Some ways of protecting yourself when buying property abroad include:

- Get all documents translated. This has become much easier with the ubiquitous availability of online tools like ChatGPT and Google Translate – however, be aware that these tools are not always completely accurate.
- If you are given something to sign, check it carefully first and ideally have a cooling-off period during which you can change your mind.
- Take the documents home to the UK and speak initially to a lawyer and financial adviser over here rather than in the country overseas (though be aware that a UK-based financial adviser may not be authorized to give you advice once you live abroad, so at some stage you may want to hire a local financial adviser).
- Make sure the lawyer you use is independent and not involved in the sale in any way.
- Do not use a lawyer recommended by the seller.
- If you are buying a repossessed property, find out what happened.

- If you are borrowing money, go to a reputable bank. The bank manager will want to be sure the deal is sound – this adds another layer of checks and protection.

UK pensions paid abroad

Both state and occupational pensions may be paid to you in any country. However, there are some pitfalls to be aware of.

If you live in the UK, your State Pension increases each year at least in line with inflation. Even after Brexit, this is also the case if you retire to an EU country or other countries with which the UK has a social security agreement. Where this is not the case, your State Pension is frozen at the rate you received when you left the UK (though if later you come back to live permanently in the UK, it will be increased up to the then current rate). In some fairly popular retirement destinations, such as Australia, Canada, New Zealand or South Africa, you will not receive any annual increases. Your frozen State Pension will, therefore, tend to buy less and less as time goes by.

You should also factor in the impact of changing exchange rates. For example, 2022 was a roller-coaster year for the pound. In March, your £179.60 a week UK State Pension was worth €218. But by September this had fallen to €207 despite the UK amount increasing to £185.15. Exchange rate fluctuations will also affect the buying power of any UK company and personal pensions paid to you abroad.

Any queries about your State Pension should be addressed to the International Pension Centre (Directory, p 34).

Taxation if you live abroad

Tax rates vary from one country to another: a prime example is VAT, which varies considerably across Europe. Additionally, many countries levy taxes that don't apply in the UK. Annual wealth tax exists in a few parts of the world, as do all sorts of property taxes. Estate duty on assets left by one spouse to another is also fairly widespread in contrast to the UK. Sometimes a special tax is imposed on foreign residents. And some countries charge income tax on an individual's worldwide income, without the exemptions that apply in the UK.

If you are thinking of retiring abroad the golden rule must be to investigate the tax situation thoroughly before you take an irrevocable step, such as selling your home in the UK. A common mistake is for people to misunderstand their UK tax liabilities after their departure.

Your UK tax position if you retire overseas

Many intending emigrants cheerfully imagine that, once they have settled themselves in a dream villa overseas, they are safely out of the clutches of the UK tax office. This is not so. You first have to acquire non-resident status.

If you have severed all your ties, including selling your home, to take up a permanent job overseas, non-resident status is normally granted fairly quickly. But for most retirees, acquiring unconditional non-resident status can take up to three years. The purpose is to check that you are not just having a prolonged holiday, but are actually living as a resident abroad. During the check period, HMRC may allow you conditional non-resident status and, if it is satisfied, full status will be granted retrospectively.

The rules for non-residency changed in 2013 and are pretty stringent. You are automatically resident if you spend 183 days or more in the UK in any one tax year, or you spend at least one continuous period of 91 days in the UK and have a UK home in which you live for at least 30 days in a tax year. Even if these automatic tests do not apply, you may be considered UK resident if you have had sufficient ties with the UK during the past three years, such as family, a UK home or UK work, and spend a specified number of days in the UK, which varies according to the number of ties you have. You can find detailed information in the HMRC guidance note RDR3 available at GOV.UK (Directory, p 34).

UK income tax

If you are non-resident, all overseas income (provided it is not remitted to the UK) is exempt from UK tax liability. Income deriving from a UK source is, however, normally liable for UK tax. This includes any director's or consultant's fees you may still be receiving, as well as more obvious income such as pensions, rent from a property you still own and interest on UK savings. However, interest paid on certain British government securities is not subject to tax and some former colonial pensions are also exempt. If you are living in a country that belongs to the European Economic Area (EEA) (the EU plus Iceland, Liechtenstein and Norway) or spent part of the tax year working for the UK government, you can claim the personal allowance to set against your UK income – see GOV.UK (Directory, p 34).

It's possible that your income may be taxed twice, both in the UK and in the country where you reside. In that case, you can usually claim some of the tax back. Alternatively, the country in which you have taken up residency may have a double taxation agreement with the UK (see the following section). If this is the case, you may be taxed on the income just in your new residence and not in the UK, or vice versa.

Be aware that tax treatment you take for granted in the UK – such as taking a quarter of your pension savings tax-free and drawing money from ISAs tax-free – may not apply under foreign tax rules. Therefore, you may want to consider taking any tax-free cash before you make the move abroad.

Your pension providers will not necessarily be willing to pay your pension into a foreign bank account, so you may need to retain a UK bank account (though not all UK banks allow this post-Brexit if you do not have a UK address) and either access your money using a debit card abroad or transfer it to your foreign account. An alternative strategy would be to transfer your private UK pensions to a pension provider in the country where you intend to live. Pension transfers are fertile ground for fraudsters, so take care: if you do fall into the hands of scammers, not only are you likely to irretrievably lose your pension savings, but you may well have to pay a hefty tax bill to HMRC as well for making an 'unauthorized payment' from your pension scheme. So, make sure that you transfer only to a genuine qualifying recognized overseas pension scheme (QROPS), recognized by HMRC to receive transfers from UK schemes. Provided you and the new pension provider are based in the same country, and your total transfers are below £1,073,100 (or a lower limit in some cases), the transfer should not trigger any tax charge. If not, there could be a hefty immediate tax bill.

Double taxation agreement

A person who is a resident of a country with which the UK has a double taxation agreement may be entitled to exemption or partial relief from UK income tax on certain kinds of income from UK sources, and may also be exempt from UK tax on the disposal of assets. The conditions of exemption or relief vary from agreement to agreement. It may be a condition of the relief that the income is subject to tax in the other country. It's important to check, before you decide on retiring abroad, if there is such an agreement and how it will affect you. You can find details of all the UK's double taxation agreements (tax treaties) at GOV.UK (Directory, p 34). Note that, if – as sometimes happens – the foreign tax authority later makes an adjustment and the income ceases to be taxed in that country, you have an obligation under the Self Assessment rules to notify HMRC.

Capital Gains Tax (CGT)

Double taxation agreements do not cover any gain you make on selling your UK home or other UK property.

Since the 2019/20 tax year, you have to tell HMRC about the disposal of UK land or property and may have to pay CGT, even if you are non-resident. You have only 60 days from the date the property sale completes to do this.

On other assets, CGT is charged only if you are resident or ordinarily resident in the UK; so if you are in the position of being able to realize a gain, it is advisable to wait until you acquire non-resident status. However, to escape CGT you must wait to dispose of any assets until after the tax year of your departure and must remain non-resident (and not ordinarily resident) in the UK for five full tax years after your departure.

Different rules apply to gains made from the disposal of assets in a UK company; these are subject to normal CGT.

Inheritance Tax (IHT)

IHT is a tax payable mainly on what you leave when you die (see Chapter 15). It generally applies to all your UK and worldwide assets. You escape IHT on overseas assets only if you are no longer domiciled in the UK – though this is due to change from April 2025. Broadly speaking, domicile is the country you consider as your permanent home. This is distinct from nationality or residence. A person may be resident in more than one country, but at any given time he or she can be domiciled in only one. Regardless of your intentions, for IHT, you will be considered domiciled in the UK if:

- you have lived in the UK for 15 of the past 20 years; or
- you had a permanent UK home at any time during the last three years before death.

If you live abroad and count as domiciled abroad, only your UK assets will be subject to IHT. Even if you have been resident overseas for many years, if you do not have an overseas domicile, your estate will have to pay IHT on your worldwide assets as if you lived in the UK, and the same assets may also be subject to the equivalent taxes in the country where you lived, unless a double taxation agreement specifies otherwise.

CHAPTER EIGHT

Leisure activities

Whatever amount of leisure time you have available in retirement, there is almost certainly something you will be looking forward to doing. Whether you tend towards studying, sports or crafts, there are loads of suitable activities for everyone's tastes on offer locally or nationally. You may need to do a bit of research and one of the easiest ways is using the internet. For example, many areas have online neighbourhood communities – such as nextdoor.co.uk – where you can find kindred spirits to share your interests in walking, reading, music, craft and much more. Other sources include local newsletters, community noticeboards and your local branch of the University of the Third Age (U3A) – see Directory p 6.

Even if meeting physically is not possible, you can still have an active social life online, meeting in groups on platforms such as zoom.us, keeping in touch with individuals and groups through messaging services and playing games with friends or strangers through sites like boardgamearena.com and smart-phone apps. If you are one of the third of over-65s not yet on the internet, now might be a good time to take the plunge! For information about how to get online and use the internet confidently, contact the Age UK Advice Line on 0800 678 1602.

Adult education

Opportunities for education abound, and there are scores of subjects easily available to everyone, regardless of age or previous qualifications. You might be a leisure learner or among the many older people studying with a view to taking on a new career in later life.

Formal learning

Not all educational courses are free, and this can deter a number of people from taking the opportunity to learn. However, there is no age limit for applying for a student loan to cover university tuition fees and, because of the way the rules work, you probably will not have to pay back all or even any of the loan.

Student loans are not interest-free. They start to be repaid after you leave full-time study or after four years if you are studying part-time. Repayments stop if you are not working or your income falls below a specified threshold (which varies across the nations of the UK).

To be eligible for a student loan, you must not be studying at the same level as a degree you already have, unless your new qualification is in a STEM (science, technology, engineering or maths) subject or healthcare. While most universities require you to have some minimum qualifications (such as A-levels), the UK's largest distance-learning higher education institution, the Open University, is specifically open to learners regardless of whether or not they have prior qualifications.

The UK has two specialist distance learning universities: the Open University and Arden (both Directory, p 6). However, increasingly, traditional brick universities are also offering online distance learning, which you might find more convenient than attending a campus. Many universities offer a choice of part-time or full-time study.

You may be interested in courses that offer pre-university or professional qualifications. See *Training opportunities* in Chapter 10 for some suggestions.

Informal learning

There are also increasing opportunities for informal learning, both at university and other levels, online and in the physical world. Agencies such as Age UK (Directory, p 6) will supply information on free and subsidized educational courses. Local libraries and your council are two of the best places to obtain information on local opportunities, such as adult education and life skills courses in, for example, literacy, numeracy, digital skills and financial capability. If you are interested in learning online, here are some of the leading websites where you can study informally for free or at low cost, which can be found in the Directory, p 6:

- **BBC Bitesize**: learn with the BBC through online courses and study.
- **City Lit**: offers online adult education courses (and face-to-face in London).
- **Massive Online Open Courses (MOOCs)**: these are offered through online platforms. You can study a very wide range of courses often from leading universities around the world. See **Coursera, edX** and **Future Learn.**
- The **Open University** (OU): free courses are available on its OpenLearn platform, some of which tie in with TV programmes that the BBC and OU co-produce.

Many universities offer non-degree courses for adults and public lectures, sometimes in the evening or during vacation periods. In addition, there are non-university organizations that offer a wide range of lectures, talks and courses. Here are just a few possibilities, which can be found in the Directory, pp 6–7:

- **U3A** (the University of the Third Age): U3As are self-help, self-managed, lifelong learning cooperatives for older people.
- The **WI (Women's Institute) Learning Hub** offers online courses. Its residential venue (Denman College) has now been sold but the proceeds are being used partly to fund local WI face-to-face training and events.
- The **Workers' Educational Association** is the UK's largest voluntary sector provider of adult learning with part-time adult education courses for everyone, delivered locally through partner organizations.

Arts

Wherever you live you can enjoy the arts. Whether you are interested in active participation or just appreciating the performance of others, there is an exhilarating choice of events, including theatre, music, exhibitions, film making, and so on. Many offer concessionary prices to retired people.

Regional Arts Council offices

The Arts Council England works to get great art to everyone by champion-ing, developing and investing in artistic experiences that enrich everyone's lives. For information and details of its investment in your region, see

Directory, p 23. The equivalent bodies in the other nations of the UK are Creative Scotland, Arts Council of Wales and Arts Council of Northern Ireland (see Directory pp 23–24).

For those who wish to join in with amateur arts activities, public libraries keep lists of choirs, drama clubs, painting clubs and similar in their locality.

Films

Cinema is a hugely popular art form. Should you enjoy film, you might think of joining a film society or visiting the National Film Theatre. Here are some other ideas (see Directory, p 24):

- The **British Film Institute (BFI)** has a world-renowned archive, cinemas, festival, films (at its cinemas and to watch at home by subscription), publications and learning resources to inspire you.
- **Cinema for All** is the national organization for the development and support of the film society and community cinema movement in the UK.

Music and ballet

From becoming a friend and supporting one of the famous 'houses' such as the Royal Opera House in Covent Garden to music making in your own right, here are some suggestions, which can be found in the Directory, p 24:

- As a Friend of the **English National Opera** you support the work of the Company and enjoy privileges such as priority booking, dress rehearsals and many other events.
- Friends of the **Royal Albert Hall**, home of the BBC proms and diverse other performances, get priority booking, discounts and more.
- Becoming a Friend of Covent Garden is the best way to keep up with events at the **Royal Opera House**, attend talks, recitals, study days, master classes and some 'open' rehearsals of ballet and opera.
- Members of **Sadler's Wells** receive priority booking and up to 20 per cent off tickets.

Music making

Whatever style of music you enjoy, there are associations to suit your taste. Here are some contacts, which can be found in the Directory, p 24:

- **Handbell Ringers of Great Britain** promotes the art of handbell tune ringing in all its forms.

- **Making Music** supports and champions over 3,000 voluntary and amateur music groups throughout the UK.
- The **National Association of Choirs** represents and supports over 500 choirs and 26,000 voices, all of them amateur and voluntary, throughout the UK.
- The **Society of Recorder Players** brings together recorder players of all ages from all over the UK.

Poetry

There is an increasing enthusiasm for poetry and poetry readings in clubs, pubs and other places of entertainment. Special local events may be advertised in your neighbourhood.

The **Poetry Society** (Directory, p 24) is a charitable organization providing support and information, and aims to create a central position for poetry in the arts.

Television and radio audiences

People of all ages, backgrounds and abilities enjoy participating as members of studio audiences and contributors to programmes. For those wishing to take part, there are a couple of websites that can help (see Directory, p 26):

- The **Applause Store** is the one-stop shop for literally thousands of free television and radio audience tickets to the very best entertainment, music, comedy, chat, sitcom, reality and award shows, produced at locations around the world.
- **BBC Shows**: be in the audience – free tickets for shows.

Theatre

Details of current and forthcoming productions for national and regional theatres, as well as theatre reviews, are well advertised in the press and on the internet. Preview performances are usually cheaper, and there are often concessionary tickets for matinees (see Directory, p 31):

- **Ambassador Theatre Group** sells tickets from the UK's largest theatre group and offers annual membership discounts.

- The **Barbican** is the largest multi-arts and conference centre in Europe, presenting a diverse range of art, film, music, theatre, dance and education events.
- The **National Theatre** stages over 20 theatre productions each year in three auditoriums. Many cinemas now show livestreams or encores (repeats) of National Theatre performances; for details, see National Theatre Live.
- **Official London Theatre** is the capital's only official theatre website. It has the latest news on listings, what's on, how to buy tickets and events.
- **UK Theatre Network** is a social network and online magazine for the performing arts industry with news and features, as well as national and regional theatre listings and reviews. See X (Twitter) feed @realuktheatre.

Visual arts

If you enjoy attending exhibitions and lectures, membership of some of the arts societies offers a good choice, and they can be found in the Directory, p 31:

- The **Art Fund** exists to secure great art for museums and galleries all over the UK for everyone to enjoy. All funding is privately raised, and the Art Fund has over 80,000 members. There are art tours at home and abroad led by experts.
- The **Arts Society** is an arts-based charity with over 340 local decorative and fine arts societies in the UK and mainland Europe. It promotes the advancement of arts education and appreciation and the preservation of our artistic heritage with day events and tours organized both in the UK and abroad.
- The **Contemporary Art Society** exists to support and develop public collections of contemporary art in the UK. Members' events include visits to artists' studios and private collections, previews and parties at special exhibitions, and trips outside London and overseas.
- Friends of the **Royal Academy of Arts** receive many benefits, including unlimited access to the world-renowned exhibition programme with guests, and the award-winning *RM* quarterly magazine.
- The **Tate** is a public institution, owned by and existing for the public. Its mission is to increase public knowledge, understanding and enjoyment of British modern and contemporary art through its collections at four

locations: Tate Modern and Tate Britain, both in London, Tate Liverpool and Tate St Ives. Members have unlimited free entry to exhibitions, special events and member-only rooms with refreshments.

Painting as a hobby

If you are interested in improving your own painting technique, art courses are available at your local adult education institute. Your library may have details of painting groups and societies in your area.

The **Society for All Artists** (Directory, p 31), which exists to inform, encourage and inspire all who want to paint, whatever their ability, provides all that you need to enjoy this hobby.

Computing and IT

As mentioned at the beginning of the chapter, there are still a large number of over-65s who are 'digitally excluded' – not using computers or the internet.

However, there are now lots of opportunities to learn and often courses are free. Your local authority can provide details of adult education classes. Local libraries may run sessions and some banks offer free digital training.

For further ideas for developing and honing your digital expertise, see the section *IT skills* in Chapter 10.

Creative writing

It is said that there is a book in everyone, and many retired people have a yen to write. As this is a solitary occupation, you may find that joining a writing group is a worthwhile and pleasurable thing to do. The National Association of Writing Groups (Directory, p 25) is one place to find a local group; another is Writers Online (Directory, p 25).

If the range of writing-related options interest you, something else to check is *Writing Magazine* (Directory, p 25). This is a monthly journal designed to help aspiring and actual writers. If your writing has become more than just a hobby and you're looking for guidance on getting published, you might consider joining Jericho Writers (see Directory p 25) which offers a variety of online video courses, in-person events, mentoring and expert editing.

Dance

Clubs, classes and groups exist in all parts of the country offering ballroom, old-time, Scottish, folk, ballet, disco dancing and others. Find out what is available in your area from your library, or see the list below, which can be found in the Directory, p 25 (there are further suggestions in Chapter 12, *Health*, covering, for example, relaxation, aerobics and yoga):

- The **British Dance Council** is the governing body of all competition dancing in the UK. It can put you in touch with recognized dance schools in your area.
- The **English Folk Dance & Song Society** is one of the leading folk development organizations in the UK. It aims to place the indigenous folk arts of England at the heart of our cultural life.
- The **Imperial Society of Teachers of Dancing** is a registered educational charity providing education and training for dance teachers, from ballet to ballroom.
- The **Royal Scottish Country Dance Society** aims to preserve and further the practice of traditional Scottish country dancing. It has 170 branches worldwide offering instruction at all levels.

Games

Many local areas have their own backgammon, bridge, chess, whist, dominos, Scrabble and other groups that meet together regularly in a club, hall, pub or other social venue to enjoy friendly board games. Information on local clubs should be available from your library. Here are some national organizations which will put you in touch with local groups, which can be found in the Directory, p 26:

- The **Association of British Scrabble Players** promotes interest in the game and coordinates all Scrabble tournaments in the UK.
- The **English Bridge Union** is a membership organization committed to promoting the game of duplicate bridge. Members receive a wide range of services, including details of tournaments and bridge holidays at home and abroad.

- The **English Chess Federation** aims to promote the game of chess as an attractive means of cultural and personal advancement, providing information about chess clubs and tournaments throughout England.

Gardens and gardening

Courses, gardens to visit, special help for people with disabilities and how to run a gardening association and other interests are all catered for by the following organizations, which can be found in the Directory, p 25:

- The **English Gardening School** teaches all aspects of gardening. Courses range from one day to an academic year, at Chelsea Wharf.
- **Garden Organic** is the national charity for organic gardening and has been at the forefront of organic gardening for over half a century. Based at Ryton in Warwickshire.
- The **Gardening with Disabilities Trust** provides practical and financial help to disabled people who want to continue to garden actively despite advancing age or disability.
- The **National Gardens Scheme** has over 3,700 gardens to choose from in England and Wales, mostly privately owned. Over half a million visitors enjoy visiting gardens that open to the public just a few days each year.
- The **National Society of Allotment & Leisure Gardeners Ltd** aims to protect, promote and preserve allotments for future generations. It acts as a national voice for allotment and leisure gardeners.
- The **Royal Horticultural Society** is the UK's leading gardening charity, dedicated to advancing horticulture, promoting gardening and inspiring all those with an interest in gardening.
- **Scotland's Gardens Scheme** facilitates the opening of large and small gardens throughout Scotland that are of interest to the public.
- **Thrive** is a small national charity that uses gardening to change the lives of disabled people.

History

People with an interest in the past have so many activities to choose from – visit historic monuments, including ancient castles and stately homes, in all parts of the country; explore the City of London; study genealogy or research the history of your local area. Here are some organizations to consider, which can be found in the Directory, p 27:

- **Age Exchange** is the UK's leading charity working in the field of reminiscence, and works to improve the quality of life for older people through reminiscence-based creative workshops.
- **Ancestry** is a global network of family history websites that together form the world's largest collection of family trees. It has collections of census and many other historical data records.
- The **Architectural Heritage Society of Scotland** is concerned with the protection, preservation, study and appreciation of Scotland's buildings. Six regional groups organize local activities and carry out casework.
- The **British Association for Local History** aims to encourage and promote the study of local history as an academic discipline as well as a rewarding leisure pursuit.
- The **City of London Corporation** website has a section called 'Visit the City' with a wealth of information about London's museums and historic sites, which include, for example, St Paul's Cathedral, the Guildhall, Dr Johnson's House, the Monument, Barbican and the Central Criminal Court.
- **English Heritage** champions our historic places to help today's generation get the best out of our heritage and ensure it is protected for future generations.
- The **Family History Federation** is an educational charity that represents the interests of family historians and especially the preservation and availability of archival documents.
- The **Gardens Trust** is dedicated to the conservation and study of historic designed gardens and landscapes. It has helped save or conserve scores of important gardens.
- The **Georgian Group** exists to preserve Georgian buildings and to stimulate public knowledge and appreciation of Georgian architecture and town planning. Members enjoy day visits and long weekends to buildings and gardens, private views of exhibitions and a programme of evening lectures in London.
- **Historic Houses** represents 1,500 privately owned historic houses, castles and gardens throughout the UK. Around 300 houses are open to the public for day visitors.
- The **Historical Association** supports the study and promotes the enjoyment of history. It believes that historical awareness is essential for the 21st-century citizen.

- The **Monumental Brass Society** is for all those interested in any aspect of monumental brasses and incised slabs of all dates and in all countries.
- The **National Trust** exists to protect historic buildings and areas of great natural beauty in England, Wales and Northern Ireland. Membership gives you free entry to the Trust's many properties and to those of the National Trust for Scotland.
- The **National Trust for Scotland** cares for over 100 properties and 183,000 acres of countryside. Members also enjoy free admission to any of the National Trust properties in England, Wales and Northern Ireland.
- The **Northern Ireland Tourist Board** has a free information bulletin, *Visitor Attractions*, listing historic sites and other places of interest.
- The **Oral History Society** promotes the collection, preservation and use of recorded memories of the past for projects in community history, schools, reminiscence groups and historical research.
- The **Society of Genealogists** promotes the study of family history and the lives of earlier generations. Its library houses a huge collection of family histories, civil registration and census material.
- The **Victorian Society** campaigns to preserve fine Victorian and Edwardian buildings in England and Wales for future generations.

Museums

Most museums organize free lectures, guided tours and special exhibitions. If you join as a friend, you can enjoy certain advantages, such as advance bookings, private views, visits to places of interest, receptions and other social activities. Here are some suggestions – see the Directory, pp 27–28:

- The **Ashmolean Museum of Art and Archaeology** is a university museum and a department of the University of Oxford. Its mission is to make its collections available to the widest possible audience, both now and in the future.
- The **British Association of Friends of Museums** is an umbrella organization that acts as a national forum for friends and volunteers who support museums around the UK.
- **British Museum** members enjoy free entry to exhibitions and evening openings as well as information about lectures, study days, tours and members' room.

- Friends of the **Fitzwilliam Museum** receive regular information about its events, including exhibitions, concerts, lectures and parties in the Cambridge area and throughout the UK.
- Friends of the **National Maritime Museum** enjoy the museum complex, housed in Greenwich Park, which comprises the largest maritime museum in the world, Wren's Royal Observatory and Inigo Jones's Queen's House.
- Membership of the **National Museums of Scotland** gives regular mailings and the *Explorer* magazine, invitations to lectures and other events, and free admission to exhibitions and some sites.
- Friends of the **Victoria and Albert Museum** (V&A) have free admission to exhibitions, members' previews, a programme of events, a free subscription to *V&A Magazine* and access to the members' room.

Nature and conservation

Many conservation organizations are very keen to recruit volunteers; the majority are therefore listed in Chapter 11, *Voluntary work*. Here are a few others of interest, which can be found in the Directory, p 28:

- The **Field Studies Council** is an environmental educational charity committed to helping people understand and be inspired by the natural world. Fieldwork and cross-curricular courses inspire thousands of students each year through its countrywide network of centres across the UK.
- **Forestry England's** mission is to protect and expand Britain's forests and woodlands, and increase their value to society and the environment.
- The **Inland Waterways Association** is a national charity run by thousands of volunteers, which campaigns for the use, maintenance and restoration of Britain's inland waterways.
- The **Wildfowl & Wetlands Trust** is a leading conservation organization saving wetlands for wildlife and people across the world.
- **Wildlife Trusts** is the largest UK voluntary organization dedicated to conserving the full range of the UK's habitats and species. There are 46 local Wildlife Trusts caring for 2,600 nature reserves and campaigning for the future of our threatened wildlife.
- **Worldwide Opportunities on Organic Farms** brings together people who want to learn about ecological farming and sustainable practices with organic farmers. You volunteer your work for one to two weeks or more at a time and get free board, lodging and training in return. There is

generally plenty of time for socializing, cultural exchange and sightseeing as well.

Public library service

We seldom pause to think how public libraries enrich our lives. They are a public service that gives everyone free access to online and print information, literature, music, local history archives and more. They offer alternative formats for people with visual impairment. And they also act as a hub for community groups, events and information about local societies and resources of all kinds.

But libraries are an endangered species due to more than a decade of local authority spending cuts. Although a number have been closed, many local support groups have sprung into action to save their local libraries, with – in some cases – volunteers taking over their running.

Sciences and other related subjects

If astronomy, meteorology or geology fascinate you, there are several societies and associations that may be of interest, which can be found in the Directory, p 28:

- The **British Astronomical Association** is open to all people interested in astronomy.
- The **Geologists' Association** organizes lectures, field excursions and monthly meetings at Burlington House.
- The **Royal Meteorological Society**, which includes among its membership both amateurs and professionals, exists to advance meteorological science.

Special interests

Whether your special enthusiasm is stamp collecting or model flying, most of the associations listed (which can be found in the Directory, p 29) organize events, answer queries and can put you in contact with kindred spirits:

- **BirdLife International** is full of information for those interested in bird life across the globe.

- The **British Association of Numismatic Societies** helps to coordinate the activities of the many local societies, whose members are interested in the study or collection of coins and medals.
- The **British Beekeepers Association** aims to promote the craft of beekeeping and educate the public on the importance of bees in the environment.
- The **British Model Flying Association** is responsible nationally for all types of model flying, organizing competitions and fun-fly meetings and advice and guidelines on model flying.
- The **Miniature Armoured Fighting Vehicle Association** is an international society providing advice and information on tanks and other military vehicles and equipment.
- The **National Association of Flower Arrangement Societies** has over 50,000 members who attend NAFAS events, the National Show, and take part in courses in floral art and design.
- The **National Philatelic Society** is for those interested in stamp collecting, buying and selling stamps through the society's auctions or postal packet scheme.
- The **Railway Correspondence and Travel Society** is Britain's leading railway enthusiast group for those interested in railways past, present and future.
- The **RSPCA** is the UK's leading animal welfare charity. Its website is all about animals: pets, horses, wildlife and farm animals.

Sport

Retirement is an ideal time to get fit and take up a sporting hobby. To find out about opportunities in your area, contact your local authority recreational department or your local sports or leisure centre. Website details for all the organizations listed below can be found in the Directory, pp 29–31.

Water-related sports

- The **Angling Trades Association** promotes the interests of anglers and angling, including educational and environmental concerns, where to find qualified tuition, local tackle dealers and similar information.

- **British Rowing** is the governing body for the sport of rowing both indoors and in water.
- The **Outdoor Swimming Society (OSS)** campaigns for the rights of everyone to swim in clean and safe rivers, lakes and seas. It also helps members connect with others to find welcoming wild swimming groups.
- The **Royal Yachting Association** has thousands of affiliated clubs and recognized training centres throughout the UK. It provides comprehensive information for boat owners, with advice on everything from moorings to foreign cruising procedure.
- **Seavets**, affiliated to the Royal Yachting Association, aims to encourage the not-so-young of all abilities to enjoy the challenge of windsurfing.
- **Swim England** is the national governing body for swimming in England. To contact Swim England or one of the other countries' governing bodies (**Swim Ireland, Swim Scotland** or **Swim Wales**), see Directory, pp 30–31.

Racquet or ball sports

- **Badminton England** is the sport's governing body in England. Many categories of membership are available. Most sports and leisure centres have badminton courts and give instruction.
- The **Bowls Development Alliance** is the united body of Bowls England, the English Indoor Bowling Association, the English Short Mat Bowling Association and the British Crown Green Bowling Association. It is a game that is available to everyone from the age of 8 to 80.
- The **Croquet Association** runs coaching courses and can advise about clubs, events, purchase of equipment and other information.
- Contact the **England and Wales Cricket Board** to get in touch with your county cricket board or your local club, if you want to play, watch or help at cricket matches. The **Kia Oval** membership entitles you to free or reduced-price tickets for the Members' Pavilion to watch international matches as well as county events. **Lord's Cricket Ground** offers a conducted tour of Lord's that includes the MCC Museum, where the Ashes urn is on display. Senior citizens can attend County Championship matches and the National League matches for half price.
- **England Golf** is one of the largest sports governing bodies in England, looking after the interests of over 1,900 golf clubs and 651,000 members. See also **Golf Ireland** (bringing together the Golfing Union of Ireland and the Irish Ladies Golf Union), **Scottish Golf** or **Wales Golf.**

- The **Lawn Tennis Association** provides information about anything to do with tennis, from advice on choosing a racquet to obtaining tickets for major tournaments. **Seniors Tennis GB** promotes competitions for older players in various age groups from 35 years up, with information on club, county and international events.
- **Table Tennis England** is the association for this sport, enjoyed by people of all ages and all levels of competence. The **Veterans English Table Tennis Society** holds regional and national championships including singles and doubles events for players of various ages over 40.

Other sports

- The **Association of Running Clubs** is the governing body for running clubs. Their website gives information on road-running clubs and their activities throughout the UK.
- The **British Darts Organisation** organizes hundreds of darts events throughout the country each year.
- The **Clay Pigeon Shooting Association** is an association of individual shooters and a federation of clubs. As a member you have public liability insurance, your scores are recorded in the national averages and you can compete in national events.
- **Cycling UK** protects and promotes the rights of cyclists. There is also a veterans' section.
- The **Ramblers** provides comprehensive information on all aspects of walking, and can advise on where to walk, clothing and equipment, and organized walking holidays, as well as details of the hundreds of local groups throughout the country.

Women's organizations

Despite greater awareness of gender equality, women typically still undertake the majority of caring and unpaid work in the home. This often gives women different experiences and perspectives on life. Unsurprisingly then there are women's clubs and organizations that continue to enjoy enormous popularity, which can be found in the Directory, p 31:

- The **Mothers' Union** promotes Christian care for families internationally in 84 countries, with over 4 million members.

- The **National Association of Women's Clubs** has around 130 clubs with nearly 5,000 members nationally, open to women of all ages, faiths and interests.
- The **National Women's Register** has groups across the UK of 'lively minded women' who meet informally in members' homes to enjoy challenging discussions. The groups choose their own topics and many also arrange a varied programme of social activities.
- The **Scottish Women's Institute** is one of the largest women's organizations in Scotland and has thousands of members of all ages who enjoy social, recreational and educational activities.
- **Soroptimist International**. A global volunteer movement that advocates for women's issues and their human rights. Local clubs fundraise and promote grassroots projects, while enjoying companionship. Also, opportunities to travel to international events.
- **Townswomen's Guilds** is one of the UK's leading women's organizations, providing fun, friendship and a forum for social change since 1929. Over 10,000 women nationwide are members.
- The **Women's Institute** (WI) is the largest national organization for women, with nearly 170,000 members in local WIs across Britain. It plays a unique role in providing women with educational opportunities and the chance to take part in a wide variety of activities and campaigns. If you live in Northern Ireland, there is the **Federation of Women's Institutes of Northern Ireland**.

For people with disabilities

In large part due to legislation, facilities for people with disabilities have improved dramatically in recent decades, so there are fewer activities from which disabled people are now excluded. Fencing is one that is fun and exciting, and a good way to keep in shape. It involves panache, style and grace, and can be done in a wheelchair. To find out more about wheelchair fencing, see the para fencing zone on the British Fencing website (Directory, p 29).

For blind or partially sighted people, the following may be of interest, as they feature talking books (websites can be found in the Directory, p 25):

- **Calibre Audio Library** has audio books that bring the pleasure of reading to people who have sight problems, dyslexia or other disabilities that prevent them from reading a print book; this service is entirely free.

- **Listening Books** is a UK charity providing a large collection of audio books to thousands of people nationwide who find it difficult or impossible to read due to illness or disability. Audio books are sent through the post on CD, or can be downloaded or streamed from the website.
- **RNIB**'s Talking Book Service offers over 40,000 audio books. It's a free service and offers a choice of formats from downloads to CDs or USB stick delivered to your door. The RNIB's library has books available in audio, digital, braille and giant print.

CHAPTER NINE

Starting your own business

Retirement as a time of endless leisure is not necessarily an appealing prospect – in fact, the latest popular acronym is CHILL (Career Happiness Inspires Longer Lives). And, while you perhaps cannot wait to leave your current job, retirement can be the opportunity to try something different that happens to involve self-employment or to fulfil a long-held ambition to start your own business. Of course, working in retirement may be a necessity if income is short or you are bridging a gap until your pension starts, and in that case you should seriously weigh up the option of taking a paid job working for someone else versus working for yourself. Running your own business can seem to offer an attractive flexibility over how, when and where you work, but it is no soft option. If your business is to be a success, it may require a great deal of mental, physical, emotional and time input, though this will vary with the type of business you choose.

Nevertheless, self-employment is a popular choice for mature workers. Government data shows that, in 2022, 3.5 million people over 60 were in work, with 919,000 (just over a quarter) of them being self-employed.

Taking stock

The range of business opportunities is limitless. Some of the areas you might be thinking of are:

- Consultancy work, selling specialist knowledge and skills built up over your career to a range of clients, who might include your former employer.
- Turning an existing hobby into a business, for example, carpentry, metal-work, sewing, jewellery-making or baking. This might entail selling things you make, holding workshops where you train others in these skills, or both.
- Selling skills you already have, such as gardening, catering, a handyperson service, teaching languages, tutoring or coaching, musical and performance arts, driving, housekeeping, care or companionship services.
- Acquiring new skills that you can sell, such as plumbing, web design or book-keeping.
- Running a location-based business, such as a café or shop.
- Starting a social enterprise, where the aim is not to make profit for yourself but to benefit your community – for example, giving debt advice, running an animal rescue centre or providing support for the homeless.

Different types of business require different levels of commitment from you and have different financial requirements. The sections that follow aim to get you thinking about how well you and your business idea marry up.

Time and flexibility

A major attraction of being your own boss is choosing when you work, and some types of business lend themselves well to this, for example arranging your own workshops and classes to teach a skill, building up a small clientele for regular gardening services or taking on contracts that simply specify delivery deadlines. However, being able to flex your hours does not necessarily mean you can work short hours, and some businesses will struggle if you are too flexible. For example, if you run a shop or café where you rely on customers dropping in without an appointment or booking, you will rapidly lose custom if your business is only open at random and unpredictable times. Nobody will want to make the effort of travelling to your premises only to find you closed.

There are similar issues if you work as a consultant. Firms often use consultants and freelancers to deal with lumpy or unexpected workloads. As such, you will often be contracted to deliver your work to tight and possibly very short deadlines. This may mean burning the midnight oil to meet a deadline, even though once it's done you can take time out. A further issue with consultancy is that much of your work may come from repeat contracts from happy clients or referrals because of the great job you did. Thus, while you're building your reputation, turning down a job because you'd prefer some free time could mean that you lose not just that one contract but also repeat work from that client and others. Once you are established, this may be less of a problem. Similar issues may apply if you are building up a business such as catering for, or performing at, special events – if you say no, the customer is likely to move on and find an alternative, and you may also lose referrals as a result.

If you are selling things you make, you may need to schedule your workload around peaks and troughs in your market. Will your sales be bunched in the Christmas period or during the summer? If so, you will need to build up your stock ahead of these periods. How you sell can also create the rhythm for your work – if, say, you sell at a monthly craft fair, you will want your stock to be highest just before each sale. If, on the other hand, you sell mostly online, your sales might be more evenly spread and you might even be in the happy position of being able to make items to order.

Be aware too that there is a fair amount of admin that goes with running a business: keeping records of sales and everything you buy; drawing up accounts; dealing with tax; complying with regulations, such as waste disposal; and so on. You may be able to hire others to take on some of these tasks, though that has to be arranged and monitored too. In many areas, from catering to finance, there are additional regulations, and, if you provide professional services, you may have continuing professional development (CPD) requirements to comply with. These will all require time on top of what it takes to run your core business.

Your skill set

Knowledge and skills you already have or plan to develop may be at the heart of your core business idea. However, as noted in the last section, there is a wide range of peripheral tasks involved in starting and running a business. Some tasks can be outsourced to experts, such as an accountant, whose fees will be a cost to the business. Maybe you have a partner or other family member who is willing to take on some aspects. Generally, though, there will be a range of non-core business tasks that you will have to undertake yourself.

It's worth thinking through all the elements involved in running your chosen business and conducting a skills audit on yourself to see which tasks you can readily take on and which might be a challenge. You could use a traffic-light system in your skills audit – green for tasks where you already have the necessary skills, amber for areas where you could get by but would benefit from updating or further developing your skills, and red for any skills gaps. Decide how you will tackle the gaps – for example, tool yourself up through training, or outsource to someone else who does have the skills. If you decide on training, decide what sort of training you need, where you can access it and by when you need to have done it. See Chapter 10 for some ideas on adult learning and check out the National Careers Service Skills Toolkit for a wide range of courses, including business and finance, marketing and professional development (Directory, p 45).

Financial resources

Some businesses require very little money (capital) to set up. For example, if you are selling your skills as a gardener locally, you could operate from home and simply advertise on neighbourhood websites or local public noticeboards to find customers, with very little outlay beyond some gardening tools (which you might already have). Launching other businesses may not be possible at all without substantial upfront finance, for example, to buy premises, fittings and machinery, meet regulatory requirements, pay for marketing or buy an existing business from the outgoing owner.

Whatever your business, you are likely to need some working capital. This finances the delay between your spending on raw materials, equipment and other inputs and receiving the proceeds from selling your services or products. The length of the delay will vary with the type of business, the conditions it faces and the terms you have with your customers. For example, if you provide consultancy work, it is typical to require payment within 30 days of presenting your invoice. In practice, clients are often much slower to pay. (The law allows you to charge business customers interest if they are late paying, but in practice you might be reluctant to do this if you want to foster an ongoing relationship with that customer.) If you are selling things that you make, you normally get revenue as soon as you make a sale, unless you offer customers credit. However, if sales are slow, you may instead see your stocks pile up and have a long wait to recoup the cost of making the items. You may be in a position to fund the working capital you need from your own savings or non-business income. If not, you may need to agree an overdraft or loan from your bank.

Your access to capital can be a defining factor in whether you can afford to start your chosen business.

Buying a franchise

An alternative to setting up your own business from scratch is to buy a franchise, where you buy the right to run an outlet based on a tried-and-tested business format for a specified term of years (often 10), after which you may be able to renew for further periods. The franchise is your own business, but you do not have total freedom because you are constrained to run it in the way set out by the franchise agreement. Moreover, you do not keep all the money you make because some of it will go back to the franchisor (the seller of the franchise). But you should be investing in a proven business format, which should increase the chance of your business succeeding.

There is a wealth of information and guidance about franchising and the franchising opportunities available on the BFA and other websites. See, for example:

- **British Franchise Association** (Directory, p 44)
- **Franchise Direct** (Directory, p 44)
- **Whichfranchise** (Directory, p 46)

Getting organized

Occasionally businesses spring spontaneously to life – you leave an employer who then asks if you'll continue a project on a freelance basis, or a friend asks if you'll make them one of the seats you built for your own garden, and it snowballs from there. However, in most cases, you will need to do some serious planning to convert your business idea into reality. Creating a business plan will help you – and others – see if your idea is financially viable, and you need to make other key decisions, such as the structure of your business, your business name, where you will work and what insurance you need.

Your business plan

If you need to raise finance, you will need to show your bank or backers a business plan so they can gauge how sound their lending or investment will be. Even if you will not be seeking finance, you are still well advised to draw up a business plan because the process of doing so will help you to make a realistic appraisal of your business viability and where you might face challenges. It will also establish a baseline to compare against later when you are reviewing the progress of your business. Your business plan should contain the following elements:

- The name of your business, what you will sell and its unique selling proposition (USP). The USP is essentially what will make you succeed against the competition. For example, you may have a novel product, cheaper costs, better quality or a special location.
- The experience and skills you and anyone else involved will bring to the business.
- The market you will operate in, who the customers are and who your competitors are.
- How you will get your customers and your pricing strategy.
- How your business operates – for example, where it's located, your suppliers, equipment you need, how you get your goods or services to market, significant risks and how you will manage compliance requirements (such as data protection).
- Financial projections, including expected revenue, profit and cash flow.
- Financing requirements.
- Business targets for the short, medium and long term.

If you will be presenting your plan to your bank or potential backers, you should include an executive summary at the start of the plan that concisely draws together the key points from the whole plan. This summary should ideally be no more than a couple of pages, and its function is to excite and interest the potential financier enough to want to know more. This is important because, if the summary does not grab their attention, they might never read the rest of your plan.

You can draw up your plan from scratch yourself, or there are many business plan templates that you can buy online – just search for 'business plan'. Even better, some templates and guidance are available free, for example from The Prince's Trust (Directory, p 46). Although this organization exists to support young people, its resources are available to all.

Your business structure

There are three main ways to structure your own business: sole trader, partnership or company. Small-scale or casual self-employment might not need to be formally structured at all. A note of caution: HM Revenue & Customs (HMRC) will only accept that you are running a bona fide business if you are doing so with a view to making a profit (even if in some years you actually make a loss). It will not accept that a hobby you do for fun, not profit, is a business.

SMALL-SCALE AND CASUAL SELF-EMPLOYMENT

Since April 2017, you can have up to £1,000 of trading income each year tax-free and without having to declare it on a tax return. The £1,000 limit applies to revenue, not profit, and you cannot claim tax relief for any expenses. This so-called trading allowance might be enough to cover your business if it is very small-scale. Similarly you can have £1,000 of property income tax-free without the need to declare it. This could cover, for example, money you make from letting out your driveway as a parking space, or from occasionally renting out your home through an internet platform.

In either case, if the revenue you get is more than £1,000, you can choose to deduct either the £1,000 allowance or your actual expenses. You then pay tax on what remains. The allowance cannot be used to create a loss, but deducting expenses can. Trading income of more than £1,000 must be declared each year on a tax return – see Chapter 4. There is a section of the return for 'Other income', and this also includes casual earnings from, say, occasional freelance work that falls short of running a business.

SOLE TRADER

This is the simplest business format. Legally, there is no separation between you and your business; you are one and the same (though you may choose a business name that you trade as). This has the disadvantage that, if something goes wrong in your business, all your personal wealth could be in the firing line and, in the extreme, lost. But the advantage is simplicity in accessing the money you make and a minimum of bureaucracy and admin.

To start up, you simply start trading. You must register with HMRC as soon as possible, which will ensure that you are on the system for the various taxes you need to pay – the main tax is income tax on your business profits. While there is no fine for a delay in registering your business, there will be interest and penalties if you fail to deal with tax correctly. You must keep records and draw up your accounts each year. These will form the basis of your tax bills. There is more information about tax later in this chapter in the section *Dealing with tax*.

Sole trader status can be particularly suitable for trades (such as plumbing or carpentry) and vocations (for example, writing or music) when they are small-scale.

PARTNERSHIP

For tax purposes, partnerships are essentially a group of two or more sole traders working together, and for tax purposes each partner is treated as if their share of the partnership is their own business.

There is no absolute requirement to draw up a partnership agreement, but you would be wise to do so. However well you and your partner(s) feel you get on, business and money disagreements can quickly turn any relationship sour. Therefore, it's best to be very clear right from the start how the partnership will work, such as how you will share its management, workload, income and expenses. A solicitor or accountant can help you draw up an agreement.

Partners are jointly and severally liable for the expenses and debts of the business and, like sole traders, partners' personal wealth can be called on to pay off any debts of the business. 'Jointly and severally' means that, even if the partnership agreement says you intend to share everything equally, if one partner cannot pay his or her way, then the remaining partner(s) must normally pick up the liability. The exception is where you set up a limited liability partnership (LLP). An LLP is a sort of halfway house between an ordinary partnership (sole-trader-type status) and limited company.

While you can just start trading as a partnership, a more normal route is to get the help of an accountant, solicitor or specialist company formation agent (see *Sources of help and advice* at the end of this chapter). If you are interested in an LLP, there is guidance available at GOV.UK (Directory, p 45).

LIMITED COMPANY

A company has a separate legal identity from the people running it. This means, for example, that it is the company, not you directly, that enters into contracts with customers and suppliers and receives the money earned. The company issues shares and the shareholders are the ultimate owners of the company. This is the basic structure of companies quoted on a stock exchange (public companies), as well as a small business that you set up for yourself where all the shares are privately owned (private company).

Day-to-day running of a company is the responsibility of the company's directors (who may also hold some or all of the shares).

As a director, you are an employee of your company. The company must pay corporation tax on its profits and, as an employee, the main tax you pay is income tax on any earnings you draw. Some or all of the company's profits can be paid out as dividends on the shares and these, too, are subject to income tax (see *Dealing with tax* later in this chapter for more information). You may also be able to borrow money from the company through a director's loan account, in which case you owe your company the money and must repay it at some stage.

If you set up your business as a limited company, you have the advantage of limited liability. This means that, provided you do not trade while knowingly insolvent, the maximum loss you can incur is the cost of the shares you hold, so your personal wealth is not at risk. That said, if the company needs to borrow money from a bank, the bank may insist that the loan is secured against your personal assets, often your home, and in that case, if the loan could not be repaid, the assets used as security could be seized. In return for limited liability, companies must be registered with Companies House (Directory, p 46) and must file various documents, including, for example, details of the director(s) and annual accounts, which can be inspected by the public.

You can deal with the form-filling required to set up a company yourself, but most people get help from an accountant or company formation agent (see *Sources of help and advice* at the end of this chapter).

Your business name

There are relatively few restrictions on what you call your business if you set up as a sole trader or an ordinary partnership. You can trade under your own name or choose something different, in which case, you will need to include your own name as well as your business name on your invoices and correspondence. There are a few restrictions, for example, you cannot include words that would suggest you are a company or have limited liability, such as 'Limited', 'Ltd', 'LLP', and so on.

If you set up your business as an LLP or company, there are rules about the name you can give to your business. You must register your business with Companies House and it cannot have a name that is the same or close to the name of any other business already on the register. Companies House has an online tool where you can check if the name you are thinking of has already been taken (Directory, p 46). The name of a private company with limited liability must end in 'limited' or 'Ltd' (though you may instead choose the Welsh equivalent, 'cyfyngedgig' or 'cyf', if your company is registered in Wales). An LLP's name must end with 'Limited Liability Partnership' or 'LLP' (or Welsh equivalent if registered in Wales).

Whatever your business structure, your business name must not be offensive, or suggest a connection with government or a public authority. Moreover, unless you have official permission, the name must not include any words or expressions that have been designated in legislation as being sensitive. These include, for example, 'association', 'bank', 'Britain', 'dental', 'mutual', 'king' or 'queen' and 'trust'. For more information, see GOV.UK (Directory, p 47).

Another issue to think about if you intend to have a website is whether a domain name is available that matches your business name or the trading name you intend to use. You can check this using the UK official domain name registry firm (Directory, p 47).

Where you will work

For many small businesses, there is a choice: work from home or from dedicated business premises. With some service businesses, such as hairdressing, there is a third option of operating out of your home, but delivering the service at your customers' own homes or other premises.

Working from home has a number of advantages: it keeps your costs low, you don't lose time travelling to a workplace, it may be easier to combine work with family commitments, you may have more control over making your working environment a pleasant place to be and home may be ideal if you have a disability that restricts your capacity to travel or operate from another space. However, there are drawbacks too: your home might lack the space you need, home services such as broadband may be less efficient and reliable than you need, working from home can be lonely, it can be hard to close the door on work leading to excessive hours or, on the other hand, family distractions may make it hard to get enough time and focus for work.

In addition, there may be legal constraints on your ability to work from home. If you have a mortgage or you rent, you should get permission from your lender or landlord before setting up a business at home. As a homeowner, with or without a mortgage, you should check your deeds for any covenants that restrict working from home or the types of business that can be located there. You might decide to go ahead even if there are covenants restricting home-working, since covenants are effective only if someone – typically a neighbour – decides to take legal action to try to enforce them.

This may be likely if your business intrudes in some way on your neighbours' enjoyment of their own properties, for example, because your business is noisy, creates a lot of waste or means that there is a string of delivery vans parking outside. If you are just quietly beavering away at a computer or sewing machine, it's unlikely your neighbours will notice or want to complain.

If you decide to work in dedicated business premises, you will need to buy, lease or rent space suitable for your particular business. If your work will be desk-based, you might consider renting in a shared-office-space complex. There are a variety of options: your own office, your own desk or hot desking. Some of these complexes also have meeting rooms you can book and shared refreshment areas. There are often small locally based complexes, but also large multi-location providers. Some sources and providers that can help you find business property include:

- local estate agents
- property websites, such as **Rightmove** and **Zoopla** (Directory, p 43)
- local craft centres – they may have workshops for rent
- firms that provide shared office space, such as: **Official Space, Regus** and **Workspace** (Directory, p 43)
- **Expert Market** (Directory, p 42) – a search engine to help you find business services, including office space.

Be aware that some spaces that have previously been free may no longer be so if you are using them for commercial purposes. This includes many local parks. If you are thinking of setting up as a fitness coach holding sessions in the park, first check out with your local council or park operator whether there is a charge.

Insurance

There are not many types of insurance that are compulsory. However, there are several that you would be wise to consider if you run a business – and some clients may insist you have certain types of cover before they will do business with you. The types of insurance you may need include:

- **Motor insurance:** this is compulsory if you are going to drive or park a vehicle on public roads. The minimum cover required by law is third-party cover to compensate other people if you injure them or damage their property.

- **Employer's liability insurance:** you must by law have this if your business has employees. It is designed to pay out if employees are injured or become ill because of the work they do for you.
- **Business premises insurance:** the equivalent of home buildings insurance but for your office, shop, café or other business premises. It covers damage to, or destruction of, the fabric of the building and its fittings against a wide range of perils, such as fire, flood, storm damage, subsidence, break-in damage, and so on. This insurance is not required by law but, if you have taken out a mortgage or other loan secured against the premises, the lender will normally insist that you have insurance cover.
- **Business contents/equipment insurance:** this covers your office furniture, computers, copiers and other equipment, books, journals, raw materials, stock of finished goods, and so on against perils, such as fire, flood and theft. If you work from home, your normal home contents policy is unlikely to automatically cover business possessions, so you may want to seek an extension to your home policy.
- **Public/product liability insurance:** cover for legal costs and compensation should a customer, client or any member of the public suffer injury or loss because of using your products or services or due to accidents on your premises, or damage you cause while carrying out your services at customers' premises. Not compulsory, but essential if you are selling products, have premises that clients or the public visit, or you work at other people's premises.
- **Professional indemnity insurance:** this covers legal costs and compensation if a client claims they have suffered loss because of a problem with your work, for example, regarding accuracy, late delivery, incompleteness or infringing someone else's copyright. Especially useful for consultants, advisers and tutors.
- **Professional treatment liability insurance:** optional cover for legal costs and compensation should a client claim that your services or advice have led to the client suffering an injury. Useful for, for example, personal trainers and hairdressers.
- **Key man insurance:** this pays out if a partner or employee who is vital to the success of the business has to leave because of illness or dies.
- **Cyber insurance:** this covers the financial consequences of data breaches, malicious hacks and similar IT-related threats.

A business insurer or broker can typically put together a package of the different types of insurance relevant to your business, so that you just have one policy rather than several different ones to worry about. Some useful contacts include:

- **British Insurance Brokers' Association** (Directory, p 21). The trade body for insurance brokers. It has a searchable database of members and you can specify the type of insurance you are seeking, for example 'commercial'.
- **Direct Line for Business** (Directory, p 21). Part of the Direct Line insurance group, specializing in insurance for small businesses and professionals. Like the rest of the group, it deals with customers direct so is not usually included on price comparison sites.
- **Hiscox** (Directory, p 21). An international broker and leading provider of business insurance to UK professionals, consultants and small- and medium-sized firms in all sectors.
- **Price comparison websites.** Some have sections where you can compare quotes for business insurance, such as **Compare the Market** and **MoneySuperMarket** (Directory, p 32).
- **Simply Business** (XBridge Limited) (Directory, p 21). A UK-based broker specializing in business insurance across 1,000 different trades.

Finding customers

Without customers you have no business, so it is essential to have a sound plan for how to reach them. The strategies you adopt depend very much on the type of business that you have.

If yours is a very local business, for example, providing gardening, plumbing or other services or trades provided in people's homes, your focus will be on how to make your local community aware of your existence and building a good reputation which will help you to get further business through word of mouth. Some possibilities include putting printed flyers through people's doors, placing ads in community magazines and on community noticeboards, and joining and posting on online community sites, such as Gumtree and Nextdoor (Directory, p 43). There are also a number of websites that you could join, where would-be customers either search for traders in their area or post their job requirements which the site then matches to traders. Typically, these sites are free for customers to use, but you pay a fee to be listed, agree to abide by a code of conduct or ethics, and agree to provide information that enables the website operators to check you comply with their standards. Customers can leave feedback which can help you to build your reputation. It's important that you check the terms and conditions before joining a site to ensure that it caters for your type of business, you are happy with how the site works and the fees it charges, and you can meet its requirements. For example (Directory, pp 42–43):

- **Checkatrade** (Vetted Limited)
- **Rated People**
- **TrustaTrader**
- **Trusted Traders** (part of the consumer advocacy group, Which?)
- **TrustMark** (a government-endorsed scheme)

If you will be selling things you make from a stall or food van, your main outlet may be local craft fairs and events, such as festivals and agricultural shows. You typically pay a fee for your stall or pitch, and gain access to all the visitors as potential customers. You can find information about local craft fairs and events from your local council, community Facebook pages, local churches and schools. You can search for events by location on event websites, such as Eventbrite, Stall & Craft Collective, Stallfinder, The List and UKCraftFairs (Directory, pp 42–43).

If you plan to sell beyond your local community, the easiest route for many small businesses is through online sites, such as eBay and Amazon Marketplace. You may previously have sold items privately on eBay, in which case your listing would have been free and you paid eBay a percentage of the price you received. The fees are different if you are selling as a business, and there are a variety of options, including creating your own virtual shop. You can find details on eBay's website (Directory, p 42). For details of how to advertise and sell on Amazon, see Directory, p 42.

Where you are selling your expertise as a consultant, your approach to finding clients is likely to be very different. Contracts with the government or other public bodies normally have to go through a tendering process. You typically pitch for the business by responding to an invitation to tender (ITT), which will usually be posted on a tendering website. Your first step is to register with relevant websites and check regularly for contracts that may be of interest to you. You can find guidance on how to sell your goods and services to the public sector at GOV.UK (Directory, p 43).

Outside the public sector, you could contact potential clients direct to find out what opportunities might be available and how to bid for them. There are also many intermediary websites that you can join for a fee that offer tender-finding services and provide automatic alerts when relevant contracts come up, such as B2B Quote (tenders) and Creative Tenders (Directory, p 42).

However, in the consultancy world, invitations to bid for, or take on, pieces of work often come through people you know or have worked with before or through referrals. Therefore, it is important to develop and maintain a good business network. Invitations to bid for work can also come through social media. For example, joining LinkedIn (Directory, p 43), and keeping your profile up to date can attract contact from businesses looking for people with your areas of expertise. Some organizations will tweet about opportunities, so it's worth having an X (formerly Twitter) account (Directory, p 43) and following the firms you would be interested in working with.

Dealing with tax

The taxes you pay as a result of running a business depend mainly on your business format, but can also be affected by the size of your business, and your age. You may have to collect tax on your sales and pay tax related to your business premises, profits and any gain you make on the sale of your business.

Tax on sales

Whatever the format of your business, you must by law register for Value Added Tax (VAT) if your annual turnover (revenue from sales) will be more than £90,000. VAT is a tax on sales that is ultimately paid by the final consumer, but it is collected by each business in the supply chain. If you are registered for VAT, you must normally charge VAT on your sales (called your outputs in the language of VAT) by adding 20 per cent (2024/25 rate) to the price you charge your customers, but you can claim back VAT you paid on your purchases (inputs). Regularly (usually once a quarter), you complete a VAT return in which you report the VAT you've collected and the amount you are claiming, and hand over the difference to HMRC.

There are some exceptions because some goods and services are exempt from VAT, and others are charged at a lower rate. The lower rate may even be zero. The distinction between exempt and zero-rated might seem a bit academic. However, an exempt supplier cannot claim back VAT on inputs, while a zero-rated supplier can.

If your turnover does not exceed £90,000, you can if you choose voluntarily register for VAT. This might be worth doing if, for example, your customers are other businesses (since unlike retail customers they can claim back the VAT you charge) and you pay VAT on most of your supplies, which you could reclaim if registered. Being registered for VAT might also lend extra credibility to your business in the eyes of clients or customers.

All VAT-registered businesses are now part of the Making Tax Digital (MTD) scheme for reporting and paying VAT – see Chapter 4. You need to use accounting software that is compatible with HMRC systems, and HMRC has an online search tool of suppliers at GOV.UK (Directory, p 43). Exceptionally, you can apply for an exemption from MTD if you cannot manage the system, for example, because of your age, disability or living in an area with poor broadband – see the GOV.UK website (Directory, p 42).

For more information about VAT, see gov.uk/vat-businesses. For guidance on how to register, see GOV.UK (Directory, p 47).

Business rates

The new government has pledged to replace business rates with a fairer system, but for now business rates are a tax due on most non-domestic properties, such as shops, offices, workshops, holiday rental homes, guest houses and stables. They may also apply to any part of your home that you use exclusively for business, such as a converted garage or a shop beneath your flat, or if customers visit your property or you have employees. But business rates do not usually apply if you simply use an existing room as your office. Business rates are administered by your local council.

Business rates are calculated by multiplying the rateable value of the property by a multiplier, although the detail of business rates differs depending on which nation of the UK you live in. However, you may qualify for one of several business rate reliefs which reduce or eliminate the bill. In particular, you might be able to get small business rate relief if the rateable value of your property is fairly low, and you might be able to get hardship relief if you are facing financial difficulties. For a full list of the various reliefs available, see GOV.UK (Directory, p 46).

If you think business rates will apply to you, contact your local council when you first start up in order to be included in the rating system and to apply for rate relief: gov.uk/find-local-council.

Tax for sole traders and partners

As explained earlier in this chapter, there is no separate legal identity for a business run by a sole trader or partner. The profits from the business are part of their personal income and subject to income tax along with all their other income. You might also have to pay National Insurance contributions, but not if you have reached State Pension age – see Chapter 3 for when that is. The income tax rules for sole traders and partners are more generous than for employees (allowing the self-employed, for example, to claim tax relief for a wider variety of expenses and also for losses), so you may need to satisfy HMRC that you are genuinely self-employed.

ARE YOU SELF-EMPLOYED?

Whether or not you count as genuinely self-employed for tax purposes depends on the facts of your relationship with each client or customer. The sort of facts that will tend to indicate you are genuinely self-employed, rather than an employee, include:

- having right to turn down work
- choosing where you work
- choosing the hours you work
- being paid a fixed sum for the work
- risking your own money
- having to put right mistakes at your own cost
- providing the main equipment needed to do your work
- having the right to provide a substitute to do the work
- employing others to help you carry out the work
- having more than one customer or client

HMRC is also concerned to distinguish self-employment from activities that do not amount to running a business, such as hobbies or one-off transactions. HMRC uses 'badges of trade' to help it make these judgements, and you are more likely to be deemed to be genuinely in business if your intention is to make a profit, the activity is systematic and repeated, the things you are selling have value mainly through being sold, the way you sell them is typical for a trading organization and the things you are selling are normally in your possession for only a short time.

GOV.UK has an employment status indicator tool that can help you work out if you are likely to be accepted as self-employed (Directory, p 44).

REGISTERING YOUR BUSINESS

To ensure that you pay the right taxes on time and so avoid any penalties, you should register your business as soon as possible after starting up. You are, in any case, required to let HMRC know of any untaxed source of income within six months of the end of the tax year in which you received the income, so the very latest you should register is 5 October in the tax year after the one when you started up. You can register your business either through HMRC's online services system or by completing form CWF1. For details, see GOV.UK (Directory, p 47) or phone the Self Assessment helpline on 0300 200 3310. Note that previous HMRC plans to close the helpline for six months each year were abruptly halted because of a public backlash. Nevertheless, HMRC is encouraging people to 'self-serve' using its online information and tools or use the webchat function. In mid-2024, helpline response times were extremely slow.

NATIONAL INSURANCE

Business people who are sole traders or partners, who are under State Pension age, must usually Class 4 National Insurance (and used to pay Class 2 contributions but this is now voluntary).

In 2024/25, Class 4 contributions are paid at a main rate of 6 per cent (previously 9 per cent) on earnings between a lower profits limit (£12,570) and an upper profits limit (£50,270) and 2 per cent on earnings above the upper limit. Class 4 contributions are purely a tax – they do not help you build up State Pension.

Since 6 April 2024, the requirement to pay Class 2 contributions has been abolished – contributions paid in the past do count towards your State Pension. But, now, if you have profits of £6,725 or more, you instead get National Insurance credits towards your State Pension. If your profits are lower, you will (as in previous years) be able to pay Class 2 contributions voluntarily. These are paid at a flat rate of £3.45 a week. You need 35 years of contributions or credits to get the maximum pension. So, if you are currently under State Pension age and on track for less, it could be well worth paying the voluntary contributions. But bear in mind you will need at least 10 years of contributions or credits to get any State Pension at all (see Chapter 3).

In any case, Class 2 contributions or credits cease from the start of the week in which you reach State Pension age. Class 4 contributions stop from 6 April following the tax year in which you reach State Pension age.

Class 4 contributions are collected through the Self Assessment tax system that applies to income tax (see the following section).

INCOME TAX

Your business profits are added to your other income for the tax year, and income tax is then calculated as described in Chapter 4. However, there are many adjustments you can make.

Your profit is basically your sales revenue less expenses, so your profit and loss account is the starting point for calculating your profit for tax purposes. For tax, you are allowed to deduct all expenses that you incur 'wholly and exclusively' for business purposes. In practice, where mixed expenses can be transparently split between private and business, you can also deduct the business part. For example, if you work from home, you can deduct a proportion of the cost of energy bills, basing the proportion on the number of rooms in the home and the percentage of time that one or more rooms are used for business. You will not need to apportion by time if you use part of your home exclusively for business. However, exclusive business use could mean that you have to pay capital gains tax (CGT) on part of any profit you make when you sell your home (see Chapter 4) and might mean you are liable for business rates on that part.

Some expenses are disallowed, including the cost of capital items and depreciation. Instead, you claim capital allowances which are, broadly speaking, depreciation calculated according to standardized tax rules. If you make a loss, you usually have several options, including, for example, carrying the loss forward to set against future profits or carrying the loss 'sideways' to set against other non-business income for the same tax year. If you use an accountant, he or she can advise you on what you can claim. If you want to check the rules yourself, there is a wealth of information at GOV.UK (Directory, p 47).

The tax year runs from 6 April to the following 5 April, but businesses can have accounting years that end on any date. For example, a business might draw up its accounts every 31 December. Under the rules that applied up to and including the 2022/23 tax year, income tax was normally charged on the business profits for the accounting year that ended during the tax year. So, in the example, the 2022/23 tax bill was based on profits made from 1 January to 31 December 2022. However, different rules apply from 2023/24 onwards.

If you start a new business from 6 April 2023 onwards, you are taxed each tax year on the profits you make during the tax year. This is very simple if your accounting year is also the same as the tax year. (Accounting years that end between 31 March and 4 April, inclusive, are treated as if they are the same as a tax year with the few non-aligned days being carried forward into the next tax year.)

If you have an existing business, the new rules apply from 2024/25 onwards. The tax year 2023/24 is a transitional year (so relevant for the tax return you send in by 31 January 2025) – the GOV.UK website has details of this 'basis period reform' (see Directory, p 44).

Under the new rules, if your accounting year is not the same as the tax year, each tax year you have to apportion profits from the two accounting years in order to estimate how much tax to pay. This is further complicated because, for businesses with profits over £50,000, from April 2026 (and £30,000 from April 2027), you will have to pay your income tax quarterly under the new Making Tax Digital (MTD) requirements – see Chapter 4. Thus, there is a very clear encouragement from the government to set, or change, your accounting year to match the tax year.

Currently, you must fill in a tax return each year in which you declare all your income, including your business profits. Once you have registered your business, HMRC will automatically contact you to remind you to do this. Chapter 4 has details of how you report and pay income tax through the Self Assessment system. Under current rules, you pay tax in two payments on account: the first on 31 January during the tax year; the second on 31 July following the end of the tax year, unless your last Self Assessment bill was less than £1,000. For example, the tax you owe for 2024/25 is paid on 31 January 2025 and 31 July 2025. These are estimates which are set at half the income tax for the previous year less any part paid through PAYE and half the National Insurance bill for the previous year. Once your tax return is filed (by 31 January 2026 for the 2024/25 tax year), the exact bill can be calculated and you will either have a balancing charge to pay by 31 January (2026 for 2024/25 tax return) or receive a refund if you have overpaid.

Tax if you operate as a company

If you set up your business as a company, it has a separate legal identity from you. Your company and you have different taxes to pay.

CORPORATION TAX

As explained earlier in this chapter, you must register your company with Companies House. Normally, this automatically triggers its registration for tax, but if you need to make a separate registration for corporation tax, you should do this within three months of starting to do business to avoid any penalty. Further information is at GOV.UK (Directory, p 46).

For tax purposes, the profits a small company makes are calculated in broadly the same way as described for a sole trader above. The company must pay corporation tax on these profits at a rate of 19 per cent (2024/25) provided it counts as a small company (annual profit up to £50,000) and on a sliding scale up to 25 per cent for larger companies. The after-tax profits may be retained within the company or all or part may be paid out to shareholders.

Corporation tax has to be paid no later than nine months and one day after the end of the company's accounting year. For example, if the accounting year end is 31 December, the tax must be paid by the following 1 October. Most small companies hire an accountant who will deal with corporation tax reporting, payment details and annual filing commitments.

NATIONAL INSURANCE

As a director of your company, you are an employee. You may decide to draw a salary from the company, in which case both you and the company normally have to pay Class 1 National Insurance.

Chapter 4 describes the National Insurance you pay as an employee. Once an employee reaches State Pension age, they stop paying National Insurance.

Your company has a number of obligations as your employer. It must pay employer's National Insurance contributions at a rate of 13.8 per cent on any of your pay above a secondary threshold of £175 a week (2024/25). This applies even where the employee is over State Pension age. Unless all employees (including you) earn less than the lower earnings limit, the company must also set up a PAYE system to collect any income tax and National Insurance you (the employee) owe, and pass all the National Insurance and income tax to HMRC. There is information at GOV.UK

(Directory, p 45). However, many small companies contract this task out to their accountant or a specialist payroll company. To find a payroll company, search online for 'payroll services'.

Any earnings your company pays you count as expenses of the business and so reduce the amount of corporation tax the company pays.

INCOME TAX

As an employee, if you draw earnings from your company, these are taxable in exactly the same way as earnings from any other job would be (see Chapter 4).

As a shareholder, you may receive dividends paid out by your company. Dividend income is also subject to income tax, but at different rates from those applicable to earnings. Chapter 4 explains how the income tax personal allowance and tax bands are applied to different types of income in a strict sequence. The tax you pay on dividends depends on the tax band into which they fall and in 2024/25 the situation is:

- no tax on dividends covered by your personal allowance;
- no tax if covered by your Dividend Allowance (£500 from 2024/25);
- remaining dividends are taxed at 8.75 per cent, 33.75 per cent and/or 39.35 per cent, according to whether they fall into the basic, higher or additional rate band(s).

Whether you and your company combined pay more or less tax on earnings or dividends depends on the amounts involved, your age and other income. There is no alternative but to work through the sums.

Tax when you sell your business

If your business involves simply selling your skills – whether as, say, a consultant or a gardener – there might not be any business as such to sell when you decide to stop working. However, other types of business may have substantial value, in their premises, brands, patents for unique products, stock of raw materials and finished goods and other assets. This means that you may be able to sell your business as an ongoing concern or sell off assets if the business is to close down. If you make a profit from the sale, you may have to pay CGT. However, you can usually claim Business Asset Disposal Relief.

CGT is a tax on any gain made when you dispose of an asset (although some assets and disposals are exempt – see Chapter 4). 'Disposal' extends beyond just selling an asset, so would also cover giving your business away (for example, to your adult children). Gains are added to any taxable income made in the same year to determine the rates at which CGT is charged. The normal rates of CGT on gains (other than from residential property) are 10 per cent for gains falling into the basic-rate band of tax and 20 per cent for anything more. Business Asset Disposal Relief reduces the rate to 10 per cent on the whole gain (up to a lifetime limit of £1 million).

The relief is available whatever the format of your business (sole trader, partnership, company). For sole traders and partners, to be eligible you must have owned the business for at least two years before you sell it. In the case of a company, you must have been an employee or office-holder (meaning an unpaid director or company secretary) for at least two years, and the company's main activities must be trading (as opposed to simply holding investments, say).

There is further information at GOV.UK (Directory, p 44).

Other rules and regulations

Depending on the type of business you have and the activities it involves, there may be a whole range of other rules and regulations that you will need to be aware of and abide by. It is not possible to cover every possibility here, but this section highlights a few of the most common areas.

Data protection

There are laws to protect people's personal data, which means any data by which an individual can be recognized, such as their name, address, email address and, depending on how data is used and combined with other information, could include many other aspects too. See the Information Commissioner's Office (ICO) for more information (Directory, p 45). You are likely to be handling and processing personal data in relation to your customers and any employees that you have.

You must have a lawful purpose for needing personal data. This might be, for example, that the data is essential for you to carry out the contract you have with the individual, or you are legally required to have the information. Before gathering personal data, you must make clear to the person involved why you need their data, how it will be used, how long you will keep it and whether you will be sharing the data with others – details such as these should be set out in a 'privacy notice'. You must obtain the person's explicit consent to collecting and using their data and, in most cases, they can withdraw their consent at any time, in which case you should normally erase their data. You must use the data only for the purposes you stated and store it no longer than necessary. The data must be stored securely and destroyed safely when no longer required and, if a data breach does occur, you must report it promptly to the ICO. Individuals have a right to request a copy of the personal data you hold about them. Anyone in your business who handles personal data needs to understand their responsibilities and obligations under the data protection legislation.

The ICO has a variety of guides to help you understand your obligations under the law (Directory, p 45).

Hiring employees

Of the 4.25 million people (of all ages) recorded in government statistics as being self-employed, the majority work on their own or with a partner but have no employees at all. Moving from working alone to employing someone is a big leap both in costs and administration.

Among the issues you will need to consider are:

- Making sure you do not discriminate – even indirectly or unwittingly – against job applicants and employees on the grounds of any 'protected characteristic', such as age, race, sex, pregnancy, and so on.
- Checking that employees have the right to work in the UK – you can be fined up to £20,000 per employee if you don't.
- Taking out employer's liability insurance to cover employees being injured or made ill by the work they do for you.
- Ensuring you comply with the law on employees' rights about, for example, minimum wage, holidays, sick pay, maternity pay and leave, and so on.
- Setting up and contributing to a pension plan for your employees.
- Providing each employee with a written statement of their employment terms.
- Making sure you – or a firm you hire – operates PAYE so that you and your employees pay the tax due on their earnings.
- If you do need to dismiss an employee, making sure that you go through the correct procedures.

A good source of information on these issues is Acas (Advisory, Conciliation and Arbitration Service) (Directory, p 44). For information about employers' pension obligations, see The Pensions Regulator (Directory, p 46).

Licence to practise

In some areas of work, it is illegal to offer your services to the public unless you have particular qualifications, abide by code of conduct rules, undertake regular continuous professional development and/or are recorded on a register of practitioners. For example, this applies throughout much of the financial services industry and the health industry if you will be in a public-facing role.

In other areas, while having a licence may not be a legal requirement, your standing may be enhanced if you are qualified or belong to a recognized professional body.

Waste disposal

If you spent most of your life as an employee, where discarded paper, old computers and other business waste magically disappears, it may come as a shock to find how difficult it can be to organize waste disposal as a small business.

Over the years, increasingly tough regulations have been introduced to ensure that waste is disposed of responsibly and recycled where possible. A domestic household taps into this system through local council kerbside collections and household recycling centres. However, you can be fined heavily for putting business waste into the household system. Businesses need alternative arrangements, and must usually pay to use these.

Some councils run schemes whereby local businesses can buy trade refuse sacks which are suitable for certain types of waste, such as paper. Other councils expect businesses to take out contracts with commercial waste handling firms. Council-run recycling centres will also usually accept business waste for a fee but, if you take waste there yourself, you will need a waste carrier's licence. Alternatively, you will need to hire a firm that does have a licence to take your waste there. You can find out about getting your own licence at GOV.UK (Directory, p 43). The licence is usually free if you are just transporting your own waste.

It is worth considering waste disposal at the time you buy supplies and you may wish, for example, to buy printer supplies from makers that run recycling schemes. Also check with your local council to see what arrangements it has for business waste (Directory, p 45). Use a search engine to find commercial waste contractors serving your area – try searching for 'business waste'.

Working with children or vulnerable adults

If your self-employment involves working with children or vulnerable adults – for example, because you tutor children, run children's dance classes or provide care services – your clients may want to be sure you have no unspent criminal convictions that would make you unsuitable for this work, by asking you to have a Disclosure and Barring Service (DBS) check. Even if not a requirement, you may feel that being able to provide the results of such a check will enhance your customers' or clients' confidence in you.

The DBS system is not really designed for the self-employed. Its main purpose is for employers to check whether employees and job applicants are suitable for roles that involve children or vulnerable adults. However, it is possible to request a basic check on yourself, which will result in a certificate that you can show to customers or clients. To do this, see GOV.UK (Directory, p 45). A basic check costs £18 (in 2024). There are more detailed DBS checks which you could obtain by going through an intermediary called a 'responsible organization' – for a list of these, see GOV.UK (Directory, p 45).

Sources of help and advice

For help setting up and running a business, including the tax implications, consider using an accountant. The following professional bodies can provide a list of members (Directory, pp 44–45):

- **Association of Chartered Certified Accountants**
- **Chartered Accountants Ireland**
- **Institute of Chartered Accountants in England and Wales**
- **Institute of Chartered Accountants of Scotland**

If you will be entering into a partnership, you are strongly advised to get legal advice from a solicitor. You can search the member lists of the following bodies:

- The **Law Society** – use its Find a Solicitor service to find legal advice in England, Wales and Scotland (Directory, p 45)
- The **Law Society of Northern Ireland** (Directory, p 45)

Information on tax and the laws applicable to small business is available at GOV.UK.

There are several membership bodies that represent small businesses, for example lobbying government to promote small business interests, and often provide members with access to a range of benefits, such as guidance, membership events, legal advice, insurance deals, and so on. They are typically funded through annual membership fees. Organizations include (Directory, p 44):

- the **Association of Independent Professionals and the Self Employed**, which specializes in representing independent contractors, freelancers and consultants
- the **Federation of Small Businesses**
- the **Forum of Private Business**
- your **local chamber of commerce** – find it through the website of the national body, British Chambers of Commerce, which includes a searchable directory of local chambers

CHAPTER TEN

Looking for paid work

Money is not the only benefit from work. Studies show that work can also be a source of identity, self-esteem, social contact and even improved health. Many people enjoy moving into a phase of life where work continues but on a part-time or otherwise less frenetic basis, either with their existing employer or a new one.

Points to consider when choosing retirement employment should include:

- previous employers who might consider you for part-time jobs if you have enjoyed working for them;
- researching temporary job recruitment websites;
- learning new skills that can lead to wider job options;
- when retirement is about to happen, asking present employers for part-time hours to help the transition;
- if money is not a factor, considering volunteer work or teaching and lecturing to pass on previous skills.

Note that this chapter looks at work in retirement where you take on a job with an employer. Another option is to do freelance work or start your own business, and you'll find ideas on that in Chapter 9. See Chapter 11 for ideas about volunteering work.

Financial considerations

Continuing to work can be a way of increasing your income, but there are some other financial aspects to consider.

Decisions about your State Pension

Your entitlement to State Pension depends purely on reaching State Pension age, and is not affected by whether you continue to work or how much other income you have. However, if you're still working, you might not need your State Pension yet and it may be pushing you into a higher tax bracket, so it may be worth deferring your State Pension – in which case it will be higher once it does start. For further details, see Chapter 3.

Decisions about your private pensions

Normally, employers cannot these days impose any particular retirement age. However, pension schemes can still set a normal pension age at which your full pension starts. If you start your pension earlier than the normal pension age, your pension will usually be lower and, if you start it later, it may be increased. (Chapter 3 has more details.)

In the past, some higher earners have retired early specifically to avoid heavy tax charges that have been triggered by their pension entitlements (typically from company schemes) breaching the limits for tax-free pension savings. The same reason has acted as a disincentive to rejoining the workforce. However, to remove those problems, the previous government changed the pension rules – see Chapter 3. Its aim was to encourage retired people back into work. At the time of writing, it was unclear whether the new Labour government would reverse the changes.

COMPANY PENSION SCHEMES

In many cases, you can start drawing your retirement pension even while continuing to work for the same employer. However, in some cases drawing a (partial) pension may be conditional on reducing your hours. In other cases your pension payments stop or are reduced if you go back to work, particularly in public sector jobs. Check the rules of your scheme carefully and note any particular steps you need to take if you want to have both your pension and earnings from that job. If you retired early on health grounds with an ill-health pension, this is likely to stop if you recover enough to return to work, but could be replaced with your normal pension if you have reached the normal pension age for your scheme. If you received an enhanced early pension on taking voluntary redundancy, there may be restrictions on your coming back to work for the same employer.

You may be able to decide to put off starting your pension, in which case the pension might be higher when it does start – but check what rules apply in your scheme. If you start taking your full pension, it's unlikely that any earnings you then get will count as pensionable, so you will not build up any further pension (and no pension contributions will be deducted from your pay). However, with a partial pension, you may still be contributing to the undrawn part. And, whatever your situation, you could still save through a personal pension if you wanted to.

There is nothing to stop you drawing a pension from a previous employer's scheme and taking on work with a different employer.

PERSONAL PENSION SCHEMES

Whether workplace schemes or ones you arranged for yourself, with personal pensions you can decide when you want to start drawing your money out. You can draw a pension whether you are still working or not. There are more details about pensions in Chapter 3 and more about investments in Chapter 5.

National Insurance contributions (NICs)

Under current rules, once you reach State Pension age, you no longer pay National Insurance contributions (NICs) even if you carry on working – see Chapter 4.

Redundancy

If you have just been made redundant, or fear this is a possibility, see the information in Chapter 2, *Money and budgeting*.

Where you will work

Travelling to and from a workplace can be tiring, not to say expensive. However, increasingly, many jobs can been done partially or fully from home.

If you are required by your employer to work from home, then you can claim tax relief for any additional home-related expenses you incur because of your work that your employer has not reimbursed. But you cannot get the relief if you simply choose to work from home and your employer lets you do that but it's not a requirement of your job.

The sort of extra costs that qualify for relief include, for example, the cost of heating and lighting your work area and business calls. You'll need to be able to identify or work out the work proportion of the relevant bills that's due to working from home. However, instead of claiming the actual extra costs, you can simply claim tax relief on a flat-rate allowance which is set at £6 a week (in 2024/25).

You cannot get relief on costs that are due to private as well as work use where it's not possible to evidence the work part or the cost would have been the same regardless of working from home, for example, broadband and your rent or mortgage.

The expenses you claim are set against your taxable income, so you'll get relief up to your top rate of income tax. For more about tax, see Chapter 4.

Special measures to assist disabled people to work

Disability, like age, is a 'protected characteristic'. This means that, under the Equality Act 2010, it is illegal to discriminate in the workplace either directly or indirectly against someone with the characteristic. Direct discrimination can happen where you are deliberately excluded, for example from recruitment, training or promotion, because the employer decides you could not manage. Indirect discrimination can occur when your employer fails to make reasonable adjustments, such as making all general areas accessible for wheelchair users. You have these rights whether your disability is a physical or mental condition. It has been established that someone living with cancer has the same rights as anyone else with a disability.

The mental health charity Scope suggests that reasonable adjustments at work might include, for example, adapted equipment such as special chairs and voice-recognition software, lowered desks, modified entrances, changing your responsibilities, transferring tasks to a colleague, flexible working, working from home, reduced hours or training colleagues to support you (for example, through deafness awareness training). If you are caring for someone with a disability, there is no requirement for your employer to make reasonable adjustments, but they must still not treat you less favourably than other employees because of the disability – if they do, it is called direct discrimination by association.

If you feel you are disadvantaged at work because of a disability, contact your human resources department to discuss measures that would help you. You might like to take a colleague, union representative, family member or friend with you to the meeting. If you're unhappy with your employer's response, seek advice, for example from your union if you belong to one or the Acas (Advisory, Conciliation and Arbitration Service) helpline: 0300 123 1100 or via online chat on the website (Directory, p 44). If Acas cannot help you reach agreement with your employer, you have the right to take your complaint to an employment tribunal.

Age discrimination and equality

Anti-age-discrimination legislation came into force in October 2006, and was enshrined in the Equality Act 2010. Under the Act, age is a 'protected characteristic' and it is illegal, except in a few situations, for employers to discriminate directly or indirectly against candidates or employees on account of age. Such discrimination might affect, for example, decisions about recruitment, training, pay, promotion or redundancy. The exception is where there is an objective reason for taking age into account, for example, the requirement for a young person to act the part of a youth in a theatrical production.

Provided individuals are capable of doing their job, an employer cannot normally require them to retire at a specific age. However, upper age limits are permitted in some jobs, such as the police, Fire Brigade and the Armed Forces, because of the physical demands of the job. There is also an exception for pension schemes so that they can set a normal pension age at which a person's full pension usually starts. But, in general, capacity to do the job should be based on the same objective factors, whatever the age of the employee and, if an older worker is underperforming, they should be given the same opportunities for improvement as any other employee.

Employees also have a right to request flexible working and, if (say) that option is available to younger workers with children, it might be discrimination if similar working arrangements were denied to older workers. Previously, you needed to work for your employer for at least 26 weeks before being eligible to request flexible working. But, since April 2024, this waiting period has been abolished so that you have this right from day one in your job. However, while an employer must consider any request for flexible working, they can refuse if there are business grounds for doing so.

If you feel you have been discriminated against at work, raise the matter with your line manager, your trade union or the human resources department. If the issue cannot be resolved informally, you could pursue it further through your employer's formal grievance procedure. If that does not produce a satisfactory outcome, the next step is the Acas conciliation service and finally you could go to an employment tribunal. There is useful information on the Acas website (Directory, p 44).

You have the same rights to complain and, if necessary, take your case to a tribunal, if you believe you have been unfairly treated during a recruitment process because of your age. However, it can be difficult to obtain evidence that age was a factor. Under data protection legislation, you have the right to request and see any notes made about you during the recruitment process if they are held on computer or in a structured filing system.

Assessing your abilities

Some people know exactly what job they want. But, if you are not one of those few, knowing what you have to offer is an essential first step. Make a list of everything you have done, in both your formal career and ordinary life, including your outside interests. In particular, consider adding any practical or other skills, knowledge or contacts that you have acquired over the years. These could now prove especially useful. If, for example, you have done a lot of public speaking, fundraising, committee work or conference organization, these would be excellent transferable skills that would make you attractive to a prospective employer. As a result of writing everything down, many people find that they have far more to offer than they originally realized.

In addition to work skills, you should include your personal attributes and any special assets that would attract an employer. The list might include organizational abilities, a good telephone manner, communication skills, the ability to work well with other people, access to a car or willingness to do flexible hours.

Although this area is new and evolving, you might consider how you could enhance your skills through learning to work with generative artificial intelligence (GAI) using tools such as ChatGPT and DALL.E 2 (Directory, p 44).

GAI is also rapidly being embedded into new versions of existing commonly used software, such as Word, and search engines, such as Google and Bing. GAI has the potential to transform many existing areas of work, such as communications, writing and coding. It probably will not displace human beings, but you might be expected to generate and use GAI materials as a time- and labour-saving step.

As a general rule when job hunting, the more accurate and targeted you can be in the application process, the more likely you are to succeed. Many people find this extraordinarily difficult. After years of working in one occupation, it takes quite a leap of imagination to picture yourself in another role, even if it is in the same or a related area. Talking to other people helps. Friends, family, work colleagues or business acquaintances may have useful information and moreover will quite likely be able to appraise your abilities more objectively than you can yourself. It could also be sensible to consult outside experts who specialize in adult career counselling. If you are claiming Jobseeker's Allowance or means-tested out-of-work state benefits, you will have a 'work coach' whose role is, in theory, to identify your skills and help you find suitable work. But in practice, like so many public services, this area tends to be under-resourced; your work coach may have too little time to advise you fully and may be more concerned to ensure that your claim for benefits is valid rather than advise you on finding a job. Whatever you decide to do, remember that with age and experience comes wisdom. You have the power to negotiate and you have the power to decide what you want to do next. Make sure you take a job that is right for you.

Training opportunities

Knowing what you want to do is one thing, but before getting a new job you may want to brush up existing skills or possibly acquire new ones. Most professional bodies have a full programme of training events, ranging from one-day seminars to courses lasting a week or longer. Additionally, adult education institutes run a vast range of courses or, if you are still in your present job, a more practical solution might be to investigate open and flexible learning, which you can do from home.

From 2021, for England, the government launched a Lifetime Skills Guarantee, promising free courses for people without A-levels. There is guidance on the scheme, now called 'Free courses for jobs' and a link to a course finder on the GOV.UK website (Directory, p 45).

Open and flexible learning

Open learning is available to all regardless of prior qualifications and flexible (usually distance) learning lets you study at your own time, place and pace.

The following organizations offer advice and courses (see Directory, p 6):

- **Distance learning universities** offer the opportunity to study to degree level. Specialists in this area are: the **Open University**, which is open to all regardless of prior qualifications; and **Arden University**, which has non-standard entry criteria, for example taking account of past experience, not just prior qualifications. Bear in mind that many brick universities increasingly offer distance learning too.
- **Massive Online Open Courses (MOOCs)**: these are offered through online platforms. You can study a very wide range of courses, many from leading universities around the world. Often the basic course is free, but you can pay to receive a 'badge' or certificate for your studies. See **Coursera, edX** and **Future Learn**.
- **National Careers Service**: includes a range of resources, including a skills assessment tool and a database (called The Skills Toolkit) where you can search for courses, some of which are free.
- The **National Extension College** offers a vast range of home study courses, leading to GCSEs, A-levels and professional qualifications.
- The **Open & Distance Learning Quality Council** is an independent guardian of quality in UK open and distance learning and includes a list of accredited providers on its website.
- **OpenLearn** from the Open University offers a wide range of free short courses, both subject-based and specific to work skills. With some you can pay for a 'badge' for your studies.
- **Professional qualification course providers**: these range from management and finance to healthcare and psychology. **BPP** is a major provider. To check out a wider range, see **Find courses**.

IT skills

If you are considering a change in direction, some new qualifications may be advantageous. IT skills are essential, so if you are not confident about your computer literacy and don't have much IT experience or specialist knowledge, here are some useful websites to look at (Directory, p 6):

- **Alison.com:** a MOOC platform that includes digital literacy from the basics onwards.
- **Digital Skills Scotland:** free online courses for individuals and business.
- **Future Learn:** courses available on this MOOC platform include a suite from Accenture on digital skills mainly for business and career development.
- **Google Free Digital Skills Training:** mainly aimed at businesses and career developers.
- **Home and Learn** offers a free computer courses and tutorials site. Courses are aimed at beginners: all you do is click on a computer course that interests you and start.
- **Microsoft:** the basics, including safety online, netiquette and accessing digital content.
- **OpenLearn:** includes courses such as 'Digital skills: succeeding in a digital world' that introduce skills such as staying safe online and finding information online.

Help with finding a job

If you plan to work in retirement, the best way is to start looking while you still have a job. Prospective employers may prefer applicants who are actively working rather than those who have been out of the market for a while. However, whether you are hoping to go straight from one job to another, or have had an enforced period of not working, this should not affect the way you approach your job search. If you have been retired for some time and want to return to work, you might consider doing some voluntary work in the meantime. This would provide a ready answer to the inevitable interview question 'What have you been doing?'.

When starting to look for work, make sure you tell your friends and acquaintances that you are in the market for work, and include your present or recent employer. Some firms encourage consultancy links with former employees, or at least are prepared to respond to a good idea. Many are more than happy to take on previous employees over a rush period or during the holiday season. Social media is also an increasingly important part of job searching. Use your LinkedIn (Directory, p 43) account and, if you don't have one, consider setting one up. Similarly, if you don't yet tweet, now is a good time to open an X (formerly Twitter) account (Directory, p 43) and follow the organizations you would like to work for – it is common these days for companies to tweet about their key vacancies.

If you are a member of a professional institute, talk to them and tell them of your availability. Many institutes keep a register of members wanting work and, encouragingly, receive a fair number of enquiries from firms seeking qualified people for projects, part-time or temporary work, interim management or sometimes even permanent employment. Any clubs to which you belong could provide useful leads, as well as any committees you sit on, or any other group with which you are involved.

A direct approach to likely employers is another possible option. Do your research carefully both on the internet and among your personal network. If possible, find out the name of the appropriate person to contact and the best method to reach them. If someone you know can prepare the ground in advance by way of introduction, and act as a referrer, this is far more likely to get you noticed. Some other tips:

- Making the most of previous employment skills is another important point when hunting for retirement jobs.
- Widen the job search: the more employment sources searched, the greater the amount of opportunities and contacts.
- Contact previous employers to enquire about part-time work.
- Search online job boards on sites such as Craigslist or Gumtree for local jobs (Directory, pp 42–43).
- Local job centres should provide good results, and jobs can be sourced on online job centre websites, including the GOV.UK Find a job service (Directory, p 44).
- Contact local colleges and universities who are often looking for teachers with a wide variety of employment skills.

There are many online recruitment websites, but the following websites may be particularly useful for more mature workers:

- **Prime Candidate** is the employability arm of the Age Diversity Forum, which campaigns against age bias, and includes a job search section for older workers (Directory, p 45).
- **Redundancy Expert** was formed to provide comprehensive information and advice on redundancy and a section of its website is dedicated to finding work and getting a job (Directory, p 46).

- **Vercida** is a job search site specializing in helping employers to have diverse workforces, including employees over 50 (Directory, p 46).

CV writing

Regardless of whether you use contacts, advertisements or agencies – or preferably all three – a prime requirement will be to have a well-presented CV. This is your personal sales document and it will be helpful if it can be emailed to prospective employers. It should contain:

- your name and contact number(s)
- email and website addresses
- key achievements to date
- qualifications and work experience, past employers, positions held and responsibilities
- referees

Recruitment agencies advise that your CV should ideally be no longer than two pages of A4 and maximum four pages, which after a long career means being selective about the information you include. While some CVs are highly professional, one that is too long is often counterproductive – it should be targeted to the job on offer, emphasizing those elements of your experience and skills that are relevant. It is customary these days to include a brief summary either as part of your CV or in your covering letter showing how you meet the specific job and person specification that was advertised. This is the place where you need to really grab the attention of whoever is trawling through possibly hundreds of applications. There are companies that will professionally produce CVs, and although this can be worthwhile, there will be a fee attached. There are plenty of websites where CV templates can be downloaded for free, such as myperfectCV (Directory, p 45).

Interview technique

If you have worked for the same employer for a number of years, your interview skills may be a little rusty. It is a good idea to list all the questions you expect to be asked (including those you hope won't be brought up) and then get a friend to rehearse your answers with you. In addition to questions about your previous job, have answers prepared for the following: what you have done since leaving employment, why you are interested in working for this particular employer and, given the job requirements, what you think you have of special value to offer. You may also be asked what you know about the organization, so do your research. Obvious mistakes to avoid are claiming skills or knowledge that you do not possess, giving the impression that you have a series of stock answers to problems and criticizing your former employer.

Be prepared to have an answer to the question: how much money would you expect? You may have to strike a balance between what you would like and what is realistic given going rates.

Employment ideas

Interim management

An interim manager gives a company instant access to a 'heavyweight yet hands-on executive' with a proven track record. Typically hired for three to nine months, interim managers help organizations undergoing major change, implement critical strategies or plug a crucial management gap. Many of the best jobs go to those who have recently taken early retirement or been made redundant. Assignments could be full-time or involve just one or two days' work a week.

EO and New Street Consulting Group could also assist (Directory, pp 44–45).

Secondment to another organization

Secondment from your current employer to another organization, often charitable, is something worth considering. This can be part-time for a few hours a week or full-time for anything from a few weeks to two years. It can also often lead to a new career. Normally only larger employers are willing to consider the idea since, as a rule, the company will continue to pay your salary and other benefits during the period of secondment. If you work for a smaller firm it could still be worth discussing the suggestion, as employers benefit from the favourable publicity the company attracts by being seen to support the local community.

Business in the Community (Directory, p 42) is a business-led charity which works with businesses to build a sustainable future for people and the planet. It has secondment opportunities for both employers and individuals.

Public appointments

Opportunities regularly arise for individuals to be appointed to a wide range of public bodies, such as tribunals, commissions and consumer consultative councils. Many appointments are to local and regional bodies throughout the country. Some are paid, but many offer an opportunity to contribute to the community and gain valuable experience of working in the public sector on a part-time, expenses-only basis. Public appointments vacancies in the UK at local, regional and national levels are found on publicappointments. cabinetoffice.gov.uk and you can be alerted to new opportunities by following the government X (formerly Twitter) account (Directory, p 43).

Non-executive directorships

Many retiring executives see this as the ideal solution; however, these appointments carry heavy responsibilities. If you are able and committed and have the necessary experience, see these websites (Directory, pp 42–43):

- **First Flight**
- **NED Exchange**

Paid work for charities

Although charities rely to a very large extent on voluntary workers, most charitable organizations of any size have a number of paid appointments. Other than particular specialists that some charities may require for their work, the majority of openings are for general managers or administrators, fundraisers and those with financial skills. Salaries have been improving, but in general are still considerably below the commercial market rate. Anyone thinking of applying for a job in a charity must be sympathetic to its aims and style.

Agencies specializing in charity recruitment advise that it is a good idea to work as a volunteer before seeking a paid appointment, as this will provide useful experience. The following organizations may help (see Directory, pp 42–43):

- **CharityJob**
- **Charity People**
- **Harris Hill**
- **NCVO**
- **Prospectus**
- **TPP**

Market research

Surveys are going on all the time – to inform business, politics, academic research and more. There are several ways in which you could get involved. The first is to be a panel member. The big market research firms all conduct regular 'omnibus surveys' – large-scale surveys that bring together questions from many clients on a diverse range of topics. The results are then often statistically treated to predict how the country as a whole would respond to those questions. The raw data for those predictions comes from a large standing panel of respondents. Typically, omnibus surveys are online, so you will need a computer and internet connection. It's up to you which surveys you opt into, and you receive a small payment for each one you complete. Market research companies also recruit people to gather data as mystery shoppers and to conduct phone surveys and face-to-face surveys on the street or in people's homes. If this all sounds interesting, try these companies (which can be found in the Directory, pp 45–46):

- **Ipsos**
- **NatCen**
- **Y Live** (owners of Populus)
- **YouGov**

Sales

Almost every commercial firm in the country needs good sales staff. Many people who have never thought of sales could be excellent in the job because of their specialist knowledge in a particular field combined with their enthusiasm for the subject. Also, some firms employ demonstrators in shops or at exhibitions for special promotions. If the idea of selling fires you with enthusiasm, there are many opportunities to tempt you.

Tourist guide

Tourist guide work is something that will appeal to extroverts and the super-fit with oodles of stamina and a liking for people. It requires an academic mind as well, since you will need to put in some fairly concentrated study. While there are numerous possible qualifications, some are easier than others – training for the coveted Blue Badge takes up to two years. The Blue Badge itself is no guarantee of steady work, since openings are largely seasonal. In fact, most tourist guides are self-employed and the field is highly competitive, but opportunities are greatest in London, especially for those with fluency in one or more foreign languages. See the national membership association for British Guild of Tourist Guides (Directory, p 44).

You could sign on as a lecturer with one of the growing number of travel companies offering special interest holidays. To be eligible you need real expertise in a subject, the ability to make it interesting and an easy manner with people. Pay is fairly minimal, although you may receive tips – plus of course the bonus of a free holiday. See Chapter 13, *Holidays*, for the names of tour operators that may be worth contacting.

Teaching and training skills

If you have been a teacher at any stage of your career, there are a number of part-time possibilities.

CHILDREN AND YOUNG PEOPLE

With examinations becoming more competitive, demand has been increasing for ex-teachers with knowledge of the public examination system to coach youngsters in preparation for A- and AS-levels, GCSEs and common entrance exams. Contact local schools, search the internet or contact a specialist educational consultancy.

Gabbitas Educational Consultants (Directory, p 42) is one of the UK's leading educational consultancies offering advice and support in all aspects of independent education. It also maintains an extensive register of appointments for teachers and tutors.

Retired teachers, linguists and others with specialist knowledge can earn good money from tutoring – see, for example, EducationJobs (Directory, p 42). Alternatively, you could oversee exams as an invigilator. The British Council may have work – check out the British Council and FE jobs (Directory, pp 42 and 44, respectively).

A formal teaching qualification is required to teach in state-maintained schools. See the Teaching Regulation Agency website (Directory, p 43).

Before engaging with children, you will need a Disclosure and Barring Service (DBS) check (formerly called a Criminal Records Bureau or CRB check) – see *Caring for other people* later in this chapter.

UNIVERSITY TUTORS

Many universities employ tutors, often called associate lecturers, to work directly with students, delivering tutorials either online or face-to-face and marking their work. There is no general requirement to have a formal teaching qualification to tutor at university level, but you will usually have an advantage if you have a teaching certificate and/or fellowship of Advance HE (Directory, p 42). With more vocational subjects, your experience and professional qualifications will be valued. Jobs in this area may be part-time or full-time. Contact universities directly to find out about their tutoring vacancies and try specialist recruitment sites such as Times Higher Education unijobs (Directory, p 46).

ENGLISH AS A FOREIGN LANGUAGE

There is an ongoing demand for people to teach English to foreign students. Opportunities are concentrated in London and the major academic cities such as Oxford, Cambridge, Bath and York. Good English-language schools require teachers to have an initial qualification in teaching English to those who have a different first language. For more information see TEFL Org (Directory, p 46).

Caring for other people

With an ageing population, there are growing opportunities for paid work in this field. If you are considering working with vulnerable people (young or old), you will be required to have a full DBS check with enhanced disclosure, designed to protect those who need to rely on other people and to ensure that no one unsuitable is appointed to a position of trust who is likely to abuse it. These checks are extremely thorough and can take several weeks or even months to process, so be patient. For further information about DBS checks and why they are required, see GOV.UK (Directory, p 42).

Your employment status will depend on the facts that apply in your case. You may be employed by a council, other organization or an agency. Alternatively, if you work directly for the person or family who needs help, you may be their employee (and they will be responsible for operating PAYE to deduct tax from your pay, and so on). If you work direct but have multiple clients, you might count as self-employed.

DOMESTIC WORK

A number of private domestic agencies specialize in finding temporary or permanent companions, housekeepers and extra-care help for elderly and disabled people or for those who are convalescent. Pay rates vary depending on which part of the country you live in and the number of hours involved. The following agencies may be of interest:

- **Consultus Care & Nursing Agency Ltd** (Directory, p 44)
- **Country Cousins** (Directory, p 42)
- **Universal Aunts Ltd** (Directory, p 43)

The Lady magazine, published every Wednesday and online (Directory, p 43), has classified advertisements for domestic help.

HOME HELPS

Local authorities may be able to direct you to vacancies for home helps, to assist disabled or elderly people in their own home with cleaning, light cooking and other chores. Ask your local social services department.

CHILDCARE

If you work as a childminder, you will normally be self-employed. However, if you work as a nanny on either a daily or live-in basis, you will be an employee of the family for whom you work. Some useful sites for finding nanny positions include (see Directory, pp 44–46):

- **Care.com**
- **Childcare.co.uk**
- **Nannyjob**
- *The Lady* magazine

Busy parents may need someone reliable to meet children at airports, stations or even travel with them. See Universal Aunts Ltd (Directory, p 46) or enter 'children's escort' in job agency websites.

Nursing

Qualified nurses are in great demand in most parts of the country and stand a good chance of finding work at their local hospital or through one of the many nursing agencies. Those with suitable experience, although not necessarily a formal nursing qualification, could apply to become a care support worker for the charity Carers Trust (Directory, p 44).

Home sitting

Taking care of someone else's home while they are away on holiday or business trips is something mature, responsible people, usually non-smokers with no children or pets, can do. It is a bit like a paid holiday, and you get paid every week (extra if care of pets is involved), depending on the responsibilities and on the size of the house or flat. Food and travelling expenses are normally also paid. It is useful to have your own car. Firms specializing in this type of work include (Directory, pp 44–46):

- **Homesitters Ltd**
- **The Home Service Ltd**
- **Universal Aunts Ltd**

CHAPTER ELEVEN

Voluntary work

There are so many problems and disasters in the world today. The urge to help is very strong, but it can be hard to know the best course of action. When earthquakes and floods hit places abroad, it can be tempting to gather and ship out second-hand clothing and household items. But charities working on the ground report that, sadly, the logistics and costs of distributing in-kind donations don't add up. Often, donated items simply end up rotting by the wayside and can even clog up supply chains making it more difficult to get vital aid to the people who need it. So, government advice is that the best form of aid is cash donations to the relief charities who have the expertise to efficiently organize the right kind of help. Don't forget to use the government Gift Aid scheme when you donate cash – Chapter 4 has details.

However, donating money is not the only way to do a bit of good in the world. The other valuable commodity you can give is your time by doing voluntary work.

Volunteering is not just about giving back; it can enhance your own life too. A quarter of people say they volunteer so they can meet new people and make friends, almost the same proportion see it as a way of using their existing skills and one in six welcome it as a chance to learn new skills, according to a government survey. So if this appeals to you, why not give it some thought? Here are some suggestions as to what you might do.

Types of work

Clerical

Any active group is likely to need basic administrative help, from typing and stuffing envelopes to answering the telephone and organizing committees. This may involve a day or so a week or occasional assistance at peak times. Many smaller charities in particular would also greatly welcome hearing from individuals with IT expertise to assist with setting up databases, a website, etc.

Fundraising

Every voluntary organization needs money, and when donations are static or falling, more creativity and ingenuity are required to help bring in funds. Events are many and varied, but anyone with energy and experience of organizing fundraising events would be welcomed with open arms as a volunteer.

Committee work

This can cover anything from very occasional help to a virtually full-time commitment as branch treasurer or secretary. People with business skills or financial or legal backgrounds are likely to be especially valuable, and those whose skills include minute-taking are always in demand.

Direct work

Driving, delivering 'meals on wheels', counselling, visiting the housebound, working in a charity shop, helping with a playgroup, respite care for carers; the list is endless and the value of the work incalculable. While certain qualifications and experience – financial, legal, nursing and social work – have particular value in some circumstances, there is also a multitude of interesting and useful jobs for those without special training or with abilities like driving or computer skills. Similarly, the time commitment can vary to suit both helper and organization. It is far better to give just one morning a month and be reliable than to promise more time than you can spare and end up cancelling or letting people down. Equally, as with a paid job, before you start you should be absolutely clear about all the terms and conditions:

- What sort of work is involved?
- Who will be working with you?

- What is expected?
- When will you be needed?
- Are expenses paid? What for? How much?

If you have all this mapped out in the beginning there will be less chance of any misunderstandings. You will find that voluntary work is not only very rewarding in its own right, but also allows you to make a real contribution to the community.

You will be required to have a full Disclosure and Barring Service (DBS) check (formerly called a Criminal Records Bureau or CRB check) with enhanced disclosure if you are considering working with vulnerable people (young or old). For further information about DBS checks and why they are required, see GOV.UK (Directory, p 42).

Choosing the right voluntary work

Once you've decided that you might take on some volunteering, the next question is what to do. You will need to find out where the opportunities are in your local area and what particular outlet would suit your talents.

Friends and neighbours, especially if they volunteer themselves, may have some ideas. However, if you don't know where to start, the following list has signposts to help you find some of the many thousands of possibilities (see Directory, pp 38–39):

- **Do It** is a digital charity that operates an online hub bringing together volunteers and organizations that need them.
- The **National Council for Voluntary Organisations** (which has taken over the previous role of Volunteering England) is a member organization for charities and similar organizations. Its website includes a directory for finding your local volunteering centre.
- **Reach Volunteering** is the skilled volunteering charity, encouraging people to take on new challenges and make a difference to their community.
- The **Royal Voluntary Service** is an 86-year-old organization that mobilizes volunteers to work particularly in hospitals and the community.
- Volunteer centres. Most towns have a body of this kind that aim to match up volunteers with local organizations seeking help. Ask your local council for contact details.

- **Volunteer Scotland** is the national centre for volunteering in Scotland.
- **Volunteering Matters** (formerly Community Service Volunteers) lets you search for local volunteering opportunities, with separate sections for the different British nations.
- **Volunteering Wales** is the website of Third Sector Support Wales, bringing together volunteering support across the Welsh local councils and third-sector organizations.
- The **Wales Council for Voluntary Action** is an umbrella body for voluntary activity in Wales.

If you do have an idea of a cause to which you would like to donate your time and expertise, here are some more specific places to start. Websites for all of these can be found in the Directory, pp 38–42.

- **General:** The British Red Cross; Citizens Advice; Lions Clubs British Isles; REMAP; Royal Voluntary Service; Toc H.
- **Animals:** Cinnamon Trust; Guide Dogs for the Blind Association; PDSA; Pet Fostering Service Scotland; Pets As Therapy; Royal Society for the Prevention of Cruelty to Animals (RSPCA); Wildfowl & Wetlands Trust.
- **Bereavement:** Cruse Bereavement Support; Good Grief Trust; War Widows Association.
- **Children and young people:** Barnardo's; Children's Society; Children's Trust; Girlguiding; Marine Society & Sea Cadets; Save the Children UK; Scouts Association.
- **Conservation outdoors:** Architectural Heritage Society of Scotland; Campaign to Protect Rural England; Friends of the Earth; Greenpeace; Ramblers; Royal Society for the Protection of Birds; The Conservation Volunteers.
- **The elderly:** Abbeyfield; Age UK; Carers Trust; Carers UK; Reengage.
- **The family:** Marriage Care; Relate.
- **Health and disability:** Attend; Backcare; Blind Veterans UK; British Heart Foundation; Calibre Audio Library; Cancer Research UK; Disability Snowsport UK; Leonard Cheshire Disability; Mind; Riding for the Disabled Association; Royal National Institute of Blind People; Scope; St John Ambulance; Thrive.
- **Heritage and the arts:** Council for British Archaeology; English Heritage; National Trust; National Trust for Scotland; Society for the Protection of Ancient Buildings.

- **Offenders and the victims of crime:** Change Grow Live; Nacro; New Bridge Foundation; Victim Support.
- **Politics:** Conservative Party; Green Party; Labour Party; Liberal Democrats; Plaid Cymru; Reform UK; Scottish National Party; Social Democratic and Labour Party (SDLP); UKIP; Ulster Unionist Party.
- **Service personnel and veterans:** Army Benevolent Fund; Combat Stress; Help for Heroes; Royal Air Force Benevolent Fund; Royal Alfred Seafarers' Society; Royal British Legion; SSAFA.
- **Those in need:** Citizens Advice; local foodbanks; Oxfam; Samaritans.

CHAPTER TWELVE

Health

People retiring today are often younger in looks and behaviour than previous generations, and may enjoy many healthy years of life. But, remember, bodies do require care and attention if they are to function at their best. There is no need to get out of shape: making time for the changes that help you to feel good should mean you are likely to have a far longer and more enjoyable retirement.

Keep fit

Emphasis on and availability of every type of keep fit activity are on the increase. This can range from brisk walking every day to more organized – and often social – exercise routines. It is a welcome innovation, as there are a growing number of opportunities for older people, including those with disabilities. Information should be available online, or in your local newspaper or library. The following organizations may be able to help you (see Directory, p 13):

- **Extend Your Health** provides gentle exercise classes for older people, and anyone of any age who has a disability, throughout the UK.
- **FLexercise** is a nationwide exercise network for people of all ages, with an emphasis on friendship as well as fitness.

- **Keep Fit Association** offers 'fitness through movement, exercise and dance' classes. There are hundreds of classes throughout the UK for all ages and abilities.
- The **NHS** has excellent guidance and videos on exercise on its website, including advice for older people and those with disabilities. For tips on staying healthy, keeping fit and maintaining your independence, see the NHS's *Practical Guide to Healthy Ageing*.

Pilates and yoga

Pilates is an invigorating form of exercise for your mind and body that can improve your strength, flexibility and overall mobility. See the Pilates Foundation website (Directory, p 13).

Yoga is suitable for all ages and is a means of improving fitness and balance, and helping relaxation:

- **British Wheel of Yoga, Iyengar Yoga (UK)** and **Yoga Alliance Professionals** can all help you find yoga teachers and classes in your area (Directory, p 13).

Strength training

Relatively new guidance suggests that older people should regularly practice weight or resistance training to counter loss of muscle tissue during the ageing process. The NHS physical activity guidelines (Directory, p 13) have a collection of videos on strength exercises you can do without special equipment. Alternatively, you might want to invest in some handheld weights or even join a gym. Here are some other sources of guidance on maintaining your muscle strength and tone (Directory, p 13):

- **Centre for Disease Control and Prevention** (part of the US government) has a comprehensive booklet, *Growing Stronger: Strength training for older adults*
- **Keeping Strong** draws on research to create free specific training programmes that you can do at home or in the gym.

Sensible eating

While regular exercise is important, so is sensible eating. Advice on healthy eating seems to change so fast, it's hard to keep up. But more than one in four adults in Britain are obese and a further two-fifths are overweight according to the National Health Service (NHS). The more excess weight you carry, the greater the risks to your health. In particular, there is an increased risk of type-2 diabetes, heart attack and stroke, as well as surgery being made more difficult. As age increases, there is greater likelihood of restricted mobility, which is only exacerbated if you are overweight.

The *Eat Well* section of the NHS website has lots of advice on food and eating a balanced diet, including recipes and, should you need it, a weight-loss plan (Directory, p 15).

If weight loss is your goal, crash diets are no solution for long-term fitness – you need to permanently shift your eating habits. Many people need a boost to get started, and whatever method you choose is fine as long as it works. Two excellent websites are (Directory, p 15):

- **Livestrong.com**, which believes that everyone has the power to change their lives, is a holistic health, fitness and lifestyle destination.
- **WW** (formerly known as Weight Watchers), whose aim is to help members establish a healthy, balanced approach to weight loss, with emphasis on making small, lifetime changes that can be maintained for the long term.

Keeping healthy in the heat

With climate change, our UK summers are getting hotter, as are many popular tourist destinations, so it's increasingly important to be aware of heat safety. The older we get the more conscious we need to be of the sun and how it affects us. The NHS warns that anyone over the age of 65 is in the 'high-risk' category for heat-related illness. Too much sun or getting overheated can induce sunstroke and dehydration, while also causing other issues – such as exacerbating existing health problems like heart disease and high blood pressure. These guidelines should help you keep your cool:

- *Stay hydrated.* One of the most common effects of prolonged periods in the heat is dehydration. The hotter months are definitely the time you should keep a bottle of water with you, especially when travelling, and remember that alcohol can dehydrate you.
- *Wear sunscreen.* The older we get, the more susceptible to certain types of skin cancer we are. Find the right sunscreen for you, and top up regularly.
- *Protect your eyes.* Protecting eyes from the brightness and UV rays of the sun will promote better eyesight and can help to prevent (or slow the development of) cataracts. Wear wrap-around sunglasses and a wide-brimmed hat.

- *Lower your temperature.* Even when out of direct sunlight your temperature can be too high. If you're feeling too hot, take a cool shower. If you often feel discomfort from the heat, aim to spend the warmest parts of the day in air-conditioned areas.
- *Exercise carefully.* Limit exercise to the cooler parts of the day, usually early morning or late evening. Wear loose, light clothing. Take frequent breaks and stay hydrated.

Food safety

As most readers will know, basic rules on food safety are important. Elderly people who are afflicted by food poisoning will typically suffer much more severe symptoms than younger people. Dehydration can become a serious factor and can lead to decreased blood pressure. This in turn affects the blood supply to vital organs such as the kidneys. It is very important that fluids are replaced as soon as possible should dehydration occur.

Some ways to guard against food poisoning include:

- not eating food products that are past their use-by dates and, where there is no date, use the 'sniff-test' to check that food still smells good to eat;
- making sure your fridge and freezer are working at the right temperatures and their doors are firmly closed;
- following cooking instructions carefully;
- not eating raw or undercooked meat products or eggs;
- always washing hands and work surfaces that have been used to prepare meat, seafood and eggs;
- always washing raw vegetables thoroughly, especially vegetables that are not going to be cooked;
- ensuring that frozen foods are completely thawed before cooking and never refreeze thawed foods;
- never eating undercooked foods in restaurants. Always send undercooked food back to be cooked completely;
- having two chopping boards: one for meat and one for everything else;
- covering the food in your fridge with shrink-wrap or beeswax wraps;
- never keeping cooked and uncooked food together, as they can contaminate each other;
- keeping all parts of your kitchen clean;
- not reheating food more than once and not keeping cooked food longer than two days.

Drink

Retirement is no reason for giving up pleasures, but more recent studies dispute earlier claims that small amounts of alcohol can be good for heart health, so the watchword is moderation. Bear in mind that alcohol-related deaths have been increasing in the UK and are highest among men aged 55 to 59 and women aged 60 to 64, according to the Office for National Statistics. Alcohol dependency is far more likely among those who are bored or depressed, who drift into the habit of having a drink to cheer themselves up or to pass the time. Because the early symptoms appear fairly innocuous, the danger signs can often go unnoticed.

Whereas most people are resilient enough to be able to control the habit themselves, others may need help. Your doctor will be the first person to check with for medical advice and the following self-help groups can help (see Directory, p 13):

- **Al-Anon Family Groups UK & Eire** provides support to anyone whose life is, or has been, affected by someone else's drinking. There are over 800 support groups in the UK and Republic of Ireland.
- **Alcohol Change UK** (formed by the merger of Alcohol Research UK and Alcohol Concern) is the national agency on alcohol misuse, campaigning for a society free from alcohol harm through an effective alcohol policy and improved services for people whose lives are affected by alcohol-related problems.
- **Alcoholics Anonymous (AA)** is a fellowship of men and women who share their experience, strength and hope with each other so that they may solve their common problem and help others recover from alcoholism.

Smoking

Any age is a good one to cut back on smoking, or preferably to give up altogether. Smokers are 20 times more likely to contract lung cancer; they are at more serious risk of suffering from heart disease and stroke, and they are more liable to chronic bronchitis and other ailments. One aid to quitting smoking is to switch instead to vaping. But, while less damaging than smoking, vaping is not harmless. So, once you're confident that you have conquered smoking, you may also want to try giving up vaping. For help, see (Directory, p 15):

- The **NHS** which offers advice, links to expert support and a personalized plan for quitting on its Quit Smoking site. The site also includes advice on quitting vaping.
- **Quit** which aims to reduce unnecessary suffering and death from smoking-related diseases, and aims towards a smoke-free UK future.

Accident prevention

One of the most common causes of mishap is an accident in the home. The vast majority of these could be avoided by taking normal common-sense precautions, such as repairing or replacing worn carpets and installing better lighting near staircases. For a list of practical suggestions, see Chapter 6, *Your home*.

If you are unlucky enough to be injured outside the home and you think an organization or someone else may have been at fault, you might consider claiming compensation. Consider getting advice from a solicitor – you can find one through the Law Society's website (Directory, p 11).

Aches, pains and other abnormalities

There is nothing about becoming 50, 60 or even 70 that makes aches and pains inevitable. Age itself has nothing to do with the vast majority of ailments. Many people ignore the warning signs when something is wrong, yet treatment when a condition is still in its infancy can often cure it altogether, or at least help to delay its advance. The following should always be investigated by a doctor:

- any pain that lasts more than a few days
- lumps, however small
- dizziness or fainting
- chest pains, shortness of breath or palpitations
- persistent cough or hoarseness
- unusual bleeding from anywhere
- unnatural tiredness or headaches
- frequent indigestion
- unexplained weight loss

Health insurance

One of the most treasured UK public services is the NHS. However, previous government policies (for example, around staffing and social care), the Covid-19 crisis and an ageing population have put tremendous strain on the NHS's ability to provide the care we need when we need it. The high cost of the alternatives – paying for private treatment either direct or by taking out medical insurance – brings home the value to each of us personally of having a properly funded, efficient and effective public health service. For example, paying direct, a 15-minute in-person consultation with a private GP could cost around £80, while cataract surgery could set you back over £3,000. So, the new government's plans for restoring the NHS's own health are important to us all.

Private medical insurance

This type of insurance covers the cost of private treatment if you need hospital care. People with private medical insurance often get a nasty shock when they reach retirement age, particularly if they were previously covered under a company scheme. Their premiums start to rocket – just at the point when their income has been reduced to a pension. However, switching to a cheaper scheme often gets more difficult as we get older. Some policies have maximum age limits, but a more frequent problem is that if you have already developed a health condition, you will lose cover for it if you switch insurers, since pre-existing medical conditions, including associated complaints, will normally be excluded from a new policy.

Nevertheless, if your current policy has become unaffordable, you may feel that you have no alternative but to look for something cheaper. Things to watch out for with lower-cost policies are that they provide less cover, such as limited outpatient cover, and may have a higher excesses (the amount you have to contribute yourself). More positively, some insurers offer discounts if you exercise regularly and encourage this by providing gym-membership discounts and free fitness trackers. Premiums are also sometimes cheaper if you agree to a restricted list of hospitals or consultants. Another variant is a six-week waiting policy, where you claim for private treatment only if the NHS waiting period for treatment is longer.

Be aware too that private medical insurance only covers 'acute' conditions, meaning health problems that can be cured or alleviated. It does not cover chronic conditions – the sort of health problems that can often be managed to some extent, but are not curable. With ageing, unfortunately, chronic conditions are more likely to develop, so not all of the health issues you experience will be covered by your health insurance.

We are lucky to have a free-at-the-point-of-use NHS, meaning that in the UK medical insurance is not usually a necessity. That said, if you have insurance to pay for private medical care you will probably get faster treatment, as well as greater comfort and privacy in hospital. Here are just a few of the organizations that provide cover (see Directory, pp 21–22):

- **AXA PPP Healthcare**
- **BUPA**
- **Saga Services Ltd**
- **Vitality**

With so many plans on the market, selecting the one that best suits your needs can be quite a problem. An independent financial adviser or specialist insurance broker could advise you, such as a member of the Association of Medical Insurers and Intermediaries (Directory, p 21).

Private patients – without insurance cover

If you do not have private medical insurance but want to go into hospital in the UK as a private patient, there is nothing to stop you, provided your doctor is willing and you are able to pay the bills. The choice if you opt for self-pay lies between the private wings of NHS hospitals or hospitals run by private-sector organizations, such as (Directory, p 22):

- **Circle Health Group**
- **Nuffield Health**
- **Spire Healthcare**

Some private hospitals run their own credit schemes, so you can pay for treatment plus interest by instalment. Do check that you can afford the repayments before you go ahead. Self-pay is also an option if the procedure you need is outside the scope of NHS-funded treatments.

Hospital cash plans

These are inexpensive alternatives to medical insurance policies. They are not intended to cover the cost of private treatment. Instead, they pay out a cash sum in the event that a wide range of health-related events happen to you. These include, for example, having to go into hospital (NHS or private) and receiving routine care, such as visiting the dentist, optician, physiotherapist, and so on. You use the cash in any way you like – for example, if you go into hospital, the cash could help a family member visit you. There is an annual limit on each pay-out. The higher the monthly premium you pay, the higher the cash limits. In effect, cash plans are not so much insurance but a way of spreading the cost of healthcare through the monthly payments. To make them worthwhile, make sure you claim each time you can.

Different cash plans cover different ranges of treatment, so choose whichever best matches the healthcare that you use. Some providers (see Directory, p 14) to check out include:

- BHSF (originally the Birmingham Hospital Saturday Fund)
- **Orchard Healthcare**
- **Simplyhealth**
- **Sovereign Health Care**
- **WHA Direct**

Medical tourism

Medical tourism, or 'global healthcare' as it is now known, involves travelling to a foreign country for a medical procedure, and has been growing rapidly over recent years. While the medical procedures needed can be urgent, the majority are elective treatments such as cosmetic surgery or dental care. One way to find out about this growing market and some of the providers of such services is to search the following websites (Directory, p 15):

- **Medical Tourism**
- **Treatment Abroad**

Make sure you are confident about the standards of treatment and care you will receive before going down this route.

Critical illness cover

Critical illness insurance pays a lump sum if you are diagnosed with a life-threatening condition such as some cancers or a stroke. However, the cost of cover increases with age and there is usually an age limit above which you cannot get cover – say, 65 or sometimes 70. Pre-existing health conditions will not be covered.

Income protection insurance

Income protection insurance is a replacement-of-earnings policy for people who are still in work and who, because of illness, are unable to continue with their normal occupation for a prolonged period and in consequence suffer loss of earnings. Full policies pay out until retirement (or recovery if earlier); budget policies pay out for a set period of time, such as two or five years. If you are close to retirement, this insurance is unlikely to feature in your plans.

Health screening

Prevention is better than cure, and these days once you are aged between 40 (50 in Wales) and 74 you may be offered a free health check by the NHS provided you have not already developed a health condition that needs more frequent monitoring anyway. Usually, this is repeated five-yearly. That said, these check-ups were disrupted by the pandemic and subsequent NHS backlog. Your local authority can advise on whether the free health check programme is currently running in your area. The NHS may also invite you to take part in other tests, for example, to screen for certain cancers, and some of these can be done with test kits that are posted to you to use at home. There are also a variety of private healthcare providers with whom you can pay for check-ups or that come as part of any private medical insurance that you have. Some gyms and health centres carry out routine health tests (similar to the NHS health check) when you first join. In addition to checking your general health (height, weight, blood sugar, cholesterol, blood pressure and heart function), these check-ups also provide advice on diet, drinking and smoking if these are problem areas. For more information, see (Directory, p 14):

- **BUPA**
- **Circle Health Group**
- **NHS**

The NHS

You only have to look at the statistics for the United States, where 27 million people have no medical insurance and a quarter of these go without medical care because of cost, to realize that the NHS for all its problems is a great national asset and a socially beneficial way to provide healthcare. However, funding is an issue, and increasingly the NHS does not routinely provide all the treatments that you might expect. Having a GP is important, not just to provide primary medical care but also as a gatekeeper to other treatments should you need them.

Choosing or changing a GP

If you move to a new area, the best way to choose your new GP is to ask for a recommendation. Otherwise your local primary care trust or strategic health authority can assist, or you can search the NHS website (Directory, p 12).

Points you may want to consider include how close the doctor is to your home, how its appointments or inquiry system works and whether it is a group practice and, if so, how this is organized. All GPs have websites and practice leaflets available at their premises, with details about their service. Having selected a doctor, you should complete a registration form (GMS1) which can be downloaded from the NHS website or obtained from the GP practice. You do not have an automatic right to be accepted, as there is a limit to the number of patients any one doctor can accept.

Especially since the coronavirus pandemic, you may be encouraged to have meetings and appointments online or by phone. Moreover, many routine tests, such as blood pressure, are offered free at pharmacies, who are also being given powers to write prescriptions for some common ailments (such as urinary tract infections). A pharmacy, rather than your GP, should also be your first point of call for minor ailments. The NHS website has a tool to help you find a pharmacy (Directory p 12).

If you want to change your GP, you go about it in exactly the same way as choosing a GP. You do not need to give a reason for wanting to change, and you do not need to ask anyone's permission.

When you cannot contact your own GP

If you need medical advice when you are on holiday (beyond the help a pharmacy can give) or at some other time when it may not be possible to contact your own doctor, you can contact any GP surgery and receive treatment for up to 14 days. If you'll need treatment for longer, you'll need to register as a temporary or permanent patient.

If you need urgent but non-emergency medical help out of hours or in other situations when you cannot get to a surgery, you can call the NHS number 111 or complete an online form using 111 Online (Directory, p 11).

In either case, a trained professional will give you advice, which may include arranging an immediate face-to-face appointment if you need one.

Help with NHS costs

If you or your partner are in receipt of the Pension Credit Guarantee Credit, Universal Credit (or certain benefits that Universal Credit is replacing: Working Tax Credit, Income Support, income-related Employment and Support Allowance, or income-based Jobseeker's Allowance), you will usually be entitled to free NHS prescriptions (if not already free – see below), NHS dental treatment, NHS wigs and fabric supports and routine NHS sight tests. You are also entitled to help towards the cost of glasses or contact lenses and payment of travel costs for NHS hospital treatment.

Even if you are not automatically entitled to help with the above costs, you and your partner may be entitled to some help on the grounds of low income. Complete claim form HC1 – available at NHS hospitals, dentists, opticians, GPs and chemists. See Claim form HC1 (Directory, p 12) or, if you live in Scotland, Claim form HC1 (Scotland) (Directory, p 12).

The GOV.UK website has an online tool that you can use to check if you are eligible for full or partial help with NHS costs: Help with health costs (Directory, p 11).

Prescriptions

In Scotland, Wales and Northern Ireland, prescriptions are free. England is the only nation of the UK that charges. However, there are a number of exemptions. As described above, you do not pay if you are getting specified means-tested benefits or you've been accepted as having a low income. Men and women aged 60 and over are entitled to free NHS prescriptions, regardless of income. You will also qualify for free prescriptions if you have certain health conditions, such as cancer. You can use the government's online tool to check if you are eligible: Help with health costs (Directory, p 11). Alternatively ask your pharmacist for guidance.

People who do not qualify for free prescriptions but who require a lot of prescriptions could save money by purchasing a prescription prepayment certificate. See Directory, p 11. Usually prescription charges increase in line with inflation each year. In 2024/25, single prescriptions cost £9.90 and a prepayment certificate £32.05 for three months or £114.50 for 12 months.

In 2024, new NHS guidelines barred some items from being routinely prescribed by GPs where they are available to buy from pharmacies and other outlets. These include items where there is only limited evidence of effectiveness (such as vitamin and mineral supplements unless treating a specific health condition), items for conditions that will in most cases clear up on their own (such as sore throats, cold sores and haemorrhoids) and items for conditions deemed appropriate for self-care (for example, mild dermatitis, ear wax and indigestion).

Going into hospital

Except in an emergency, your first port of call for medical help is your GP, who will refer you to a hospital if necessary. Many patients are unaware that they can ask their GP to refer them to a consultant at a different NHS hospital from their local one or even, in certain cases, help make arrangements for them to be treated overseas. Before you can become a patient at another hospital, your GP will need to agree to your being referred. A major consideration will be whether the treatment would be as clinically effective as the treatment you would receive locally.

Those likely to need help on leaving hospital should speak to the hospital social worker, who will help make any necessary arrangements.

If you go into hospital you will continue to receive your State Pension and any bereavement benefits as normal. Means-tested benefits and disability benefits usually continue in full for 28 days, but may be reduced if you are in hospital for longer. Your benefits should not be reduced if you are paying privately for your treatment. You need to tell the government office that pays your benefits if you go into hospital for one night or more and when you come out. The GOV.UK website has details of which government agency to contact (Directory, p 11).

Complaints

The NHS has a complaints procedure if you are unhappy about the treatment you have received. In the first instance, you should speak to someone close to the cause of the problem, such as the doctor, nurse, receptionist or practice manager. If, for whatever reason, you would prefer to speak to someone who was not involved in your care, you can speak to the complaints manager at your local clinical commission group (England), local health board (Wales or Scotland) or health and social care trust (Northern Ireland).

You may be able to get help with bringing your complaint, for example, from a patient support service or independent advocate. For example, this person can attend meetings with you and review the information you are given.

If you are unhappy with the response you get, an ombudsman may be able to help. The ombudsman service is independent of both government and the NHS and investigates complaints of failure or maladministration across the whole range of NHS services.

The precise details of the steps to take and who to contact at each stage vary across the UK. You can find information for England, Scotland, Northern Ireland and Wales, both for complaints and the ombudsman, on page 12 of the Directory.

Rather than proceed through the formal channels described above, an alternative approach is to contact the Patients Association – an independent advice centre that offers guidance to patients in the event of a problem with the health and social care services: phone 0800 345 7115 or see the Patients Association (Directory, p 11).

Alternative medicine

These days, there is greater awareness of the potential benefits of some types of alternative medicine. Here are some of the better-known organizations (see Directory, pp 11–12):

- The **British Acupuncture Council** is the home of traditional acupuncture in the UK. With around 3,000 members, it is the UK's largest body of professional acupuncturists, where excellence in training, safe practice and professional standards are paramount. You can find an acupuncturist in your local area on their website.
- **British Chiropractic Association** practitioners specialize in the diagnosis, treatment and overall management of conditions that are due to problems with the joints, ligament, tendons and nerves, especially related to the spine.
- The **British Hypnotherapy Association** keeps a register of professionally trained practitioners who are able to treat phobias, emotional problems, anxiety, migraine, psoriasis or relationship difficulties.
- The **General Osteopathic Council** regulates the practice of osteopathy in the UK and practitioners are required to register with the council. Osteopathy is a system of diagnosis and treatment of a wide range of medical conditions.
- **Homeopathy UK** (formerly the British Homeopathic Association) exists to promote homeopathy practised by doctors and other healthcare

professionals. For a list of practising GPs and pharmacies that stock homeopathic medicines, see the Homeopathy UK website.

- The **Incorporated Society of Registered Naturopaths**: naturopathy is concerned with the underlying conditions that may cause illness, including, for example, diet, general fitness, posture, stress and the patient's mental outlook on life.

- The **National Institute of Medical Herbalists** is the UK's leading professional body representing herbal practitioners. It promotes the benefits, efficacy and safe use of herbal medicine.

Eyes

Did you know that regular sight tests can pick up conditions such as glaucoma, cataracts, macular degeneration, dry eye and inflammation of the cornea? They can also detect signs of other diseases including diabetes, hypertension (high blood pressure), thyroid toxicosis, auto immune disorders, pituitary tumours, raised cholesterol and shingles. It is advisable to have your sight checked at least every two years.

You will qualify for a free NHS sight test if you are aged 60 and over in England, Wales or Northern Ireland; at any age if you live in Scotland; you or your partner receive means-tested benefits or have a low income; or you have specified eye problems such as glaucoma or a family history that puts you at risk of such conditions. See *Help with NHS costs*, earlier in this chapter, for how to check whether you are eligible.

People with mobility problems who are unable to get to an optician can ask for a domiciliary visit to have their eyes examined at home. This is free for those with an HC2 certificate or who are in receipt of one of the benefits listed in *Help with NHS costs*. People with a (partial help) HC3 certificate can use this towards the cost of a private home visit by their optician. The going rate for private sight tests if you do have to pay starts at around £20 to £30.

Whether you have to pay or not, the optician must either give you a prescription identifying what type of glasses you require or give you a statement confirming that you have no need of spectacles. The prescription is valid for two years. You are under no obligation to buy from the optician who tested your eyes, you can go elsewhere.

There is a voucher system for helping with the purchase of glasses or contact lenses. If you or your partner are in receipt of specified means-tested benefits or have a low income as described in the section on *Help with NHS costs*, you will receive an optical voucher, with a cash value. The amount you get will depend on your optical prescription.

People who are registered blind are entitled to a special tax allowance each year – see Chapter 4. The Royal National Institute of Blind People (RNIB) is an excellent source of general advice and information and can supply a range of special equipment, details of which can be found on the RNIB website (Directory, p 13).

Do you have a family history of glaucoma? Are you short-sighted? Do you have diabetes? Are you of African-Caribbean origin? If the answer to any of these is yes, and you're over 40, then you could be at increased risk of developing glaucoma. It has no symptoms in the early stages, but slowly and painlessly destroys sight if not detected and treated. For more information, see glaucoma.uk. Many elderly people with failing sight suffer from macular degeneration, which affects their ability to distinguish detail. Although there is no known cure, individuals can be helped to make the most effective use of their sight by special magnifiers and other aids, such as clip-on lenses that fit over normal spectacles. See the Partially Sighted Society (Directory, p 13). British Wireless for the Blind Fund (Directory, p 13) is a national independent charity providing specially modified audio equipment to all UK-registered blind or partially sighted people in receipt of means-tested benefits.

The Equality Act 2010 requires businesses to take reasonable steps to make their services accessible to customers with disabilities. This is nowhere more important than in banking and day-to-day money services. Unfortunately, with the closure of bank branches, it is now more difficult to get face-to-face help. However, there are other options, so do request statements in alternative formats, such as braille, large print or audio formats; and consider phone banking or online/mobile banking which you can access with the aid of a screen-reader. Some banks also offer talking cash machines.

Feet

Many people forget about their feet until they begin to give trouble. Corns and bunions, if neglected, can become extremely painful, and ideally everyone, especially women who wear high heels, should have podiatry treatment from early middle age or even younger. Podiatry is available on the NHS without referral from a doctor, but facilities tend to be very oversubscribed, so in many areas it is only the very elderly or those with a real problem who can get appointments.

The Royal College of Podiatry (Directory, p 14) is the professional association for registered chiropodists and podiatrists, and has a searchable directory of its members who are private practitioners across the UK and overseas.

Hearing

In the UK alone there are 11 million people living with a hearing loss, and only 2 million of them are wearing hearing aids, even though many more could benefit from them. It's estimated that people delay 10 years on average before seeking help with hearing loss. Being able to hear properly is important for a number of reasons: for safety and awareness; conversation and interaction; enjoyment and entertainment. Signs to look out for are:

- not hearing the doorbell or a telephone ring
- turning up the television too loud for the comfort of others
- failing to hear people come into the room
- misunderstanding what has been said in conversation
- not speaking clearly or speaking in a monotonous tone
- uncertainty about where sounds are coming from
- difficulty in hearing at a distance or in public gatherings

If you have noticed any of these, talk to your GP, who may refer you to an audiologist or hearing care professional. You can obtain a hearing aid and batteries free on the NHS or buy them privately. There are many other aids on the market that can make life easier. BT (Directory, p 14), for example, provides guidance on a variety of special features and equipment for when a standard phone becomes too difficult to use.

There are other specialist organizations that can give you a lot of help on hearing aids and on other matters (see Directory, p 14):

- **Boots Hearingcare** provides a 15-minute free appointment aimed at people who have not had a hearing test before.
- The **British Deaf Association** works to protect the interests of deaf people and also provides an advice service through its regional offices.
- The **British Tinnitus Association** is a world leader, with a trained team of friendly and experienced advisers for anyone who experiences tinnitus or those simply seeking guidance or information about the condition.
- **Hearing Link** is a voluntary organization providing support and information to people with hearing loss, as well as their families.

- **RNID** (Royal National Institute for the Deaf) offers a wide range of services including sign language interpreters and other communication support. The RNID has a free-to-use online hearing check that can indicate whether you have hearing loss and also an in-person test.

Teeth

Everyone knows the importance of having regular dental check-ups. Many adults, however, slip out of the habit, which could result in their having trouble with their teeth as they become older. Dentistry is one of the treatments for which you have to pay under the NHS, unless you have a low income – see *Help with NHS costs*, earlier in this chapter.

Help with the cost is all very well, but for many an even bigger problem than money is actually finding an NHS dentist in their area. You can use the NHS online search tool (Directory, p 15). This will show you the dentists in your area and indicate whether or not they are taking on NHS patients. However, NHS dentists do not always have the time to give the depth of care and advice that you might be seeking, in which case a private dentist may be a better option. Private dentists tend to focus on prevention as much as treatment, and will spend time explaining and demonstrating good oral hygiene.

Prevention is always better than cure. If you want free, independent and impartial advice on all aspects of oral health and free literature on a wide range of topics, including patients' rights, finding a dentist and dental care for older people, see the Oral Health Foundation website (Directory, p 15).

Personal relationships

Retirement, for couples, involves a major lifestyle change. With it comes fresh opportunities, and, inevitably, a few compromises. Couples can sometimes find it difficult to adjust to spending longer together, while others may feel they have little left in common. It is important in the early stages of retirement that couples work out the best way of living together in their retirement. However, for some couples it does not work out so easily, and it may be helpful to seek skilled guidance (see Directory, p 15):

- **Albany Trust** is a professional therapy service for individuals and couples needing emotional and psychological help.

- **Marriage Care** offers a similar service, plus a confidential telephone helpline, for those who are having problems with their marriage or other close personal relationship.
- **Relate**, the relationship people, offers advice, relationship counselling, sex therapy, workshops, mediation, consultations and support face-to-face, by phone and through the website.
- **The Spark** is a leading provider of couples counselling and marriage counselling in Scotland.

Help for grandparents

A sad result of today's divorce statistics is the risk to grandparents of losing contact with their grandchildren. While some divorcing parents lean over backwards to avoid this happening, others – maybe through force of circumstance or hurt feelings – deny grandparents access or even sever the relationship completely. Recourse to the law is never a step to be taken lightly and should obviously be avoided if there is the possibility that a more conciliatory approach could be successful. There are a number of organizations that have experience of advising grandparents and offer practical help and support (see Directory, p 14):

- **Gransnet**
- **Kinship**

Depression

Depression is a condition that may develop as a result of the lifestyle change from working to having time on your hands. If the condition persists for more than a few days, or seems to be more than simply feeling a bit sad or low, then a doctor should always be consulted, as depression can be a debilitating condition. These days, NHS treatment does not necessarily mean taking anti-depressants (which can be addictive). The NHS also offers talking therapies which you can access through your GP or by self-referral. There is a tool on the NHS website to help you find a therapist (Directory p 12). The drawback of the free NHS talking therapy service is that the waiting lists tend to be long. If you find yourself concerned for your mental health or that of a loved one, there are several organizations that may be able to help (see Directory, pp 12–13):

- **Mind**
- **NHS**

- **Samaritans**
- **Sane**

Other common afflictions

You may be one of the lucky ones who sails through retirement with minimal or no health problems. You can certainly increase your chances of that by committing to a healthy diet, regular exercise and avoiding becoming overweight. But, even then, genetic disposition or just bad luck can mean you are afflicted with one or more of many common afflictions, such as back pain, diabetes, heart disease, and so on.

We all get odd little symptoms from time to time and many of us worry about wasting a doctor's time, so it can be hard to know when to dismiss a niggle as trivial or to seek medical help. If you have access to the internet, a good place to investigate symptoms and find guidance on when to get help is the NHS website (Directory, p 11). Your local pharmacy is also a good source of advice (Directory, p 12).

If you have an urgent health issue but short of a life-threatening emergency, contact your GP or the NHS 24-hour helpline on 111. For emergencies, dial 999.

Disability

If you have a physical or mental disability, you will find guidance in relevant chapters throughout this book: Chapter 2 describes the main state benefits available; Chapter 6 has information about council tax; Chapter 10 considers your rights if working; and Chapter 14 looks at the options and help available for someone needing support or care.

CHAPTER THIRTEEN

Holidays

Worry about climate change may be making you question the wisdom of flying these days. However, there are alternatives and retirement may give you the time to enjoy greener but more leisurely options such as rail travel. Moreover, one thing the 2020 pandemic did remind us about is that you don't necessarily have to go abroad to get away from it all. The UK can equal anywhere for beautiful locations and activities from mountain climbing to cycling and from wine tasting to café culture. Less predictable of course is British weather, and that is a big advantage of travelling abroad. However, the intense heat in some traditional sunny holiday favourites, including parts of Greece and Spain, is causing a surge in popularity of destinations with more moderate climates, such as Scandinavia. While coronavirus is no longer top of most people's concerns, it continues to be important to check the vaccination and any quarantine rules that apply in the countries you're planning to visit – and you can check the government's guidance at GOV.UK (Directory, p 16). Needless to say, you must also check the usual entry rules and requirements – see *Visas, passports and other requirements* later in this chapter – including the new ETIAS system if you're travelling to Europe.

A word of warning: many of the sad tales of holiday woe one hears could have been avoided, or at least softened by compensation. It is essential that holidaymakers check to ensure that their travel agent or tour operator is affiliated to either the Association of British Travel Agents (ABTA) or the Association of Independent Tour Operators (AITO). Both organizations have strict regulations that all member companies must follow, and both run an arbitration scheme in the event of complaints. No one can guarantee you against every mishap, but a recognized travel company plus adequate insurance should go a long way towards giving you at least some measure of protection.

Insurance

Holiday insurance, once you are over the age of 65, is not only more difficult to obtain but also tends to be considerably more expensive, especially if you have health issues. However, were you unfortunate enough to fall ill or experience some other mishap, it would almost certainly cost you very much more than insurance. Some companies, like Saga (saga.co.uk/insurance/travel-insurance), offer insurance policies specifically for the over-50s. However, policies targeted at particular age groups do not necessarily offer the best deal, so it's worth shopping around. The easiest way to do this is using a price comparison website (Directory, p 32). With travel insurance you will need to disclose any pre-existing medical conditions fully before you can get a quote, and be aware that you will also need to declare the health conditions of anyone close to you that could cause you to cancel your trip. If your circumstances are non-standard, you may want the help of a broker, for example a member of the British Insurance Brokers' Association (Directory, p 21). If you have a pre-existing health condition, MoneyHelper has a directory of specialist firms (Directory, p 21). It is an interesting sign of the UK's ageing population that one or two of these medical specialist firms now advertise widely including on TV.

Tour operators may offer their own inclusive insurance package. This may be convenient, but you will probably be able to find as good cover more cheaply if you shop around.

You can choose between single-trip insurance policies and annual travel policies. Annual policies often cost very little extra, so, even if you're not quite sure how many trips you will make, it may be worth taking out an annual policy. However, do be aware that you may be required to tell the insurer about any changes, for example to your health, that occur within the year covered by your annual policy, and this could result in an in-year change in your cover or the cost or even cancellation of your policy.

An annual policy might also prove more convenient if the date of your trip has to change. A single-trip policy would need to be cancelled and replaced and you might not get a full premium refund (because you will already have had the benefit of some cancellation cover in the period up to the time the trip dates change).

What cover to look for

Here are some top tips when buying holiday insurance. Your policy should cover you for:

- **Medical expenses,** including hospital treatment and the cost of an ambulance, an air ambulance, flights home (which may require extra space if you are injured or ill) and emergency dental treatment, plus expenses for a companion who may have to remain overseas with you should you become ill. MoneyHelper suggests you have coverage of at least £1 million if travelling in Europe, and £2 million for travel elsewhere.
- **Personal liability cover,** should you cause injury to another person or property. At least £2 million is the norm.
- **Personal accident** leading to injury or death (check the small print, as some policies have reduced cover for older travellers).
- **Additional hotel and repatriation costs** resulting from injury or illness.
- **Loss of deposit or cancellation** (check what emergencies this covers).
- The **cost of having to curtail your holiday,** including extra travel expenses, because of serious illness in the family.
- **Inconvenience** caused by flight cancellations or other travel delays.
- **Baggage and personal effects** and emergency purchases should your baggage be delayed. Most policies cover £1,500 or more. However, there may be limits per item and there is usually an excess (the first part of a claim that you must bear).
- **Loss of personal money** and documents.

Check any coronavirus cover carefully. According to a Which? survey, most policies cover medical treatment abroad and repatriation if you fall ill with the virus. However, only some cover refunds if you cannot travel due to testing positive or needing to self-isolate. Typically, being unable to travel because of government advice, the cost of tests and quarantine in government hotels are not covered.

If you are planning to take your car abroad, you will need to check your existing car insurance to ensure that you are properly covered and may need to pay extra to extend your cover. Now the UK has left the EU, this applies to driving in Europe as well as other countries. See the section *Driving abroad* for more information.

It is essential that you take copies of the insurance documents with you, as losses or other claims must normally be reported immediately. You will also be required to quote the reference number and/or other details given on the insurance certificate. Additionally, there may be particular guidelines laid down by the policy. For instance, you may have to ring a helpline before incurring medical expenses.

The Association of British Insurers (Directory, p 21) has information on holiday insurance and motoring abroad.

Global Health Insurance Card (GHIC)

You may have a European Health Insurance Card (EHIC) that entitles you to reduced cost or free emergency healthcare during stays in the EU. Following Brexit, an existing EHIC is valid until it expires. However, most people now need to apply instead for the new global version (the GHIC) which works in the same way for Europe. If the government strikes deals on reciprocal healthcare with other countries, it may eventually cover other places as well.

Travel insurers often require you to have an EHIC or GHIC. You can apply on the NHS website (Directory, p 11).

Cancelled or overbooked flights

Also useful to know about is the Denied Boarding Regulation, which is European legislation (written into UK law post-Brexit) that entitles passengers who cannot travel because their flight is overbooked to some immediate cash payment. This applies even if the airline puts them up in a hotel or books them onto an alternative flight. To qualify, passengers must have a confirmed reservation and have checked in on time. Also, the airport where they were 'bumped off' must be in an EU country. (It may sometimes also be possible to get compensation in the United States.)

If, as opposed to being overbooked, your flight is cancelled, you are entitled to get a refund if you decide not to travel. Alternatively, you can request to be re-routed. You may get compensation depending on the length of your journey and how long you are delayed. If the delay is more than two hours, you will also be entitled to meals or refreshments plus two free telephone calls, emails or faxes. If it is overnight and you have more than five hours' wait, you will be put up in a hotel and given free transfers. Compensation is not, however, obligatory if the cancellation is due to 'extraordinary circumstances which could not have been avoided'. See the Civil Aviation Authority's consumer guidance (Directory, p 16).

If you miss your flight or have to cancel your trip, you may be able to get a refund on at least part of the ticket cost. Most airlines will reimburse non-fliers for the air passenger duty and overseas government taxes. This applies even to normal non-refundable tickets. However, you have to make a claim, and in most cases there is an administration charge. If you booked through a travel agent, there could be a second administration charge.

Travel and concessions

Buses, coaches, some airline companies and especially the railways offer valuable concessions to people of retirement age. And let's hope that the new government's plans for bus and rail travel in the UK improve the reliability of these important public services.

Trains

Some of the best-value savings – typically one-third off – that are available to anyone aged 60 and over are provided by train companies. These include (see Directory, p 24):

- **Disabled Persons Railcard:** costs £20 for one year or £54 for three years and entitles the holder and one accompanying adult to reduced train fares.
- **Family and Friends Railcard:** costs £30 for one year or £70 for three years and entitles up to four adults and four children to travel on one card.
- **Network Railcard:** costs £30 and is valid for 12 months, available only in London and the south-east. On weekdays it is restricted to travel starting after 10am. Up to three adults can travel with you and up to four children.
- **Senior Railcard:** for those aged 60-plus, costs £30 for one year or £70 for three years. As well as reduced fares, it offers discounts on hotels, restaurants and days out.
- **Two Together Railcard:** for two named adults travelling together. You don't have to be a couple – it could be you and a friend or one of the family. It costs £30 for a year.

An excellent website to help you plan and book your rail journeys, whether in the UK, Europe or further afield, is The Man in Seat Sixty-One (Directory, p 24).

Buses and coaches

In England, around a fifth of eligible older people have not applied for their free bus pass. Nevertheless, some 7.8 million do have a pass and are able to enjoy the travel benefits it brings.

If you live in England, and you are either over State Pension age or have a disability, you can travel free on local buses anywhere in England between 9.30am and 11pm on weekdays and all day weekends and public holidays. However, if you live in London, you can also get a free travel pass from age 60 that covers London buses, tubes and other public transport in the capital. To apply for a bus pass, contact your local council (Directory, p 24).

If you live in Scotland, over-60s and people with a disability can travel free on local buses and scheduled long-distance coach services in Scotland at any time – no time restrictions. To apply, contact your local authority. For further information, see Bus pass (Scotland) (Directory, p 24).

If you live in Wales, over-60s and people with a disability can travel free on local buses in Wales at any time. People living in Wales can also use their passes to travel free on cross-boundary journeys into and out of England, provided the journey starts or finishes in Wales. To apply, contact your local council – see Bus pass (Wales) (Directory, p 24). If you live in Northern Ireland and you are aged 60 to 64 you can apply for a travel pass that entitles you to concessionary fares on public transport in Northern Ireland. When you reach 65, you can switch to a pass that covers the whole of Ireland. See Bus pass (Northern Ireland) (Directory, p 24).

There are often reduced rates for senior citizens and people with disabilities on long-distance buses and coaches. For example, National Express has a Senior Coachcard for people aged 60-plus, and a Disabled Coachcard, both of which offer savings of a third and cost £15 (plus £3 postage) for a year – see National Express (Directory, p 24).

Overseas

Many countries offer travel and other reductions to older holidaymakers including, for example, discounts for entry to museums and galleries, day excursions, sporting events and other entertainment – so it's always worth asking. As in Britain, provisions are liable to change, and for up-to-date information probably the best source to contact is the national tourist office of the country to which you are travelling.

Many European countries offer discounted rail travel for older travellers who have an appropriate railcard. The railcard you need varies from one country to another. The website or operator through which you book your tickets can advise on what cards may be available and how to get them.

Airport meet-and-greet services

If you hate the hassle of parking your car in the long-stay car park and collecting it again on your return after a long journey, BCP (Directory, p 23) offers a better choice for parking – it operates a meet-and-greet service at a variety of airports across the UK. Another option is to stay over the night before your flight in a hotel that allows you to leave your car in its car park until your return.

Driving abroad

A number of organizations, including in particular some ferry operators, offer packages for the motorist that include ferry crossings, accommodation and insurance. While these often provide good value, some people prefer to make all their own arrangements. Here are some of the major operators (see Directory, p 25):

- The **AA**: for all your motoring needs, at home and abroad, including route planning, maps, guidance on driving abroad, breakdown cover and insurance.
- **Brittany Ferries**: sail and holiday choices, planning your trip, ferry bookings, holiday bookings, routes and timetables.
- The **RAC**: for overseas single-trip or annual travel insurance, plus international driving permits and roadside assistance.

Since Brexit, there is a return to the old rules that you might remember from the time before the UK became part of the EU. So you will need to have your driving licence with you when driving abroad (but for the EU you will not normally need an international driving permit). You will need a 'green card' which is proof that your car insurance cover has been extended to driving abroad. And you will need to put a UK sticker on the back of your car. There is more EU guidance on the government website (Directory, p 25).

Here are some top tips when motoring abroad, if taking your own vehicle:

- Have your car thoroughly serviced before you go.
- Make sure your UK sticker is clearly visible.
- Have headlight converters if driving in Europe.
- Find out about speed limits and if you require any specific equipment.
- Invest in a good guide book on your destination that advises on local customs and laws.
- Check you have packed your driving documents and green card.
- Check whether your breakdown cover provides roadside assistance while abroad.
- Take the following with you: a tool kit, the manual for your car, spare fuses, a fuel can, a mechanic's light that plugs into the cigarette lighter socket, at least one extra set of keys and any extras required by local laws such as a reflective tabard and warning triangles.
- Always lock your car and park it in a secure place overnight.

Other sources of advice and services are (Directory, p 25):

- **Association of British Insurers**
- **Europ Assistance**
- **Green Flag**

If instead of taking your own car you plan to hire a vehicle overseas, you will probably have to buy special insurance at the time of hiring the vehicle. Typically, you will have to agree to an excess (the first part of any claim that you will pay) unless you buy additional insurance to cover the excess.

If you are not used to driving a left-hand-drive vehicle, consider hiring an electric vehicle or an automatic. And, if you have not driven one of these before, you might want to book a lesson in one with a driving school before you set out on your holiday.

Health tips for travellers

Remember to pack any regular medicines you require: even familiar branded products can be difficult to obtain in some countries. Also take a mini first-aid kit, including plasters, disinfectant, tummy pills, and so on.

If you are going to any developing country, consult your doctor as to what medicines (and any special precautions) you should take. Have any inoculations or vaccinations well in advance of your departure date.

One of the most common ailments among British travellers abroad is too much sun. In some countries it really burns, so take it easy, wear a hat and apply plenty of protective lotion. The other big travellers' woe is an upset stomach, which unhappily can occur in most hot countries, even within Europe. Be wary of water, ice, salads, seafood, ice cream and any fruit that you do not peel yourself. Always wash your hands before eating or handling food, particularly if you are camping or caravanning.

When flying, wear loose clothes and above all comfortable shoes, as feet and ankles tend to swell in the air. To avoid risk of deep vein thrombosis, which can be fatal, medical advice is to do foot exercises and walk around the plane from time to time. For long-haul travel especially, wear compression stockings. On long journeys, it helps to drink plenty of water and remember the warning that 'an alcoholic drink in the air is worth two on the ground'. If onboard meals are included with your ticket and you have a special diet, inform whoever makes your booking.

Flying with medicines

Airlines normally have a strict ban on taking sharp objects onto a plane and the rules against travelling with liquids in containers exceeding 100ml which were abolished have been temporarily reintroduced at some UK airports. You should in any case check whether the airport you're flying into has more limited restrictions. So you will run up against extra rules if you will be flying and need to carry medicines that come prepacked with an auto-injector, such as EpiPens®. You should declare the auto-injectors at the security checkpoint and they will be examined. You will be required to show a certificate from your GP confirming the prescription. Similar rules apply if you need to carry other liquid medicines in quantities larger than 100ml.

The UK does not place any limits on the quantity of pills that you travel with, but because of concern over drug trafficking countries you visit may be suspicious if you try to bring in large amounts of pills.

Health and safety advice

This sometimes changes and the best advice is to check the foreign travel advice for the countries you will be visiting at GOV.UK (Directory, p 16). For the over 200 countries listed, this site gives you information about safety and security, terrorism, local laws and customs, entry requirements including coronavirus restrictions, health, money and where to get emergency help while abroad. Check the site several weeks before departure, to allow time for any inoculations, and again just before you leave.

Visas, passports and other requirements

Don't get caught out by not keeping up to date with the visa and other requirements of the countries you will be travelling to or through. These sometimes change without much warning and, at worst if you get it wrong, can result in your being turned away on arrival. So check the GOV.UK site (Directory, p 16) under 'Entry requirements'. This will give you information about, for example:

- how much time you need left on your passport (often a minimum of three months though, to be on the safe side, six is better);
- be aware that, for travel within Europe, your passport must also have been issued in the last 10 years (so any extension will not be recognized);
- whether you need a visa. Since 2024, for travel to EU countries, a new online European Travel Information and Authorisation System (ETIAS) starts (Directory p 16). Apply for ETIAS before you book your holiday;
- coronavirus requirements, such as any need to self-isolate on arrival, rules about public transport usage and mask wearing;
- any vaccination certificates you must have. There may also be other vaccines that you are recommended to have and you can find country-specific information on the Travel Health Pro site (Directory, p 16).

If you do need to order a new passport, allow plenty of time. In mid-2024, the government was advising that you should allow at least three weeks for your application to be processed.

Finally, make sure you are aware in advance of any departure and re-entry (to the UK) requirements. For example, some countries impose a departure tax. And check that you do not exceed the customs limit for importing duty-free items like cigarettes and alcohol – you will need to declare and pay tax on anything over those limits. Also take care not to bring in any banned substances, such as souvenirs made from ivory. For details, visit the GOV.UK sites on duty-free goods and banned goods (Directory, p 15).

CHAPTER FOURTEEN

Caring for elderly parents

As anyone who is helping and supporting elderly parents will know, not only is it often difficult and confusing to access care, it is hard to know how good that care is and the coronavirus experience has made us all justifiably anxious about the safety of care homes. In addition, care can cost a fortune, and provision varies depending on where you live – a veritable postcode lottery. The undoubted preference for most elderly people is that they remain in their own homes for as long as possible. With a bit of support from friends, relatives or local care organizations, many can, and the main focus of this chapter is on helping aged parents remain as independent as possible. It also looks at care home practicalities if this becomes necessary. In addition, see Chapter 2 for information about state benefits available for people with disabilities and carers, and Chapter 3 for how building up your State Pension may be protected if you have a disability or you are a carer.

Ways of adapting a home

Many elderly people will not require anything more complicated than a few adjustments to their home. Many of these adaptations are changes you could make yourself if you are up to a bit of DIY, or can be carried out by local contractors. In the case of equipment, such as grab rails, hoists, accessible showers and other aids, there are many suppliers both online and bricks-and-mortar shops where you can buy what you need. It is also possible to borrow equipment. The following organizations, which can be found in the Directory, pp 3–5, may be helpful:

- **Age UK**: local branches can often loan equipment, such as wheelchairs, in the short term and may also be able to advise on local stockists.
- **Boots**: online or at larger branches, Boots sells a wide range of special items for people with disabilities, including bath aids, wheelchairs and crutches.
- **British Red Cross** local branches make short-term loans of wheelchairs and other equipment, such as toileting aids. Sometimes there is a charge or you may be invited to make a donation. Its online shop also sells a variety of aids.
- **CAE** (Centre for Accessible Environments) offers a range of access consultancy services customized to the needs of clients.
- **DEMAND** (Design & Manufacture for Disability) is an independent charity that transforms the lives of disabled people through the provision of bespoke equipment. It does not charge clients for its services.
- **Disability Wales/Anabledd Cymru** is another helpful source of advice.
- **Focus on Disability** is a website covering a wide range of information and advice. It includes a catalogue of mobility aids and equipment as well as directories of Disabled Living Centres across the UK where you can see and try out equipment.
- **Independent Living** has information about equipment and adaptations and a list of suppliers.
- **Living made easy** (also known as The **Disabled Living Foundation**) is one of the UK's leading health charities, providing impartial advice and information to people of all ages, to help them find equipment to assist with everyday tasks essential to independent living.
- **Remap** is a special charity working through volunteers who use their ingenuity and skills to enable people with disabilities to achieve much-desired independence. It has panels across the country, and helps thousands of people each year, including through the loan of equipment free of charge.

However, should such arrangements not really be sufficient, you may be able to access advice and possibly financial help from the elderly person's local authority.

Local authority help

The state system in England and Wales is governed by the Care Act 2014 and is designed to support the elderly in their own home for as long as possible. Similar legislation applies in Scotland and Northern Ireland. Regardless of the person's needs or finances, local authorities normally have a legal duty to assess the support an elderly person may need. Then, depending on what is required and the individual's ability to pay, it may assist with the cost.

To request a care needs assessment, contact the adult social services department of the local authority. There should be a number to call on your local council's website: gov.uk/find-local-council. The request should be made either by the person needing care or, with their permission, you can make the request. If you or somebody else is already providing informal care, they will be included in the assessment. A carer may also request their own assessment to consider what support they need to carry on providing care. Unfortunately, the waiting time for these assessments, which varies from one council to another, can be quite lengthy – ask your local authority how long you might have to wait.

The assessment will determine whether the person's wellbeing is reduced because of a physical or mental condition that means they cannot manage two or more aspects of normal daily living without help. The local authority will then identify what care and support would help, and, while they can ask the local authority to arrange the support, the person receiving help may have to pay for part or all of it. The range of solutions is very wide and can include equipment and adaptations to the home aimed at preventing or reducing the need for care services.

Financial help with home repair and adaptations

Following a needs assessment, even if you could afford to pay, you may find your local authorities will without charge provide equipment such as a raised toilet seat or a hoist, and make minor adaptations to your home, such as grab rails or an access ramp. Equipment may be provided on a long-term loan and will eventually need to be returned. Alternatively, you might be given a prescription for equipment and you then buy it yourself from the suggested suppliers.

However, if you need major adaptations to your home, financial help is means-tested. One possibility is a local council disabled facilities grant to help towards the cost of adapting a home to enable a disabled or elderly person to live there. It can cover a wide range of improvements to help the occupants manage more independently. This includes work to facilitate access either to the property itself or to the main rooms, like the widening of doors or the installation of ramps or a lift; the provision of suitable bathroom or kitchen facilities; the adaptation of heating or lighting controls; improvement of the heating system, and various other works where these would make a home safe for a disabled person. Home improvement agencies (HIAs) are also a source of housing-related support. See *Improvement, repair and adaptations* in Chapter 6 for further information.

Alarm systems

Alarm systems for the elderly are many and varied, but the knowledge that help can be summoned quickly in the event of an emergency is reassuring and can enable many people to remain independent far longer than otherwise. Typically the alarm is a button worn around the neck which, when pushed, links to a control centre. They will then alert a nominated relative, neighbour or friend or, if need be, the emergency services.

Your parents' local authority social services department will have information and may even run an alarm service itself. There will usually be a charge. You can find contact details for your council at gov.uk/find-local-council. You could also try the TEC Services Association – a body representing a wide variety of organizations involved in providing and advising about technology-enabled care, including alarm systems. Its website (Directory, p 5) has a searchable directory of providers. The Living made easy website (Directory, p 5) also has useful guidance in the section on telecare.

Some of the many commercial systems you might consider include (Directory, pp 3–5):

- **Age UK Personal Alarm Service**
- **Careium**
- **Helpline Limited**
- **Saga**

See *Personal safety* in Chapter 6 for information about the switch-over of landlines from analogue to digital and how this may affect alarm systems.

Main local authority services

Free social care in Scotland and Northern Ireland

If, following a local council needs assessment, your parent requires personal or nursing care in their own home, this will be free in Scotland if your parent is aged 65 or over. It will either be provided directly by the local authority or your parent will receive payments they can use to choose and buy the care themselves.

The services that will be free include, for example, help with personal hygiene, continence, mobility, transferring to and from bed, preparing food and taking medicines. However, there is normally a charge for other services such as help with housework, laundry and shopping, day centres and providing pre-prepared meals unless your income and savings are low. You can find more information at Scottish Government (Free personal and nursing care: questions and answers) (Directory, p 5) and Care Information Scotland (Directory, p 4).

In Northern Ireland, if your care needs assessment shows you need social care in your home, this is provided free if you are aged 75 or over or you are getting means-tested benefits. You can, if you prefer, receive payments that enable you to choose and arrange your own support.

Financial help with care services in the rest of the UK

Local authorities have the discretion to charge for most of the social services they can provide, but are bound by the principle that no one should be charged more than they can afford. So, after a needs assessment, and quite separately, the local authority will carry out a financial assessment. This could be quite light-touch if it's clear that either you have very few resources or that you are sufficiently well-off that you will not qualify for help. In other cases, it will be a detailed look at your income and capital to determine whether you can receive the services at no charge or should contribute at least something towards the cost. For care in your own home, the value of your home is not included in this means test. Only the income and savings of the person in need of care are taken into account, but included is their share of any joint income and joint savings.

In England, a guiding rule is that, after paying for the services the person should not be left with less than a minimum sum, called the Minimum Income Guarantee. In 2024/25, this is £228.70 a week for a single person or £174.60 a week if they are part of a couple. You qualify for maximum financial help if your capital is less than £14,250. If you have capital of more than £23,250, you will not get any financial help and will have to bear the full cost yourself. These limits have not increased lately, despite inflation.

In Wales, local authorities may not charge more than the cost to the authority of providing the service and there is a maximum collective charge for all services (£100 a week in 2024/25) in addition to being left with a minimum income broadly in line with the Guarantee Credit portion of Pension Credit (see Chapter 2). However, if you have capital of more than £24,000, you will have to bear the full cost yourself.

Key voluntary organizations

Voluntary organizations complement the services provided by statutory health and social services in making life easier for elderly people living at home. The particular organization providing these services depends on where your parents live, but the best organization to advise you is the local Citizens Advice or your local council. These are the key agencies likely to be acting as providers (see Directory, pp 3–5), but many areas also have their own smaller local charities providing similar services:

- **Age Cymru (Wales)**
- **Age Northern Ireland**
- **Age Scotland**
- **Age UK**
- The **British Red Cross** supplies important services to elderly people such as helping sick, disabled or frail people make essential journeys, loaning medical equipment for short-term use, easing the transition of patients to their own home after discharge from hospital and pointing vulnerable people towards statutory or voluntary services
- **Centre for Independent Living, Northern Ireland**
- **Disability Wales**
- The **Royal Voluntary Service** runs many local projects: books on wheels; social transport; meals on wheels; good neighbour schemes; lunch clubs; a meal delivery service for those not qualifying for meals on wheels

Other sources of help and advice include:

- The **Civil Service Retirement Fellowship** (Directory, p 4) is a charity dedicated to helping former civil servants, their partners, widows, widowers and dependants.

- **Disability Rights UK** (Directory, p 4) is a national registered charity that provides help and information including the *Disability Rights Handbook*, which is a mine of information on benefits and rights for the disabled.
- **Good neighbour schemes** where volunteers provide befriending and other help, such as shopping. To find out whether such a scheme exists locally, ask social services, health centres or Citizens Advice.
- HousingCare (part of Elderly Accommodation Counsel) (Directory, p 19). Its site includes a searchable database of a very wide range of services to help older people in all aspects of life.
- **Independent Age** (including the former Counsel and Care) (Directory, p 4) is a national charity working with older people, their families and carers to get the best care and support. It provides personalized, in-depth help and advice.
- **Jewish Care** (Directory, p 5) provides services for elderly Jewish people, including those who are mentally ill, in London and the south-east of England. Principal facilities include special day-care centres, residential and nursing homes, community centres, a home care service for the housebound and short-term respite care.
- The **National Council on Independent Living** (Directory, p 5) is run by disabled people for disabled people and recommends reliable local people including 'support brokers'. It can give you details of independent living schemes in your county.

Transport

Difficulty in getting around is often a major problem for elderly and disabled people. In addition to the facilities run by voluntary organizations already mentioned, including local councils and small local charities running their own community accessible transport (CAT) schemes, there are several other very useful services (Directory, pp 4–5):

- **Driving Mobility** is a network of independent organizations throughout the UK helping individuals who have a medical condition that may affect their ability to drive.
- **London Taxicard** provides subsidized door-to-door transport in taxis and private-hire vehicles for people who have serious mobility or visual impairment.

- **Motability** is a registered charity set up to assist recipients of the mobility allowance part of state disability benefits to use their allowance to lease or buy a car or a powered wheelchair or scooter.

Driving at older ages

All drivers aged 70 are sent a licence renewal form to have their driving licence renewed. The entitlement to drive will need to be renewed by the DVLA; the new licence will normally be valid for three years. See Renew driving licence (Directory, p 5). Note that there is no charge for renewing your licence with the DVLA. Don't be taken in by websites offering renewal for a fee.

If you've recently travelled in a car and been frightened by a relative's driving, or you think you might be starting to scare others with your driving skills, it is simple enough to get checked. RoSPA Advanced Drivers and Riders has an Older Drivers website (Directory, p 25). Through this you can search for mature driver assessments in your area available to anyone wanting to check their driving skills and confidence. It takes about an hour with a tactful and helpful examiner. If your relative passes, they will receive a certificate and in all cases a written report and practical suggestions for improvement. Depending who runs the assessments, there may be a modest charge or the assessment might be free.

Power of Attorney

Giving another person Power of Attorney authorizes someone else to take financial decisions on the donor's behalf. This can be a temporary arrangement – for example, while your parent is in hospital – or set up in advance so that someone can take over in the event that your parent loses their mental capacity. This second type of power has different names in the different nations of the UK. In England and Wales, it is called a Lasting Power of Attorney (LPA) and there are two types – one to cover property and financial affairs and the other regarding health and welfare decisions. In Scotland, there are similarly a Continuing Power of Attorney to cover property and financial matters and a Welfare Power of Attorney for health and welfare – although they can be combined. In Northern Ireland, there is just an Enduring Power of Attorney for both property and financial matters.

A Lasting Power of Attorney (and its equivalents) can only be made while the donor is still of sound mind, and then comes into effect if they cease to be able to make their own decisions. It then continues, if necessary, throughout the remainder of the individual's life. To protect the donor and the nominated attorney, the law clearly lays down certain principles that must be observed, with both sides signing a declaration that they understand the various rights and duties involved. The law furthermore calls for the power to be formally registered with the relevant public office, which can also provide information and the forms you need (Directory, p 23):

- **Office of Care and Protection, Northern Ireland**
- **Office of the Public Guardian (England and Wales)**
- **Office of the Public Guardian (Scotland)**

If your parent has not made a Lasting Power of Attorney but becomes unable to make decisions for him or herself, you can apply to the Court of Protection for a similar power to act, called being a deputy, guardian or controller. For England and Wales, there is more information on becoming a deputy (Directory, p 23). For Scotland, see becoming a guardian (Directory, p 22). For Northern Ireland, see becoming a controller (Directory, p 23).

Living-in help

Temporary

Elderly people living alone can be vulnerable and if you have reason for concern – perhaps because you are going on holiday and will not be around to keep a watchful eye on them – engaging living-in help can be a godsend.

VOLUNTEERING MATTERS
Volunteering Matters, formerly Community Service Volunteers, is the UK's leading training and volunteering charity. It engages 20,000 volunteers a year to work with 85,000 beneficiaries across the UK, providing practical assistance in the home and also offering companionship. Usually a care scheme is set up through a social worker, who supervises how the arrangement is working out. For more information contact your parents' local social services department, or see Volunteering Matters (Directory, p 38).

AGENCIES

The agencies listed (see Directory, p 38) specialize in providing temporary help, rather than permanent staff. Charges vary, but in addition to the weekly payment to helpers there is normally an agency booking fee:

- **Consultus Care & Nursing Agency Ltd**
- **Country Cousins**
- **Universal Aunts Ltd**

For a further list of agencies, see *The Lady* magazine, or search the internet under the heading 'Nursing agencies' or 'Care agencies' (Directory, p 38).

NURSING CARE

If one of your parents needs regular nursing care, the GP may be able to arrange for a community or district nurse to visit him or her at home. This will not be a sleeping-in arrangement, but simply involves a qualified nurse calling round when necessary. If they need more concentrated home nursing, you will have to go through a private agency. Some of the agencies listed above can sometimes supply trained nurses. Additionally, there are many specialist agencies that can arrange hourly, daily or live-in nurses on a temporary or longer-term basis. Fees and services vary considerably. The local health centre or social services department should be able to give you names and addresses of local agencies, or search the internet for 'nursing agencies'.

Permanent

There may come a time when you feel that it is no longer safe to allow one of your parents to live entirely on his or her own. One possibility is to engage a companion or housekeeper on a permanent basis; such arrangements are normally expensive. If you want to investigate the idea further, many domestic agencies supply housekeeper-companions. Alternatively, you might consider advertising in *The Lady* magazine (Directory, p 38), which is probably the most widely read publication for these kinds of posts.

Flexible care arrangements

One of the problems for many elderly people is that the amount of care they need is liable to vary according to the state of their health. There are other relevant factors including, for example, the availability of neighbours and family. Whereas after an operation the requirement may be for someone with basic nursing skills, a few weeks later the only need may be for someone to act as a companion. Under normal circumstances it may be as little as simply popping in for the odd hour during the day to cook a hot meal and check all is well. Few agencies cater for all the complex permutations that may be necessary in caring for an elderly person in his or her own home, but here are some that offer a flexible service (see Directory, p 38):

- **Autumna** is a digital platform providing a searchable directory of home care and live-in care providers (as well as care homes and sheltered housing).
- **Christies Care** is the largest independent specialist provider of live-in care, providing a professional and dedicated service tailored to clients' individual requirements.
- **Corinium Care** is a specialist organization able to provide care and support seven days a week, 52 weeks of the year, as much or as little as required.
- The **Homecare Association** is the professional association for home care providers, and has a searchable database of its members.
- **Miracle Workers** offers both long- and short-term care. It looks after clients in all sorts of situations. Live-in carers provide practical assistance, support and companionship.

Although any of these suggestions can work extremely well for a while, with many families it may sooner or later come down to a choice between residential care and inviting a parent to live with you. Sometimes, particularly in the case of an unmarried son or daughter or other relative, it is more practical to move into the parent's (or relative's) home if the accommodation is more suitable.

Emergency care for pets

For many elderly people a pet is a very important part of their lives. But in the event of the owner having to go into hospital or through some other emergency being temporarily unable to care for the pet, there can be real problems. Two organizations that can help are (Directory, pp 19–20):

- The **Cinnamon Trust** offers permanent care for pets whose owners have died, as well as respite care while the owners are in hospital. Animals either stay at the Trust's havens in Cornwall and Devon or are found alternative loving homes with a new owner.

- **Pet Fostering Service Scotland** focuses on temporary care. The only charges are the cost of the pet's food, litter (in the case of cats) and any veterinary fees that may be incurred during fostering.

Practical help for carers

If your parent is still fairly active – visits friends, does his or her own shopping or enjoys some hobby that gets him or her out and about – the strains and difficulties may be fairly minimal. This applies particularly if your parent is moving in with you and your home lends itself to creating a granny flat, so everyone can retain some privacy and your parent can continue to enjoy maximum independence. However, this is not always possible, and in the case of an ill or very frail person far more intensive care may be required. It is important to know what help is available and how to obtain it. The many services provided by local authorities and voluntary agencies, described earlier in the chapter, apply as much to an elderly person living with a family as to one living alone. If there is nothing there that solves a particular problem you may have, it could be that one of the following organizations could help or provide useful information (see Directory, pp 3–5):

- **Age UK**
- **British Red Cross**
- **Carers Trust**
- **Carers UK**
- **Royal Voluntary Service**

Most areas have respite care facilities to enable carers to take a break from their dependants from time to time. Depending on the circumstances, this could be for just the odd day or possibly for a week or two to enable carers who need it to have a real rest.

Holiday breaks for carers

There are various schemes to enable those with an elderly relative to go on holiday alone or simply to enjoy a respite from their caring responsibilities. A number of local authorities run fostering schemes, along similar lines to child fostering. Elderly people are invited to stay in a neighbour's home and live in the household as an ordinary family member. Lasting relationships often develop. There may be a charge, or the service may be run on a voluntary basis (or be paid for by the local authority). Some voluntary organizations arrange holidays for older people to give their relatives a break. Different charities take responsibility according to where you live: Citizens Advice, a volunteer centre or social services department should know whom you should approach.

Special accommodation

Elderly parents who no longer feel able to maintain a family home may decide that the time has come to move into accommodation that is smaller, easier and more economic to maintain. Purpose-designed retirement housing, with a high degree of independence and with the option to have a range of support resources as and when required, is a solution that suits increasing numbers of people. There is a wide choice available to meet individual requirements, budgets and tastes.

Sheltered housing

Sheltered housing is usually a development of independent, purpose-designed bungalows or flats within easy access of shops and public transport. It generally has a house manager and an alarm system for emergencies, and often some common facilities. These could include a garden, possibly a launderette, a sitting room and a dining room, with meals provided for residents, on an optional basis, either once a day or several days a week.

Residents normally have access to all the usual range of services – home helps, meals on wheels, and so on – in the same way as any other elderly people. Sheltered housing is available for sale or rent through private developers, housing associations or local authorities. It is occasionally provided through gifted housing schemes, or on a shared ownership basis. (Gifted housing schemes are where the older person gifts their home during their lifetime to an organization that in return provides home maintenance and care services.)

Good developments are always sought after, and can require you to join a waiting list. Although this is emphatically not a reason for rushing into a decision you might regret, if you were hoping to move in the fairly near future it could be as well to start looking sooner rather than later.

SHELTERED HOUSING FOR SALE

The following organizations can provide information about sheltered housing for sale (Directory, pp 19–20):

- **Elderly Accommodation Counsel** is a nationwide charity that aims to help older people make informed choices about meeting their housing and care needs.
- **Retirement Homesearch** has an extensive nationwide portfolio of over 2,000 retirement properties, including flats, houses and bungalows, in all price ranges.

New developments are constantly under construction. Properties tend to be sold quickly soon after completion, so it pays to find out about future developments and to get on any waiting lists well in advance of a prospective purchase. Firms specializing in this type of property include the following (see Directory, pp 16–17):

- **Churchill Living**
- **Cognatum**
- **McCarthy Stone Retirement Living**
- **Pegasus Homes**
- **Richmond Villages**

Housing associations build sheltered housing for sale and also manage sheltered housing developments on behalf of private construction companies; see Anchor (Directory, p 16).

RENTED SHELTERED HOUSING

This is normally provided by local authorities, housing associations and certain benevolent societies. As with accommodation to buy, quality varies.

Local authority housing is usually only available to people who have resided in the area for some time. You will be asked if you have any special needs so that only suitable housing is offered – for example, on the ground floor if you have mobility issues. Apply to the local housing or social services department or via a housing advice centre.

Housing associations supply much of the newly built sheltered housing. Both rent and service charges vary around the country. If your income is low you might qualify for Housing Benefit to help with the cost – see Chapter 2. Citizens Advice and housing departments often keep a list of local housing associations. There are hundreds to choose from; here are just a few (see Directory, pp 20–21):

- **Abbeyfield**
- **Anchor**
- **Girlings**
- **Habinteg Housing Association**
- **Housing 21**

BENEVOLENT SOCIETIES

These cater for specific professional and other groups, for example (Directory, p 20):

- **Royal Alfred Seafarers' Society** provides quality long-term care for elderly seafarers, their widows and dependants.
- **SSAFA** is restricted to those who have served in the armed forces (including reservists and those who did National Service) and their families.

Shared ownership for older people

Shared ownership schemes are available for first-time buyers of any age. Offered by some developers and some housing associations, these schemes involve buying part of your home and paying rent for the rest. Over time, you may be able to increase the part that you own (called staircasing) and, if you sell, you get part of the sale price in line with the proportion you own. In England, there is a government-backed shared ownership scheme aimed specifically at people aged 55 and over called Older Person's Shared Ownership (Directory, p 17). In Scotland, there is a similar scheme, New Supply Shared Equity, for the over-60s (Directory, p 17).

Almshouses

Most almshouses are endowed by a charity for the benefit of older people of reduced means who live locally or have a connection with a particular trade. There are over 1,600 groups of almshouses providing homes for 36,000 people. Although many of the homes are of considerable age, most of them have been modernized and new ones are being built. Rents are not charged, but there will be a maintenance contribution towards upkeep and heating – broadly equivalent to rent but lower.

A point you should be aware of is that almshouses do not provide the same security of tenure as some other tenancies. You would be well advised to have the proposed letter of appointment checked by a lawyer or other expert to ensure you understand exactly what the beneficiary's rights are. There is no standard way to apply for an almshouse, since each charity has its own qualifications for residence. Some housing departments and advice centres keep lists of local almshouses. An organization that could help is the Almshouse Association (Directory, p 19), which supplies information on almshouses and contact details in the county in which you are interested.

Granny flats

A granny flat or annexe is a self-contained unit attached to a family house. A large house can be converted or extended for this purpose, but planning permission is needed. Enquire with your local authority planning department. Some councils, particularly new towns, have houses to rent with granny flats.

Salvation Army homes

The Salvation Army (Directory, p 20) has a limited number of homes for elderly people in various parts of the UK, offering residential care for men and women unable to manage in their own homes. Christian caring is given within a family atmosphere, in pleasant surroundings, but the homes are not nursing homes.

Extra-care schemes

A number of organizations that provide sheltered accommodation also have extra-care sheltered housing, designed for those who can no longer look after themselves without assistance. Although expensive, it is cheaper than most private care homes and often more appropriate than full-scale nursing care. A possible problem is that tenants of some of these schemes do not have security of tenure and could be asked to leave if more intensive care were required. Among the housing associations that provide these facilities are Housing 21, Anchor Housing Association and Abbeyfield (see Directory, pp 20–21).

Care homes

While a person has a right to a care needs assessment, there is no compulsion to have one and you may in any case come to the conclusion that your parent would be better off moving into a home. This is a major decision, not just because of the emotional trauma it may cause, but because of the high cost and the difficulty in some regions of finding a care home place. Here are some suggestions before taking the decision:

· Is a care home really needed? Get advice on the housing options.
· What type of care home is wanted? Some offer accommodation and help with personal care; other care homes offer nursing care as well as the basic help.
· How to find a care home? Think of it like buying a house: you need to get a feel for what is out there before making a decision. Personal recommendations are important.
· How much will it cost? There is a lot of variation in care home fees. If the local council is paying, it will set a maximum cost that it will contribute. If the costs are higher, a relative or friend will need to top up that amount. If your parents are self-funding, make sure they can afford the fees. Care home fees vary widely across the country. Research by the consumer organization Which? using data from Lottie found that residential care home costs in 2024 varied from £1,035 a week to £1,383 a week, and nursing home costs ranged from £1,088 a week to £1,607. This means residents were paying between £54,000 and £84,000 a year.

Financial help with care home costs

If moving into a nursing home is a continuation of NHS treatment that your parent has been having for an illness – for example, he or she is discharged from hospital direct to a home – this should be paid for by the NHS. However, this is a grey area and you may have to be persistent to get their costs met in this way.

If they do not qualify for NHS continuing care, assuming the recommendation to move into a home is the result of a local authority needs assessment, they may still qualify for some state help with care home fees, provided their assessment found this was the best option for them and the subsequent financial assessment finds that their income and capital are low enough. The rules around this means assessments are complicated and vary from one nation of the UK to another.

In England and Northern Ireland, you will get maximum help if your income is low and your capital comes to no more than £14,250. If your capital exceeds £23,250, you will have to pay the full cost of care (called self-funding) until your capital drops below that limit. For capital between those limits, you are treated as if each £250 of capital above the lower £14,250 threshold produces £1 a week of income and this is added to the rest of your income for the purpose of working out what you can afford to pay. You will be allowed to keep a small amount of income (£30.15 a week in 2024/25 20 in England and £27.19 in Northern Ireland) as a personal expenses allowance.

Wales has the most generous means-test of all the UK nations. In 2024/25 you will have to self-fund if your capital is above £50,000. Below that, the help you get is based just on your income, with up to £50,000 of capital being disregarded. You are allowed to keep £39.50 a week for personal expenses.

In Scotland, you will get maximum help if your income is low and your capital comes to no more than £21,500 (in 2024/25). If your capital exceeds £35,000, you will have to pay the full cost of care (self-funding) until your capital drops below that limit. For capital between those limits, you are treated as if each £250 of capital above the lower threshold produces £1 a week of income and this is added to the rest of your income for the purpose of working out what you can afford to pay. You will be allowed to keep a small amount of income (£34.50 a week in 2024/25) as a personal expenses allowance.

For the purpose of these means tests, a home you own does not count as capital if your partner or another dependant still lives there. But, in other cases, it will be counted, which means your home may have to be sold or the local authority can put a charge against the home so that it can recover the cost of care fees it has paid once the home is sold. Another option could be to rent out the home and put the rental income towards paying the care home fees. Be aware that, if your parent gives away some or all of their wealth, this may be treated as 'deprivation of capital' and the means test can be carried out as if they still own the assets.

Changes to state help with care costs abandoned

From October 2025, the rules about state help with the cost of care in England were due to change and would have put an upper limit on the total amount you would pay over your lifetime for care services. However, previous governments consistently delayed implementing these changes and diverted funding intended to finance them to more generally ease the lack of funding for social care. The new Labour government has now announced that the reforms will not go ahead at all, but has promised a new review of social care.

Paying for a care home

If your parent has to pay some or all of the cost of a care home, their income often will not be enough and so it will be a case of looking at how they might raise money from their assets.

One option is to buy a *care fee annuity* (sometimes known as an 'immediate-needs annuity'). This is a product where you use a lump sum and in return get a regular monthly cash sum for the rest of your life to put towards your care costs. Provided the money is paid directly to a care provider, the income is tax-free. Because someone needing care is likely to have a shorter life expectancy than a person of the same age in good health, the income from this type of annuity is generally higher than the income from the types of annuity described in Chapters 3 and 5. To qualify for this higher income, you will typically need to show that you require help with a specified number of activities of daily living (ADLs), such as being able to bathe, transfer from bed to a chair, and so on.

The lump sum to buy the immediate annuity could come from your savings or by releasing equity if you are a homeowner (see *Equity release* in Chapter 6). Prices quoted by different companies to provide exactly the same annual income often differ by many thousands of pounds. You are strongly advised to get advice from a financial adviser (see Chapter 1).

Immediate care annuities and advice about them are regulated by the Financial Conduct Authority. Always check that the companies you are dealing with are authorized by checking their entry on the Financial Services Register (Directory, p 9). Provided you deal with an authorized firm, the protection of the Financial Ombudsman Service and Financial Services Compensation Scheme (Directory, p 9) apply should anything go wrong.

Residential care homes

In a residential care home, the accommodation usually consists of a bedroom plus communal dining rooms, lounges and gardens. All meals are provided, rooms are cleaned and staff are at hand to give whatever help is needed. Most homes are fully furnished, though it is usually possible to take small items of furniture. These days, most rooms have an en-suite bathroom. Intensive nursing care is not usually included.

Homes are run by private individuals or companies, voluntary organizations and local authorities. All homes must be registered with the public body responsible for ensuring minimum standards (the Care Quality Commission in England). An unregistered home should not be considered. It is very important that the individual should have a proper chance to visit it and ask any questions. Before reaching a final decision, it is a good idea to arrange a short stay to see whether the facilities are suitable and pleasant.

It could also be sensible to enquire what long-term plans there are for the home. Having to switch care home can be a highly distressing experience for an elderly person who has become attached to the staff and made friends among the other residents. Though a move can never be totally ruled out, awareness of whether the home is likely to remain a going concern could be a deciding factor when making a choice. Possible clues could include whether the place is short-staffed or in need of decoration. If it is run by a company or charity, you could check its latest accounts filed with Companies House or the Charity Commission (Directory, p 19).

Nursing homes

Nursing homes provide medical supervision and fully qualified nurses, 24 hours a day. Most are privately run, with the remainder being supported by voluntary organizations. All nursing homes in England must be registered with the Care Quality Commission, which keeps a list of what homes are available in the area. There are equivalent bodies in the other nations of the UK. Nursing homes are significantly more expensive than residential homes.

Finding a care home

For information about residential and nursing homes in the UK, contact the following (Directory, pp 19–20):

- The **Care Quality Commission** maintains a register of the homes it regulates across England. You can search for care homes and check their inspection reports and ratings.
- The **Elderly Accommodation Counsel** maintains a nationwide database of all types of specialist accommodation for elderly people and gives advice and detailed information to help enquirers choose the support and care most suited to their needs.
- **Lottie** is one of several digital platforms bringing together people seeking care and care providers. You can use it to search for and compare care homes and submit care requests to which providers may respond.
- The **National Care Association (NCA)** (with which the Registered Nursing Home Association has merged) is an organization that provides support for nursing homeowners, requiring its members to meet high levels of standards and service.

Useful reading

Read *Care Finding, choosing and funding a care home,* a free factsheet downloadable from Age UK (Directory, p 3).

Some special problems

A minority of people, as they become older, suffer from special problems that can cause great distress. Because families do not like to talk about these problems, they may be unaware of what services are available and so may be missing out on practical help and sometimes also on financial assistance.

Some problems to watch out for and sources of help are:

- **Hypothermia.** Older people are more vulnerable to the cold and may not even notice, instead becoming listless and confused. If your parent is worried about heating bills, see the section *Help with fuel bills* in Chapter 6 and the other information on help with the cost of insulation. Make sure your parent is claiming any state benefits for which they qualify (see Chapter 2), including Pension Credit if their income is low, which will then qualify them for Winter Fuel Payment.

- **Incontinence.** Bladder and bowel problems can seem deeply embarrassing but no one should suffer unnecessarily. Your GP can help and B&B (Bladder and Bowel Community) (Directory, p 3) offers advice from its specially trained nurses.
- **Dementia.** Confusion and memory loss are not necessarily signs of dementia – they could result from other problems that can be cured, such as depression or vitamin deficiency. So, it is important to consult a GP as soon as possible. If dementia is diagnosed, there are organizations that offer advice and support, including: Alzheimer Scotland (Directory, p 3), Alzheimer's Society (Directory, p 3) and Mind (Directory, p 5). A very useful book, *Caring for a Person with Dementia: A Practical Guide*, can be downloaded or ordered by post from the Alzheimer's Society website.

CHAPTER FIFTEEN

No one is immortal

Before we get too old, it is important to think for a moment about the practicalities of dying. We all know that we should write a will, but it is one of those things that many of us never seem to get around to. A great deal of heartbreak and real financial worry could be avoided if people were more open about the subject. At the earliest and most appropriate moment, if you can bring yourself and your relatives to have an honest and open discussion about mortality, it could potentially save huge amounts of trouble later on and also legitimately avoid paying unnecessary tax. By the way, the inheritance tax rules here are those that applied in the 2024/25 tax year. However, there has been much speculation that the new Labour government may reform this tax.

Inheritance tax (IHT)

Inheritance tax (IHT) is mainly a tax on what you leave when you die – although some lifetime gifts can also be taxable. Many people worry that IHT will eat into what they leave their family, but in fact only around 1 passing in 27 triggers an IHT bill.

However, the figure is low partly because married couples and civil partners often pass on their estates tax-free on the first death and tax kicks in only when the remaining partner dies. And, with the inheritance tax threshold frozen now for many years, the number of estates being drawn into the tax net is set to rise.

What is taxed?

IHT is an unusual tax because it is based on the gifts and bequests that you've made over the last seven years. Although gifts you make in your life-time are within the scope of IHT, there are many exemptions and other rules that mean they are usually tax-free. Therefore, most people come across IHT as the tax that may be payable on your 'estate'. Broadly speaking, this is everything you own at the time of your death, less any debts you have. For example, assets included in your estate include property, possessions, money and investments. If you own assets jointly with someone else, just your share counts as part of your estate. Note, though, that savings in a pension scheme and the pay-out from any life insurance policies usually go direct to whoever you nominated to receive these amounts, bypassing your estate, and so are normally free of IHT.

Tax at the time of death

Most estates are too small to pay IHT or can make use of various exemp-tions. For example, anything you leave to your husband, wife or civil partner is free of IHT, as are bequests you make to charity. Common taxable bequests are things you leave to your children or a brother or sister, and bequests to your partner if you are an unmarried couple.

The estate you leave is treated as the final gift you make in the seven years up to death. All taxable gifts over the seven years are added together, but the first slice of the total, called your 'nil-rate band' (NRB) is tax-free. Your NRB is set against the earliest gifts first, and lastly your estate. These rules may seem rather odd, but essentially they are making sure you do not avoid IHT by giving away all your possessions in the last few years before death.

Anything you leave that is not either tax-free or covered by your NRB is taxed at an IHT rate of 40 per cent (2024/25). However, if you leave at least 10 per cent of your taxable estate to charity, the rate is reduced to 36 per cent.

Your nil-rate band

Since 2017/18, there have been two parts to your NRB: the standard part which is £325,000, and a main-residence NRB, which stands at £175,000 in 2024/25.

A single homeowner can leave an estate of up to £500,000 free of IHT and couples can leave up to £1 million. There are some conditions attached to getting the main-residence NRB, mainly that the home has to be left to your children, their children or others in that direct line of descent. But, if you downsize (move to a cheaper home) or cease to own a property, the main-residence NRB can cover an equivalent amount of assets. Also, the main-residence NRB is tapered away at a rate of £1 for each £2 by which the value of a person's estate exceeds £2 million. If you are a tenant renting your home, you cannot qualify for the main-residence NRB, so the maximum you can leave tax-free is just the standard £325,000.

Each person has their own NRB and, if applicable, main-residence NRB. However, since 2007/08, married couples and civil partners can leave any unused part of their NRB to their partner. This also applies to the main-residence NRB. Unmarried couples cannot do this, so any part of their NRB unused on their own death is lost.

REAL-WORLD EXAMPLE

Jim and Emma were married and jointly owned their home. When Jim died in 2024, he left an estate, including his share of the home, worth £600,000. He left everything to Emma, so the whole amount was exempt from IHT. That meant Jim's estate didn't use any of his £325,000 NRB or £175,000 main-residence NRB. Sadly Emma died later the same year. With what she had inherited from Jim, her estate was worth £900,000 and she left this entirely to their children. The people sorting out her estate (her 'executors') were able to claim Jim's unused NRBs of £500,000. Combined with Emma's own NRBs of the same amount, this meant there was no tax to pay on Emma's estate.

REAL-WORLD EXAMPLE

Hattie and Xiang are unmarried. When Hattie died in 2024, she left an estate of £600,000 including her share of their home, with everything going to Xiang. Since they were unmarried, the bequest to Xiang was not tax-free and, since she left her share of the home to him and not their children, her estate did not qualify for main-residence NRB. Her standard NRB of £325,000 was deducted from what she left, meaning there was IHT to pay on the remaining £275,000 of what she left. At a rate of 40 per cent, the tax bill came to £110,000. Therefore Xiang inherited £490,000.

Lifetime gifts

The case studies above assumed that each person had not made any taxable gifts during the seven years before they died. That's a common situation, because many lifetime gifts are free of IHT. These include, for example:

- Gifts to your husband, wife or civil partner (though limited to a lifetime amount of £325,000 if their permanent home is not in the UK).
- Gifts to charity.
- Gifts up to £250 a year to any number of people. This covers things like birthday and Christmas gifts.
- Gifts when someone marries – parents can each make tax-free gifts to the couple of £5,000, grandparents £2,500 and anyone else £1,000.
- Gifts of any amount to one or more people if the gifts form a regular pattern, are given out of your income and do not reduce your normal standard of living. This is quite a flexible exemption. It could cover, for example, paying regular sums into a pension scheme or insurance policy for the benefit of someone else. But equally it could cover regularly giving each of your grandchildren a gift on reaching age 25. This is a very useful exemption because there is no specific limit on what you give, however, it can be quite hard to prove that the gifts came out of 'spare' income and did not reduce your living standards.
- Gifts of any amount that are for the maintenance of your children, your current partner or a former partner. This includes children still in full-time education.
- Up to £3,000 a year of any other gifts. If you do not use the full £3,000, you can carry forward the unused bit, but only for one year.

While the gifts above are definitely exempt from IHT, most other lifetime gifts that you make are potentially exempt and so are called Potentially Exempt Transfers (PETs). This means that they are treated as if they are exempt at the time you make them and, if you survive for seven years after making a PET, it actually becomes exempt. However, if you die within the seven years, it is instead reclassified as a taxable gift. This may have two effects: first, there might be tax to pay on the gift itself; second, it may use up part of your NRB, causing more tax to be payable on your estate.

REAL-WORLD EXAMPLE

Shivani died in 2024 leaving an estate of £400,000. Five years earlier, she made a gift of £13,000 to her niece. £3,000 of this gift was exempt. At the time, the remaining £10,000 was a PET, but because Shivani did not survive seven years it is now a taxable gift. The first £10,000 of Shivani's standard NRB is set against this failed PET. That leaves £315,000 of NRB to set against her estate.

Making lifetime gifts can be used to reduce the value of your estate, and so to minimize the IHT payable. However, make sure not to give away more than you can afford. You need to leave yourself with enough to live on and to cope with unexpected expenses. Be aware too that your gifts must be genuine. If, say, you give away your home but continue living in it, the home will still count as part of your estate for IHT (or alternatively you might have to pay extra income tax each year). A nasty sting in the tail is that, while the gift would not be effective for IHT, it would nevertheless count as a genuine gift for CGT purposes so the recipient would lose the benefit of gifts on death being free of CGT. Be wary, too, of contrived schemes designed to save IHT – often HMRC decides later that they do not work. If you are thinking of ways to save IHT that go beyond the simple exemptions and PETs outlined above, get professional advice (see *Information and advice about tax* in Chapter 4).

Provided you really can afford to give away some assets during your lifetime, a common reason is to help your children onto the housing ladder. This 'bank of mum and dad' is often the only way young people can accumulate a deposit these days given that house prices are so high. Some parents take out an equity release scheme (see Chapter 6) to fund such gifts. The gift will be a PET for IHT (after deducting the £3,000 annual exemption). Be aware that, if your child is married or in a civil partnership but their relationship breaks down, their partner may take a share of your gift or the home it bought. You might consider making an interest-free (or low-cost) loan to your child instead, receiving regular repayments in return – this could be suitable if, say, you have lump sum savings that you'd like to turn into an income, provided you're confident that your child will be able to keep up the payments. Unlike a gift, the loan remains part of your estate, so does not reduce IHT.

Just a few lifetime gifts are taxable at the time you make them. These are mainly gifts you make to a company or to a trust. A trust is a separate legal entity where one or more people (the trustees) are the legal owners of assets, but must use them for the benefit of other people (the beneficiaries). The person who gives assets to a trust is called the settlor, and you can set up trusts either during your lifetime or in your will. The new government has pledged to end the use of offshore trusts as a way of avoiding inheritance tax.

Wills

Planning what will happen to your money and possessions after your death helps ensure your survivors are financially secure, and that the people you want to inherit from you do so. When you retire, there are often big changes to your finances as well as to the rest of your life. It is at this stage that it is important to review how your survivors would manage financially if you were to die. Would, in fact, your money and possessions (your estate) be passed on as you would wish?

There are five rules of will making:

1 The person making the will must be of sound mind.
2 The will must be properly signed.
3 The will must be correctly witnessed.
4 Be clear about what or how much you want to leave and to whom.
5 Remember to update your will as your life circumstances change.

Having a will is especially important if you live with an unmarried partner, have remarried, need to provide for someone with a disability, own a business, own property abroad or your estate is over the IHT threshold. A will is a legal document that needs to be drawn up precisely and set out your wishes clearly and unambiguously. Although you can write your own will, it is safer to get a solicitor to do it.

Laws of intestacy

Dying without having made a will is called dying 'intestate'. The laws of intestacy are different in the different nations of the UK. However, they all follow the same basic principles:

- your husband, wife or civil partner and your own children are favoured; this includes a former partner if you are only separated rather than divorced;

- an unmarried partner and stepchildren have no automatic rights;
- your husband, wife or civil partner does not automatically get the whole of your estate;
- possessions, including your home, may have to be sold to split the proceeds between your heirs;
- if children who are minors are among your heirs, their inheritance may have to be held in a trust until they reach adulthood;
- if you have no partner or children, more distant relatives inherit;
- if you have no relatives, the state gets the lot.

Making a will

You have four choices: you can do it yourself, ask your bank to help you, hire a solicitor or use a will-writing service.

DOING IT YOURSELF

Home-made wills are not generally recommended. People often use ambiguous wording which, while perfectly clear to them, may be less obvious to others. This could result in the donor's wishes being misinterpreted, and could also cause considerable delay in settling the estate.

The wording of a will is important, including a formal revocation of any earlier wills. It's also important to think beyond your basic wishes and address questions such as what if a beneficiary dies before you, what if you and your partner (if you have one) die together or within a short space of time of each other? Few people would start writing a will from scratch – templates are available from stationers and can be downloaded from the internet. They are not perfect, however, and still leave considerable margin for error, especially if your circumstances or your estate are complicated.

Two witnesses are needed, and an essential point to remember is that witnesses and their spouses cannot be beneficiaries of a will, so if they do witness it, they will be automatically disinherited. In certain circumstances, a will can be rendered invalid. There will also be confusion if part of a will seems to be missing, so, if you need to change your will, it's best to start from scratch with a new one rather than staple an amendment (called a codicil) that might become detached.

BANKS

Advice on wills and the administration of estates is given by the trustee companies of some major banks. In particular, the services they offer are to provide general guidance, to act as executor and to administer the estate. They will introduce clients to a solicitor and can arrange other related advice on tax planning and financial advice.

As with using a solicitor (see below), an advantage of using a bank is that they can keep a copy of the will – plus other important documents – in their safe, avoiding the risk of these documents being mislaid or lost in, say, a house fire. However, the contract for services is between you and the bank, so after you have died, your heirs have very little leverage to get the bank to speed up if it is taking a long time administering the estate or to control what the bank charges.

SOLICITORS

Solicitors are the traditional professional to use to draw up a will. You can also appoint them to act as executors and administer the estate, though as with banks this is not necessarily a good idea since your heirs will have no control over the speed or cost of the solicitor's services. Like banks, solicitors will also retain a copy of your will in safekeeping and most will not charge for this.

If you do not have a solicitor, friends or family may be able to recommend one, or you can find a member of one of the legal professional bodies (Directory, p 22):

- the **Law Society**: use its Find a Solicitor service to find legal advice in England, Wales and Scotland
- **Law Society of Northern Ireland**

A simple will would normally start at about £150 (but, according to MoneyHelper could cost over £2,400, so make sure you shop around). Couples sometimes make 'mirror wills' leaving everything on broadly the same terms, and there may be a discount for doing both at the same time. However, many solicitors take part in special schemes where they partner with charities and offer free writing of simple wills. The schemes (Directory, p 22) include:

- **Free Wills Month.** During the campaign months (March and October), people aged 55 and over can have a will written by a solicitor for free. Participating charities hope you will leave them a legacy in your will although you cannot be forced to do so.
- **Make a Will Week.** Participating solicitors write your will for free in return for you making a suggested donation to a partner charity. The week has been in May in recent years, and the charities involved advertise if they are taking part.

- **National Free Wills Network** is a partnership where participating charities pay for solicitors to write free wills for their supporters. Again, the hope is that you will leave a legacy to the charity, but that is up to you.
- **Will Aid** is a partnership between solicitors and nine charities. The solicitors write your will for free, but suggest a voluntary donation to Will Aid which then supports the work of the charities.

The schemes work because solicitors earn extra where it turns out you need more than just a simple will or decide to buy other services.

Charities do this in the hope that you will include a legacy to them in your will, but they cannot make it a requirement of using their services, they do not have access to the will that you have written, and the solicitor involved is working for you not the charity.

For individuals with sight problems, the Royal National Institute of Blind People (RNIB) has produced a comprehensive guide to making or changing a will and offers a number of options, including free will writing through the National Free Wills Network. RNIB (Directory, p 22) also offers a free service to transcribe your will into large print size, braille or audio. Age UK (Directory, p 22) is a partner in the Will Aid scheme and its website has a lot of useful information about writing a will.

WILL-WRITING SERVICES

A will-writing service is a sort of halfway house that is generally more reli-able than a DIY will, but cheaper than a solicitor. Will-writers take you through a questionnaire to find out your needs and are trained to be able to draw up simple wills. But they are not professionally trained in the law as solicitors are and they are not regulated to the same degree, so do not use a will-writing service if your affairs are at all complex. Do make sure that any will-writer you use belongs to one of the following self-regulating bodies which requires members to abide by a code of conduct including having a formal complaints procedure and professional indemnity insurance (Directory, p 22):

- **Institute of Professional Willwriters**
- **Society of Will Writers**

Executors

If you die without making a will, usually your next of kin will be expected to sort out your estate. This might not be the best person for the job, and writing a will gives you the chance to say who you want to finalize your affairs when you're gone.

The duties of an executor are many, including dealing with the financial wishes made by the testator. An executor may have to settle debts, create trusts and distribute the testator's assets among nominated individuals. Executors may also have to inform the next of kin of the death, register the death, deal with house sales and tax if required. When appointing an executor, you should be sure of the person's ability to carry out these duties.

It is possible for a bank, solicitor or accountant to take on this responsibility, but note the warnings above about the fact that there is very little your beneficiaries can do if the executor that you (not they) contracted with during your lifetime turns out to take a long time executing the estate and charges a lot. Make sure you understand what the charges will be – for example, based on time taken or a percentage of the value of your estate – and that you are happy with these.

When choosing an executor of a will, the following points are worth bearing in mind:

- A spouse as a sole executor is not the best choice, especially if both husband and wife are elderly.
- You can – and it is common – to appoint beneficiaries as executors. It might be advisable not to appoint just one or two of several beneficiaries in case others claim there is a conflict of interests.
- The chosen people should be asked in advance to agree to the role.
- Legally, an executor must be over 18, of sound mind and not in prison when the executor decision is made.
- If conflicts within the family are likely to be a factor, it may be worthwhile appointing more than one executor, or even hiring a professional executor.
- If family members are chosen, they should have the time and capability to carry out all the duties. This can be difficult if an executor does not live in the same part of the country.

Other points

Wills should always be kept in a safe place – and their whereabouts known. The most sensible arrangement is for a solicitor to keep the original and for both you and each executor to have a copy.

A helpful initiative devised by the Law Society is a mini-form, known as a personal assets log. This is for individuals drawing up a will to give to their executor or close relatives. It records essential information: name and address of solicitor, where the will and other important documents (for example, share certificates and insurance policies) are kept, the date of any codicils, and so on. Logs should be obtainable from most solicitors. Alternatively, create your own log and keep it with your copy of the will.

Don't forget about digital assets. Some of these you own, such as the money in your online bank and savings accounts, shares in an online trading account and even cryptocurrencies! Make sure your asset log includes details of where these assets can be found. With many other digital assets, such as music and video streaming accounts and electronic books, you have a right to use the assets but don't own them, so they are not part of your estate. You should still leave details, so they can be cancelled. Similarly, think about your social media accounts and leave instructions about whether they should be left untouched or closed down and who should do this. Typically, this will be a job for your executors. Their job will be easier if you compile a list of all digital assets and accounts, together with log-in and security details, and keep this in a secure place (for example, with a solicitor) that your executor is aware of.

Wills may need updating in the event of an important change of circumstances, for example a divorce, a remarriage or the birth of a grandchild. An existing will normally becomes invalid in the event of marriage or remarriage and should be replaced. A will is not invalidated by divorce or dissolution of a civil partnership, but bequests to your ex-partner are automatically invalidated – however, this does not apply if you merely separate. Any changes to your will must be by codicil (for minor alterations) or by a new will, and must be properly witnessed. The witnesses of a codicil do not have to be the same people who witnessed the will.

Another reason why you may need, or wish, to change your will is in consequence of changes in the IHT rules. For example, prior to 9 October 2007, it was quite common for husbands and wives to write wills that created a trust on death to receive some of the deceased's assets in order to prevent their IHT NRB being wasted. However, since then, it has been possible for a surviving spouse or civil partner to inherit the deceased person's unused NRB, reducing the need to create these so-called will trusts.

If you have views about your funeral, it is sensible to write a letter to your executors explaining your wishes and to lodge it with your will. If you have any pets, you may equally wish to leave a letter filed with your will explaining what arrangements you have made for them.

Some related documents are best communicated with family and executors rather than stored with your will, since they are important while you are still living. Over the years there has been increased interest in advance decision making, sometimes called an 'advance directive' or 'living will'. These set out what you would like to happen in the event that you are still alive but unable to communicate your wishes, for example, because you are in a persistent vegetative state. It lets your family and medical practitioners know if you want treatment to be withheld. For those who would like more information, there is basic guidance on advance decision making on the NHS website (Directory, p 22).

Assisted dying is a troubled issue in the UK, but Dignity in Dying (Directory, p 22) is very helpful and can supply you with forms and advice. You may want to think about organ donation. All nations of the UK now have an 'opt-out' system where you are deemed to be a willing donor unless you register that you do not want this to happen. To register an opt-out visit Organ Donation (Directory, p 22).

Provision for dependent adult children

A particular concern for parents with a physically or mentally dependent son or daughter is what plans they can make to ensure his or her care when they are no longer in a position to manage. There is no easy answer, as each case varies according to the severity of the disability or illness, the range of helpful voluntary or statutory facilities locally and the extent to which they, as parents, can provide for their child's financial security long-term.

While social services may be able to advise, parents thinking ahead might do better to consult a specialist organization experienced in helping carers in this situation to explore the possible options available to them. Useful addresses are (Directory, p 19):

- **Carers Trust**
- **Carers UK**

Parents concerned about financial matters such as setting up a trust or making alternative provision in their will would also be advised to consult a solicitor.

Money and other worries – and how to minimize them

Many people say that the first time they really think about death, in terms of what would happen to their nearest and dearest, is after the birth of their first child. As children grow up, requirements change, but key points that anyone with a family should consider – and review from time to time – include life insurance, survivor pensions and mortgage protection.

During their working lives, both partners in a relationship (married or not) should have life insurance cover if anyone, such as children, is dependent on them or they are co-dependent on each other (for example, sharing household bills). If either were to die, not only would the partner lose the financial benefit of the other's earnings, but the survivor would lose the value of any unpaid work done by the deceased, such as childcare, laundry and home maintenance. A very common motive for life insurance is where a couple or single parents have a mortgage; this ensures the mortgage would be paid off in full in the event of death. People without dependants, such as single people without children, do not normally need life insurance, since no one's financial security is at risk.

Later in life, the need for insurance should be re-examined. By this stage, any mortgage is commonly paid off and children financially independent. Where couples each have their own pension income, they might be financially independent and still secure in the event of their partner's death. However, due largely to caring responsibilities, many women have much smaller pensions than their partner. In that case, the couple should consider what the financial position of a survivor would be. It may be that the pension schemes of the deceased person would pay out a survivor pension or continuing annuity income or the survivor might inherit a remaining fund of pension savings. If that's not the case or the amounts involved would not be sufficient, there may be a need for life insurance to plug the gap. However, be aware that the cost of life cover rises steeply at older ages.

A note about debts, since this can be a cause of confusion. Where a debt is jointly held, it is invariably on a 'joint and several basis' which means that each person is responsible for the whole debt. In that case, if one person dies, the remaining borrower takes over the whole debt and responsibility for continuing the repayments. Where a debt is in the name of just one person, if they die, then the debt is repaid out of that person's estate. If the estate is too small to pay off the debt in full, the remainder of the debt is written off. So these debts, while they reduce the amount of the estate left to be passed on, do not become the debts of anyone else.

Life insurance is also sometimes used for IHT planning. At its simplest, life insurance can cover a potential tax bill either on lifetime gifts that become taxable due to death within seven years (failed PETs) or on the estate. Life insurance may also form part of more complex tax avoidance schemes – be aware that these could be challenged by HM Revenue & Customs (HMRC).

Funeral plans

Many people worry about funeral costs. Burial service costs can vary, according to different parts of the country. The costs tend to rise faster than inflation, not just because of funeral directors' fees but more because of disbursements – payments to third parties including church, grave or crematorium. As a result, some people are opting for much cheaper 'direct cremation' with no funeral service. Either way, the cost can either be met by your estate or you might consider a pre-paid funeral plan where you pay now for your final arrangements. Since July 2022, pre-paid funeral plan providers must be regulated by the Financial Conduct Authority (FCA).

Before handing over any money, make sure the company is regulated by the FCA by checking the Financial Services Register (Directory, p 9). Pre-paid schemes are usually linked to a particular funeral director, which you might, or might not, be able to choose. The funeral director must then carry out your funeral with whatever money is available in the trust or insurance policy. If that is less than they are charging at the time, that is their loss.

Do check what is covered in the package you buy – there are usually exclusions. For example, the cost of cremation might be covered, but not burial. Because of the large increases in fees being charged by some cemeteries and crematoria, as well as the rising cost of other disbursements, a number of funeral plan providers are now restricting their guarantee on price to those services within the control of the funeral director. If you are considering this type of scheme, as with any other important purchase it is sensible to compare the different plans on the market to ensure that you are choosing the one that best suits your requirements.

If you are interested in taking out a funeral plan, you might check out these providers (Directory, p 10):

- **Co-operative Funeralcare**
- **Dignity Caring Funeral Services**
- **Golden Charter**

Before making any advance payment, you would be wise to investigate what freedom you have if you subsequently want to change any of the details of the plan; if you cancel the plan, whether you can get all your money back – or only a part.

Before paying, you should receive a letter confirming the terms and conditions, together with full details of the arrangements you have specified. It is important to check this carefully and inform your next of kin where the letter is filed.

An alternative, but less satisfactory arrangement, is to buy a small-premium life insurance policy designed to pay out when you die. These are targeted at the over-50s and are sometimes marketed as funeral plans, although the money can be used for any purpose and there's no guarantee it will be enough to pay for a funeral. (And your relatives will still have to make your funeral arrangements.) These are whole-of-life policies, which means you have to continue paying premiums until you die – and quite possibly will pay much more in premiums than the pay-out they promise. If you stop paying premiums, the cover stops immediately and you don't get any money back.

You do not need to have a dedicated funeral plan at all. Money can be released early from your estate for these costs. Moreover, funerals do not have to cost a fortune – there is growing interest in direct (also called simple) cremation (with no service) which cost around £1,000 to £1,500 in 2024.

Survivors in receipt of Pension Credit or other means-tested benefits might qualify for a payment from the Social Fund to help with funeral costs, if there is not enough money in your estate. For details of eligibility and how you claim, see Help with funeral costs (Directory, p 10).

Dealing with a death

A very real crisis for some families is the need for immediate money while waiting for the estate to be settled. At least part of the problem can be overcome by couples having a joint bank account, with both partners having drawing rights without the signature of the other being required. Sole-name bank accounts and joint accounts requiring both signatures are frozen. For the same reason, it may also be a good idea for any savings or investments to be held in the joint name of the couple. However, some accounts – such as ISAs – can only be held in a single name.

Additionally, an essential practical point for all couples is that any financial and other important documents should be discussed together and understood by both parties. A further common-sense 'must' is for both partners to know where important papers are kept. The best idea is either to lock them, filed together, in a home safe or to give them to the bank to look after.

When someone dies, the bank manager should be notified as soon as possible so he or she can assist with the problems of unpaid bills and help work out a solution until the estate is settled. The same goes for the suppliers of essential services: gas, electricity, telephone, and so on. Unless they know the situation, there is a risk of services being cut off if there is a delay in paying the bill. Add, too, any credit card companies, where if bills lie neglected the additional interest could mount up alarmingly.

Normally, you must register the death within the first five days (eight in Scotland). Your local registrar can be found at GOV.UK. Since the pandemic, deaths are registered by phone. You will need to tell the medical officer who attended the death which registry office you will use, so they can send in their paperwork ahead of your phone appointment. The registrar will give you:

- A certificate allowing cremation or burial to go ahead; this will normally be emailed direct to the funeral director you appoint.
- A unique reference number and contact details for the government's Tell Us Once (TUO) service (Directory, p 10).
- A leaflet with details of bereavement benefits you may be able to claim.
- One or more death certificates, for which there is a fee. You normally need to send a death certificate to each provider of pensions, life insurance, savings and investments that the deceased had. It is cheaper to buy extra certificates straight away than later.

Registering a death is upsetting, and dealing with a death involves more paperwork and phone calls than a family wants to deal with at such a time. Thankfully, the government operates a scheme in most areas called Tell Us Once. You have 28 days from registering the death to access the TUO service, using the reference number from the registrar. Having given TUO the required details, it will then pass them on to a whole range of government and local council services to deal with the deceased's State Pension, state benefits, tax, passport, driving licence, Blue Badge, and so on.

Another organization that may be able to help you after a loved one has died is the Bereavement Register (Directory, p 10). This organization has one aim: to reduce the amount of direct mail to those who are deceased. Coming to terms with the loss of a loved one takes time; receiving direct mail bearing the name of the deceased is often painful and unnecessary. The Bereavement Register puts an end to such occurrences.

For step-by-step guidance, see *What to do when someone dies* for England and Wales, Northern Ireland and Scotland on page 10 of the Directory.

State benefits and tax

The state provides an extra financial benefit for widowed people. This used to be restricted to those whose husband, wife or civil partner has died. But Bereavement Payment is now available to unmarried parents too. Some other aspects of the tax and benefit system favour married couples and civil partners, but not unmarried couples, in the event of death.

Benefits and bereavement

What help you can get from the state differs depending on whether you were under or over State Pension age at the time of death.

UNDER STATE PENSION AGE

A widowed person under State Pension age may be entitled to Bereavement Support Payment. This benefit is not means-tested and depends on your late partner (not you) having paid or been credited with sufficient National Insurance contributions or their death being work-related. You cannot get this payment if you and your late partner were divorced or you are living in a relationship with someone else. Find out more at Bereavement Support Payment (Directory, p 2).

Bereavement Support Payment has two parts, which are both tax-free: a lump sum plus a monthly payment paid for a maximum of 18 months. There is a standard rate paid to people without children and a higher rate for people who are bringing up children. In 2024/25, the standard rate is a lump sum of £2,500 and monthly payments of £100. The higher rate is a lump sum of £3,500 and £350 a month. To claim this benefit, apply online or by phone on 0800 731 0469. Alternatively, get the bereavement pack (form BSP1) either from GOV.UK, or by post by contacting your local Jobcentre Plus (England, Wales and Scotland). In Northern Ireland, download an application form from Bereavement Support Payment (Northern Ireland) (Directory, p 2), or contact the Bereavement Service on 0800 085 2463. To get the full amount, you must claim within three months of your partner's death.

Whether or not you get Bereavement Support Payment, if your income and savings are low, you may qualify for means-tested benefits, such as Universal Credit and Council Tax Reduction – and, if you have a mortgage, you might be eligible for the government's equity release loan, Support for Mortgage Interest. See Chapter 2 for more information.

If you are over State Pension age at the time your partner dies, you do not get state bereavement benefits. If you reached State Pension age before 6 April 2016, you might instead be able to get a higher state basic pension based on your late husband's, wife's or civil partner's National Insurance record, and you might inherit up to half their state additional pension. These arrangements do not usually apply if you reached State Pension age on or after 6 April 2016 because the rules for the new State Pension that started then are different. However, under transitional rules, you might inherit half of your late partner's 'protected payment' if they had one. Chapter 3 has more details.

In either case, if your income is low, you might be able to claim means-tested benefits, such as Pension Credit, Housing Benefit and Council Tax Reduction – and, if you have a mortgage, you might be eligible for the government's equity release loan, Support for Mortgage Interest. Chapter 2 has more information.

Tax and bereavement

The UK has a system of independent taxation, which means that broadly speaking, the tax you pay depends only on your particular circumstances, not those of a partner or anyone else. However, there are some exceptions and some work to the advantage of married couples and civil partners in the event of one of them dying.

ISAS

ISAs are often described as 'tax-free' (see Chapter 4), but this description has been challenged by people who point out that ISAs nevertheless count as part of someone's estate, and so may be subject to IHT on death. Moreover, the tax-free status of these savings disappears on death. Since ISAs cannot be held in joint names, this is a problem for couples who have been forced to take out ISAs independently, but view their ISA savings as being on behalf of them both.

This latter problem has been solved for married couples and civil partners, but not unmarried couples. For deaths occurring on or after 3 December 2014, a surviving husband, wife or civil partner can inherit an ISA allowance equal to the value of the ISA savings and investments their late partner owned. This is an extra allowance on top of your own normal annual allowance. The extra allowance is available for three years from the date of death or 180 days after the administration of the estate has been completed, whichever is later. You get this allowance even if the actual savings and investments left in your late partner's ISAs are inherited by someone else. However, the extra allowance means that you can continue to get the freedom from income tax and CGT if you do inherit those assets or if you choose to invest money of an equivalent value. Inheriting the ISA allowance does not affect IHT, though. Your late partner's ISAs will still count as part of their estate, and there could be IHT to pay.

THE IHT NIL-RATE BAND

It's common for couples to leave the bulk of their estate to each other so that the survivor will be financially secure. As described earlier in this chapter, not only are gifts between married couples and civil partners in lifetime and on death tax-free, the surviving husband, wife or civil partner can inherit any NRB their late partner did not use.

Gifts and bequests between unmarried partners are not tax-free, so whatever they leave to each other uses up some or all of their NRB. Moreover any unused part cannot be inherited, but is simply lost for good. Particularly for couples who have a valuable home (maybe in London where house prices are especially high), this can mean that assets, such as the family home, have to be sold on the first death in order to release enough money to pay the IHT due and any tax on the second death will typically be higher than a married couple would pay. This affects other people who live together too, such as siblings.

Tax and private pension lump sums

When you die, you may be leaving a pot of unused pension savings (in defined-contribution schemes) and these can be passed on to your heirs. Whether or not there is tax to pay depends on the circumstances.

Inheritance tax could be payable if you control who inherits the savings. In that case, the pension savings are part of your estate and so covered by the inheritance tax calculations described earlier in this chapter. However, most people give up that control and leave it to the administrators of the pension scheme to make the final decision of who inherits the savings. The administrators will ask you to complete a form where you can set out your wishes for who you'd like to inherit. In most cases the administrators will respect your wishes. But they have the discretion to distribute the savings differently, for example, if someone claimed they had been financially dependent on you at the time you died.

The other tax to be aware of is income tax. As discussed in Chapter 3, from April 2023, there have been changes to the lifetime allowance so that currently you can build up as much as you like in pension savings without suffering an extra tax charge in your lifetime. That extra tax charge has also been abolished for what you leave on death. However, your heirs might have to pay income tax under the normal rules described in Chapter 4 on any lump sum they inherit from your pension savings. Whether or not income tax applies varies with the circumstances:

- You were under age 75 at death and the savings you leave, plus the value of all other lump sums drawn in the past from your pension savings, come to less than a set limit (£1,073,100 in 2024/25). The savings are inherited tax-free.
- You were under 75 at death and the savings come to more than the limit. Your heirs have to pay tax on the excess under the normal income tax rules described in Chapter 4.
- You were 75 or older at the time of death. Your heirs have to pay tax on the whole lump sum under the normal income tax rules described in Chapter 4.

To work out the tax an heir pays, the lump sum is added to any other income they have for the tax year. Therefore, inheriting a pension lump sum can push your heir into a higher tax bracket during that year. Where you inherit a defined contribution pension pot (see Chapter 3) and decide to draw the proceeds as income (through drawdown or an annuity), the income will continue to be tax-free provided the deceased was under age 75 at the time of death. If they were older, the income you draw is taxed in the same way as other pensions and earnings you may have.

Organizations that can help

Problems vary. For some, the hardest thing to bear is the loneliness of returning to an empty house. For others, money problems seem to dominate everything else. For many older women, in particular, who have not got a job, widowhood creates a great gulf where for a while there is no real sense of purpose. Many widowed men and women go through a spell of feeling enraged at their partner for dying. Most are baffled and hurt by the seeming indifference of friends, who appear more embarrassed than sympathetic.

In time, problems diminish and individuals are able to recapture some of their joy for living with all its many pleasures. Talking to other people who know the difficulties from their own experience can be a tremendous help. The following organizations not only offer opportunities for companionship but also provide an advisory and support service (Directory, p 39):

- **Cruse Bereavement Support** offers free help to anyone who has been bereaved by providing both one-to-one and group support through its local branches throughout the UK.
- The **Good Grief Trust** is a hub that brings together details of helplines from many organizations that offer support and advice to widows and widowers.

Many professional and other groups offer a range of services for widows and widowers associated with them. These include:

- the **Civil Service Retirement Fellowship** (Directory, p 2)
- the **War Widows Association** (Directory, p 39)

Many local Age UK groups offer a counselling service. Trade unions are often particularly supportive, as are Rotary Clubs, all the armed forces organizations and most benevolent societies.

Index

Looking for another book?

Explore our award-winning books from global business experts in General Business

Scan the code to browse

www.koganpage.com/general-business

Discover our online companion resources to support this guide

Scan the code to download

Please note you will be required to sign in or register an account with us in order to access